Édith Thomas

lettres française

OCTOBRE 1942 — n°2

Crier la vérité!

déjà l'automne avec ses asters et ses dahlias, et ses feuilles roussies par
s hêtres? Est-ce la mélancolie de l'automne sur l'asphalte tiède et les peti
s marchandes de quatre saisons pleines de fruits aussi beaux que des fruits
étonnants d'exister encore?

, là-bas, à l'Est, des millions et des millions d'hommes dans le choc effroy
dans le bruit- inhumain -qui a dépassé la zone où l'oreille humaine peut enc
e jettent les uns sur les autres, en cet instant.

oche sonne, ici et là. Et plus loin encore, se répondant d'un clocher à l'au
oucoule sur les arbes du jardin. Midi. Qui pourrait parler de la douceur de

ci. Des milliers et des milliers d'hommes sont en prison ou dans les camps.
nt deux louches d'eau de vaisselle à boire par jour pour tout breuvage, et c
es de pain pour toute nourriture? Et qu'un homme d'un mètre soixante-quinze
s que trente kilogs? Il est mort tout à l'heure.

areil de T.S.F. vaguement joue
MELISANDE. J'ai vu passer un train.
wagon contenait des gendarmes
des soldats allemands. Puis, ve-
wagons à bestiaux plombés. Des
s d'enfants se cramponnaient aux
ne main au dehors s'agitait comme
dans la tempête. Quand le train
des voix ont crié: "Maman". Et
pondu que le le grincement des essieux.
re ensuite que l'art n'a pas de
peux dire ensuite que l'artiste
s'isoler dans sa tour d'ivoire,
métier, rien que son métier.

métier? Pour en être digne, il
la vérité. La vérité est totale ou
La vérité: les étoiles sur les poi-
rachement d s enfants aux mères,
qu'on fusille chaque jour, la dé-
méthodique de tout un peuple- la
interdite. La douceur de l'automne?
as la vérité. Elle est un mensonge
en parler en l'isolant de l'espoir
laisse encore. Pire, elle est un
fumée cachant la vérité, masquant
rotégeant le criminel! Elle est

D'UN FRONT A AU

Il y a huit jours, HITLER hurl
Stalingrad serait pris. Mais Stalin
tient toujours. Et la Caspienne est
loin, et Bakou encore plus loin et
ses du Caucase ne sont pas franchie
le sang allemand coule à flots par
froyables blessures.Miracle?Non. Con
héroïsme
ce/l'un peuple qui se bat comme seu
battent des hommes conscients de dé
mieux que la vie: tout ce qui rend
digne d'être vécue. C'est bien pour
que Stalingrad rappelle tant Valmy
DEAT, obsédé par cette idée, tente
sement de prouver que l'esprit
se trouve du côté des armées de KRU
LING, GOERING & Cie!

Déjà l'hiver pointe. On est é
lé devant l'intelligence de la stra
soviétique qui est passée de la tac
du recul défensif à la bataille d'
moment précis où l'armée allemande
vait dans une position stratégique

Édith Thomas

A PASSION FOR RESISTANCE

DOROTHY KAUFMANN

Cornell University Press   Ithaca and London

First published 2004 by Cornell University Press

Printed in the United States of America

Library of Congress Cataloging-in-Publication Data

Kaufmann, Dorothy.
    Édith Thomas : a passion for resistance / Dorothy Kaufmann.
        p. cm.
    Includes bibliographical references and index.
    ISBN 0-8014-4223-0 (cloth : alk. paper)
    1. Thomas, Édith.   2. Authors, French—20th century—Biography.
I. Title.
    PQ2639.H56Z735 2004
    843'.912—dc22

                                                        2004005012

Cornell University Press strives to use environmentally responsible suppliers
and materials to the fullest extent possible in the publishing of its books. Such
materials include vegetable-based, low-VOC inks and acid-free papers that
are recycled, totally chlorine-free, or partly composed of nonwood fibers. For
further information, visit our website at www.cornellpress.cornell.edu.

Cloth printing   10 9 8 7 6 5 4 3 2 1

In memory of my father
Felix Kaufmann (1890–1988)
who awakened my love
for a certain idea of France

Contents

# Acknowledgments

It is a great pleasure to thank the many people who have helped bring this project to fruition.

A Passion for Resistance would not exist without the trust and confidence of Dominique Aury. She loaned me, for as long as I needed them, Édith Thomas's diaries and memoirs, which are at the heart of this book. We met to talk about Édith Thomas on each of my trips to Paris. After Dominique's death, her son, Philippe d'Argila, kindly offered me access to his mother's correspondence with Édith Thomas.

Daniel Thomas, the legal heir of his aunt's estate, and his wife Andrée Thomas provided unfailing support and assistance over the years, while also taking for granted my complete freedom of interpretation. Throughout the research and writing of this biography, on visits to St. Marcellin and La Bâtie, in letters, e-mails, and phone conversations, I have benefited from their integrity and their knowledge of history and "la tante Édith."

Many people who knew Édith Thomas agreed to speak to me about her. I wish to thank her colleagues Michel Bouille, Monsieur Guillot, Odile Krakovitch, and Monique Pouliquen at the Archives nationales for their insights and information. I had many helpful conversations with Yvonne Lanhers, who was a close friend of Édith Thomas as well as a colleague. Other friends also offered thoughtful insights: Claude Aveline, Paulette Courchet, Joël Schmidt, and especially her good friend Anne-Marie Bauer. I appreciate the different perspectives provided by Roger Bacuet, the Thomas family caretaker at Sainte-Aulde; Julien Kravtchenko, a friend of Édith's brother Gérard during his student years; and Édith's sister-in-law, Madeleine Thomas.

The generous financial support of the Florence Gould Foundation in the early stages of this project allowed me to dedicate myself full-time for a year to uncovering Édith Thomas's life. During that year, under the inspired direction of Florence Ladd, the Bunting Institute of Radcliffe (now the Radcliffe Institute at Harvard) provided a collegial and stimulating workplace.

I am indebted to Anthony Helm, humanities technology adviser at Clark University, who expertly scanned all the illustrations in this book. Special thanks go to my computer mentor Christine Turkovich, who helped me through innumerable computer crises and sometimes succeeded in making me see my iBook laptop, "le petit," as a friend.

I wish to thank Pancho, a political cartoonist for *Le Canard enchaîné* and *Le Monde,* for graciously giving me permission to reproduce his spirited drawing of Édith Thomas that accompanied the review of my critical edition of her diaries and memoirs in *Le Canard enchaîné.*

I am deeply obliged to Marie Fort, the wise friend and helpful reader of my essays in French about Édith Thomas. For many years, the elegant desk in her apartment in Paris became an unofficial archive for all the documents given to me by Dominique Aury. Those documents are now in their appropriate home at the Archives nationales, along with Édith Thomas's other papers.

My thanks to friends here and in Paris who gave me moral support as well as advice about various aspects of the biography project and articles related to it, in particular Joe Boskin, Michel Couderc, Christian Marouby, my son Steve McCall, Nicole Racine, Martine Raud, Helen Solterer, Bert States, and Laurence Zoneliche.

I am grateful for the suggestions of friends and colleagues who read my manuscript in whole or in part at various stages: Célia Bertin, Gerhard Joseph, Dan McCall, Anne Simonin, and Susan Suleiman. The insightful recommendations of Elissa Gelfand led me to make significant positive changes. Erica Harth enhanced the manuscript in countless ways by her astute criticism and unfailing encouragement. I wish to thank John LeRoy and Ange Romeo-Hall at Cornell University Press who guided me with expert editorial judgment through the process of turning the manuscript into a book and, finally, Bernhard Kendler for the eureka of *A Passion* in my title.

Édith Thomas

Introduction

Édith Thomas (1909–70) was deeply engaged in the traumatic upheavals of her time, most crucially the Resistance to Nazi occupation and the collaborationist Vichy regime, but also the Spanish Civil War and the Algerian War. A remarkable French intellectual and woman of letters, she was driven by the need to bear witness. Her writings offer a fresh perspective on compelling questions of history and memory, of ideology and ethical values, of fiction and autobiography. A historian by training, she authored novels, short stories, historical studies, and a significant corpus of journalism, as well as diaries and a memoir that were published long after her death. She joined the Communist Party in 1942, the time of greatest danger, and publicly resigned a few years after the war, in 1949. In her thinking about women, she became what we would now call a feminist, before the rebirth of feminism as a vital political movement. Her sexual identity was one of the many paradoxes in her life. She considered herself heterosexual, but her most intense affair and enduring intimacy was with a woman, Dominique Aury, a translator and editor who was also the longtime anonymous author of *Story of O.*

During the period of Nazi occupation, when everyone in France was obliged to make a choice, the great majority chose neither resistance nor collaboration but rather accommodation. In the present moment of widespread American cynicism about France that even now focuses on the Vichy years, it is especially timely to revive the life and work of a woman whose immediate choice in response to defeat and occupation was resistance. Édith Thomas played a crucial role in what the French call the intellectual Resistance, the struggle to give voice to forbidden discourse that would counter Nazi and Pétainist propaganda. The only woman in the Paris network of Resistance writers, she was the linchpin of the group, providing headquarters in her left-bank apartment for their clandestine meetings. She wrote articles, stories, and poems for the underground press. As early as October 1942 her editorial "Crier la vérité!"—headlined in large calligraphic letters—spoke of the deportations she had witnessed firsthand. It was a passionate call to writers to be faithful to their vocation, which meant crying out the truth of what they saw happening around them. Her stories *Contes d'Auxois*, subtitled "transcribed from the real" and published in 1943 by the underground Éditions de Minuit, are tales of extraordinary and everyday courage, brief sketches of the ways in which ordinary French women and men—and even a German soldier—said "no" to the occupying Nazi forces. In 1943 Charles de Gaulle quoted one of her poems, written under the pseudonym "Anne," in his speech in Algiers that paid homage to writers of the Resistance. In the spring of 1944 Thomas spent several weeks with the maquis in the mountains of the southern zone to report on their activities for the underground press.

Édith Thomas has often seemed to me a shadow sister of Simone de Beauvoir: "sister" through their ethics of commitment, their feminism, and their affinities as intellectual women, in spite of Thomas's ambivalence about Beauvoir and her hostility to Sartrean existentialism. Although the two women do not seem to have known or even have met each other, Beauvoir and Thomas were born only a year apart into middle-class families. Both spent most of their adult lives in Paris. Thomas completed her historical anthology of women writers, "L'Humanisme féminin," in 1949, the same year that Beauvoir published her monumental and pioneering contribution *Le Deuxième Sexe*. The two women share an intimate obsession with the figure of the woman in love, a central figure not only in *The Second Sex* but in most of Beauvoir's novels and those of Édith Thomas as well. I use the word "shadow" (*ombre*) to highlight Thomas's obscurity in contrast to Beauvoir's fame and also to evoke her role in the Resistance, which the French call *l'armée des ombres*. Thomas's war writings emerge from a lived experience of the Resistance, in contrast to Beauvoir's Resistance novel *Le Sang des autres* (1945), which can be read as a "compensatory fantasy" for what she did not do during those years.[1]

The novels of Édith Thomas, apart from two early works that she considered literary exercises, focus on themes of a woman's solitude, represented in its most extreme and despairing form in *La Mort de Marie* (The Death of Marie), the narrative of a young woman's fatal illness, which won the prize for the best first novel in France in 1933. Another kind of solitude pervades *Le Champ libre* (Free and clear), which reads like a female *Bildungsroman*, almost a contradiction in terms since an individual's journey to awareness through experience of the world was culturally conceived as male. With the exception of *Eve and the Others*, a collection of playful feminist tales based on women in the Bible, and *Le Jeu d'échecs* (Chess game, but literally game of failures), her last and best work of fiction, all of Édith Thomas's novels were written before the war. After the occupation, in revolt against its pervasive mystifications, she felt the need to return to her original vocation as a historian, to confront real figures and events of the past that she found resonant with her own time.

Her first work after the war was about the present. In the impassioned chronicle *La Libération de Paris* (1945), she offers her day-to-day account as an engaged witness rather than a historian. *Jeanne d'Arc* (1947) figures as a work of transition between her involvement with issues of the Resistance and her subsequent feminist biographies. The choice of Joan of Arc was inspired by Joan's extraordinary destiny during the war, when she became a national symbol for the Resistance and for collaborators as well. Thomas's study *Les "Pétroleuses"* (1963), the name given to the women accused of setting fire to Paris during the Commune uprising, won a prestigious award and was subsequently translated into English (as *The Women Incendiaries*). *Louise Michel* (1971), her biography of the leader and symbol of the Commune, was also translated into English. *Rossel* (1963), which won a prize for the best work of history in that year, is her only biographical study of a man. Some critics compared Rossel to a de Gaulle who failed. A remarkable and surprisingly intimate work, *Rossel* explores the life of a military officer in the Franco-Prussian War who joined the Commune after France's defeat and was executed by the French government as a deserter at the age of twenty-seven.

Although Édith Thomas was beginning to emerge from relative obscurity when she died in 1970, her importance in French intellectual life has gone largely unrecognized. Her education at the École des Chartes, which prepares specialists in the deciphering and interpretation of historical French manuscripts and readily accepted women, was far less prestigious than the École Normale Supérieure, which forms the intellectual elite and counted very few women.[2] For Édith Thomas's generation, to be a woman writer and especially an intellectual woman was to intrude on a masculine domain. Moreover, she wrote as a woman alone, without any male mediator to ease her acceptance into the literary world. When I asked Dominique Aury why Édith Thomas was not better known, she replied: "She had a thundering voice, she was very headstrong, and she wasn't the wife of Aragon"—a reference to Elsa Triolet, a well-known writer of the time (and wife of Louis Aragon, literary commissar of the French Communist Party) who, like Simone de Beauvoir, became a public figure as part of a writing couple.

I prefer an explanation of a different order, however. The most significant

Drawing of Édith Thomas by Pancho in *Le Canard enchaîné,* February 22, 1995.

material for understanding the historic dimensions of Édith Thomas's life and work, especially during World War II and the postwar period, can be found in the astonishing documents she chose not to publish during her lifetime: in particular her diaries, which she kept from 1931 to 1963; her fictional diary of a collaborator, written during the first year of the occupation; and her political memoir, to which she gave the devastating title *Le Témoin compromis* (The compromised witness). In 1995 my critical edition of selected diaries of the war years, as well as the complete fictional diary and her memoir, was published in France. The three texts are of exceptional interest, both for their literary quality and their historical insights. Each testimony is written in a different genre with its own inherent constraints and possibilities, its own relation to questions of truth and memory. Together these texts offer three perspectives on the Nazi occupation of France from a woman who lived through that catastrophic period as a witness and an engaged participant.

My choice of passages from the diary notebooks in *Pages de Journal* deliberately excludes Thomas's personal entries unless they have a direct bearing on the war years. In contrast, *A Passion for Resistance* depends on all the diaries, including those written before and after the war, and on other unpublished material as well. In the second part of this introduction, I tell the story of the unexpected discovery of these documents, most of them contained in a shopping bag given to me on loan by Dominique Aury.

During the war years, the intimate genre of the diary became for Édith Thomas a refuge for forbidden speech about the occupation and Vichy France, in spite of the risk of discovery by the Gestapo or the French police. Vercors, one of the founders of the underground publishing house Éditions de Minuit, comments in *The Battle of Silence,* which he wrote many years after the war: "I have never managed to keep a diary and under the occupation it would have been out of the question anyhow, except for recording meaningless trivia."[3] But it was not out of the question for Édith Thomas, and she did not record meaningless trivia. Her diary provides rare insight into Vichy culture and daily life from the point of view of a Resistance writer. From 1935 until 1939 Thomas had worked as a journalist, reporting on domestic issues in France but also on the Spanish Civil War from Barcelona and later the Pyrenees, where refugees were crossing the border into France, and on the German-Austrian Anschluss from Austria. Her diary during the occupation years evokes the double meaning of the French word *journal,* which can mean either newspaper or diary. Since the imposition of censorship in 1940 meant that a journalist in opposition could no longer speak her mind in the public world, Édith Thomas found in the diary a private vehicle that allowed her immediate expression. In spite of the danger of arrest, she wrote with relatively little self-censorship until the fall of 1942. After she became involved in organized Resistance, she continued to record her opposition to Pétain and the occupation, although she had to keep silent about her activities and those of her comrades.

Édith Thomas's need to break through the silence imposed by Vichy censorship led to a highly improbable refuge for forbidden speech: the satiric, fictional diary of a Pétainist collaborator that she kept during the first year of the occupation, while she was writing in her "real" diary. During that period, from October 1940 to May 1941, she was recovering from illness in Arcachon, a southern coastal city near Bordeaux in the zone occupied by the Germans. *Le Journal intime de Monsieur Célestin Costedet* was written on loose pieces of paper folded in half, corresponding to one hundred and fifty pages about the size of the pages in her diary. Like her own journals, Costedet's diary is often hastily written and difficult to decipher, with no indication that it was reworked at a later time, since it was not intended for publication. As far as I know, the diary of Costedet is formally unique. In the fictional diary as a literary genre, dates function as a narrative strategy for the effect of immediacy, but the writer can conceive the diary from the beginning in its entirety. In *Le Journal intime de Monsieur Célestin Cos-*

tedet, it was not possible for Édith Thomas to know how this diary would develop or end. Actual events in the present intrude into her character's reflections, changing and disrupting his story.

To create the character of Costedet, Édith Thomas did not need to look beyond official discourse. The image of reality presented by the Vichy regime was in itself a caricature. Costedet's edifying moralism reflects Vichy ideology, whose sentimental rhetoric barely disguised its brutality. The embodiment by Costedet of a Pétainist version of reality makes this fiction a historical document as well as a literary work. Although Édith Thomas mocks Costedet's pretensions of testifying for posterity, her parodic fiction provides a wealth of real information about the period. Costedet's opinions about contemporary events and his reading of history could readily be found in the regional collaborationist newspaper *La Petite Gironde* (printed in nearby Bordeaux), programs on the radio, and scenes of daily life. At a time when Thomas was ill, when in any case there was not yet an organized Resistance in which she could participate, Costedet's diary provided a means of satirizing the mystifications of official discourse. Like her own diary, it allowed her to speak the truth, however privately, and keep her sanity.

In contrast to Thomas's two handwritten diaries, *Le Témoin compromis,* a book-length political memoir that she wrote in 1952, three years after her painful break with the Communist Party, is typewritten. Whereas one can say with reasonable certainty that she did not intend for her diaries to be published, the evidence of her intentions for *Le Témoin compromis* is far more ambiguous. From the first pages, she writes to justify herself, in her own eyes and those of an imaginary other. The *tu* whom she addresses in her narrative is communist, male, and scornful of her autobiographical project. She gives herself too much importance, he tells her; self-portraits are always self-indulgent, distorted by the bias of subjectivity. As a witness writing to attest to the truth of what she has lived, Thomas feels compromised by her role as witness in another meaning of the word: one who testifies, in this case for the accused, defending herself against the internalized judgments that have profoundly divided her. *Le Témoin compromis* is the narrative of a political trajectory and a plea for the defense, "since we are all accused, sooner or later."[4]

Thomas repeatedly insists she is writing first of all out of inner necessity, "so that the truth exists somewhere, even if it is not read by anyone." However, at the end of the manuscript, her defense plea allows her to express the small hope of being understood by an eventual reader, "whoever you are." In the final, self-doubting sentences of *Le Témoin compromis,* Édith Thomas's divided feelings about publishing her manuscript are palpable: "It is very possible that these pages are of interest only to me. It is also possible that they have the value of bearing witness to these tormented years. I don't know. Perhaps I've also written these pages to have your response, whoever you are. But I hardly believe in responses anymore."[5]

A differently oblique representation of her conflicted desire to keep her memoir private and to have it read by others can be found in her choice of an epigraph for *Le Témoin compromis*: "We abandoned the manuscript to the gnawing criticism of the mice, all the more willingly as we had achieved our main purpose—self-clarification." The quote, taken from Marx's preface to his *Contribution to the Critique of Political Economy*, is an allusion to *The German Ideology*, which he wrote in 1846 with Engels. Édith Thomas would certainly have been aware that *The German Ideology* was published for the first time in 1932, several decades after the death of its authors. It is not difficult to imagine her own hope for a posthumous publication of *Le Témoin compromis*, when the passage of time would allow a calmer perspective on the tormented years that form the subject of her memoir.

Édith Thomas's diaries reveal a feeling of singularity, of alienation and difference from others, which is inseparable from her sense of being an intellectual woman and a woman alone. "Old [Mme de] Staël used to say," she notes, "that fame is the tomb of happiness. But for a woman, consenting to her singularity is already a tomb."[6] What she calls her singularity was a source of both pride and vulnerability. On the one hand, she fiercely valued her autonomy, the determination to make choices and construct her destiny without the social mediation of a man. On the other, she yearned for the love of a man who would confirm her not only as an intellectual but also as a woman. Those conflicting needs took on another dimension through her passionate love of another woman, Dominique Aury. For Édith only a person to whom she would be the indispensable great love could break through her solitude and justify her life. Although she experienced her solitude as a curse, it was also a need and a habit. Most importantly, it was the indispensable condition for writing, the only activity whose value remained intact, whatever her doubts about herself and her work. During her worst depressions she continued to write.

The diaries give voice to a craving for wholeness that she sought sometimes in love, sometimes in revolutionary action, always in writing. She was well aware of the religious longing at the heart of her desire, although she could not believe in God. "I told you a hundred times during this long silent colloquium in the middle of the night," she writes to herself, "only God would have been great enough to suffice for you. Only God can be created to one's own measure, without verification from experience to disturb the imagination."[7] Seeking wholeness meant an active struggle to dissolve the ego into something beyond the self. In *Le Jeu d'échecs* the autobiographical narrator, a writer, describes her desire in images of combat: "I worked on my book. In moments of sadness and ennui, work saves me from everything. It is enough to give myself to it, or rather take it on like a physical battle, and fight with it until it yields. That struggle dispenses with the rest. Even living."[8]

From the outset, Édith Thomas's autobiographical impulse was inseparable from the need to resist, a need that was deeply personal before it became political. At the age of twenty-two she fell ill with tuberculosis of the bone and writing became a means to resist death. Pages torn from her diary, in which she recorded her intention to end it all, precede her first entries. In the suffering of infirmity and acute pain, she found in writing a life/line[9] that might save her from going under. Her writing self could begin to externalize the despair and enable some feeling of control, however limited and precarious. To live required a constant effort of will, impelled by the act of writing. She found an odd comfort in the sense of her existence as provisional, demanding a renewed decision to continue living so she could observe her ordeal and write about it. The choice, she felt, was hers.

In the mid-1930s, when she had recovered from her illness, Édith Thomas's diary began to record a new role. Influenced by her brother, Gérard, and his left-wing radical friends, she felt a need to enter and change the world of social reality, which took the form of a romantic attraction to communism. Like so many intellectuals of the 1930s with utopian impulses who were deeply disillusioned by the corruption and ineffectiveness that passed for democracy, she wanted passionately to believe that communism could bring about a just world. At the same time, she was not quite able to accept the unconditional justification implicit in crusading ideologies. Thomas's diary vividly portrays her ongoing efforts to keep the faith, which for the most part prevailed against her doubts. Her submerged distrust surfaced with particular anguish in the diary entries after August 23, 1939, the date of the Nazi-Soviet nonaggression pact. In spite of the rationalizations of her comrades, she remained stubbornly convinced that the end does not justify all means, that the means affect the end, that a just society cannot be achieved though injustice, lies, and crime. At times she seems to have been embarrassed by her belief that moral questions of means and ends matter, as if such thinking were a weakness. Her diary entries over the years show clearly the ethical passion that drew her to the Communist Party and would drive her to leave it after the war.

In her reflections on the diary as a literary genre, Béatrice Didier suggests that diaries are "readily born in a situation of imprisonment."[10] Édith Thomas's initial imprisonment was figured by the devastating illness that kept her confined for almost two years and left her with a permanent limp. In a situation of complete immobility, writing in her diary became a strategy to make a refuge out of "the prison of my room."[11] The feeling of imprisonment incited the need to write as a protest against things as they are, which took a number of different forms in the course of her life. In 1939 she once again fell ill, with pulmonary tuberculosis this time, which brought fatigue and melancholy but spared her the pain of her earlier sickness. She spent most of the next two years convalescing in Arcachon. During her second bout of illness, Thomas's impulse to keep a diary was increasingly impelled by the urgency of bearing witness. The political became personal. Solitary imprisonment changed into the shared imprisonment of the war years, the collective impossibility of moving and speaking freely. "To leave," she writes in September 1940. "Where can one go? We are all prisoners. To be in prison and know that one is in prison even when outside, that there no longer is an outside."[12]

The last autobiographical document contained in Dominique Aury's shopping bag is an imagined letter written on fifty handwritten pages and addressed to Gérard after his death in 1967. Writing to her brother was Édith Thomas's way to grieve, to keep his memory alive, and to construct her story of what they meant to each other. In contrast to the immediacy of the diary form, "À mon frère" becomes an intimate memoir, providing a counterpart to her political memoir by giving shape and retrospective meaning to her private itinerary. Looking back, she recreates their childhood together, his trajectory and hers, their political estrangement when she left the Communist Party—to which he continued to belong until the end of his life—and the unique place he has held in her imagination. Like the diaries, her letter to Gérard is written only for herself.

Philippe Lejeune writes of what he calls "the autobiographical pact," a project of truth telling on the part of the author that implies a promise to the reader and distinguishes the autobiographical narrative from fiction.[13] Truth telling in the diary is based on a different kind of pact. Here the author and the intended reader are one; the diarist's pact is with herself. On the inside cover of her first diary notebook, Thomas records a quotation from Stendhal: "The little details jotted down recall and make present every sensation. Such a journal is intended only for the person writing it." The secrecy of the diary provided a safe haven where she could feel protected from any judgment other than her own. Thomas's notations, almost always written in times of distress, allowed for self-expression impelled only by its urgency. Without the constraint of shaping language for another's gaze, she could give free rein to thoughts and feelings of the moment, exposing the messy contradictions of life that elsewhere she rarely allowed herself to admit. In its simplest version, the diary claims the factuality of the date inscribed, an aspect specific to the diary form. More problematically, the diarist makes a pact with herself to write the truth as she experiences it at the time of writing.

Truth telling about public matters in Vichy France was a luxury reserved only for trusted comrades and, for Édith Thomas, her diary. Yet it was primarily during the occupation that she thought critically about diary writing. Citing Vigny and Chateaubriand, she gave voice to her unease with the narcissism of keeping a diary. Apropos of Vigny's *Journal of a poet,* she scornfully points out "the intolerable pose of the 'intimate' diary in which one is constantly offering oneself to oneself as a spectacle: false pride, false humility, everything is distorted and embellished in this so-called mirror." When she quotes Chateaubriand's *Memoirs from Beyond the Grave,* she applauds the man who writes as a defender of liberty, in order to contrast his political lucidity with his lack of self-knowledge. However, she unequivocally admires the diary of Samuel Pepys: his "nakedness," his "perfect sincerity," and even his "absence of subtlety," all of which she sees as positive qualities, made possible by his turning outward to the world.[14] Without the need for self-analysis, Pepys is able to describe things straightforwardly, whether it is the London plague in 1665 or his reaction to a pornographic book. She is well aware, however, that she is not extroverted like Samuel Pepys.

In one entry during the occupation, she is both admiring and distrustful of her own truth telling. Her "letter to myself" is written in 1942, between pages describing the appalling events taking place in Vichy France. She begins: "My dearest friend, I don't often have the occasion to write to you. At the risk of appearing to be a pharisee—but that's what we are, you and I—I will say that I am pleased with you: the only terrain that has never cracked under your feet is still yourself, and I see in your life a line straight enough to be unusual, firm enough so that I can no longer doubt the uphill path it will follow."[15] She undercuts the self-satisfied tone of the "letter" by calling herself a pharisee. In its modern and figurative usage, the term suggests someone who claims to incarnate the truth by following a strict set of rules, in order to admire himself and pass harsh judgment on others. In the context of the self-description that follows in her diary entry, "pharisee" is like a negative photograph, projecting a darker self-image of the uncompromising integrity that she needed to live by.

If Thomas's pact, in all its ambiguities, is with herself, where does that leave the reader? The diary reader can only be a voyeur, bringing the gaze of an intruder on writing intended for no one but the writer herself. But although Édith Thomas clearly did not want the gaze of readers while she was alive, what she wanted for her diaries after her death is unclear, complicated by two other considerations: her desire to be known—renowned, but also understood—and her professional vocation as a historian of individual lives. Significantly, Thomas did not destroy her diaries or her memoir, nor did she make any written provisions for what should become of them when she was no longer alive. She might have imagined a reader after her death who would want to write her life story, investigating and interpreting whatever documents could be found, following her own practice as a biographer. In any case, she had little use for biographical portraits that magnified their subjects or oversimplified them. In her last biography, of Louise Michel, she writes at the very beginning of her introduction: "Hagiography is always unsatisfactory."[16]

I share that opinion. Rescuing a writer from semi-obscurity, even a writer of the Resistance, does not mean making her into a monument of virtue or even consistency.

During most of her adult life, Édith Thomas worked as a curator at the Archives nationales, a career for which she had been trained at the École des Chartes. My initial work on Édith Thomas at the Archives nationales, to which she left most of her public papers, often seemed cast in a peculiar mirror that reflected her traces in her own workplace, where she spent much of her time researching and writing biographies of women. While I was waiting for permission from her family to consult the Édith Thomas dossier and during the subsequent months I worked at the Archives, I had a number of interviews and informal conversations with people who had been her colleagues and who provided strikingly different perspectives. Those who did not like her found her cold, unapproachable, intimidating. A woman who had started working at the Archives in 1950 suddenly burst out: "I don't know if it was because I wasn't a *chartiste* or if she simply couldn't tolerate young women, but she treated me like an idiot if I made a few spelling mistakes. Every time I saw her she reduced me to tears." The man who helped readers with requests on the computer said to me: "Since we had different assignments and a different place in the hierarchy, we didn't see each other that much, but when we did, we would talk about our common misfortunes. We were both handicapped, you know. She was extremely nice."

Many of those who admired Édith Thomas spoke of her "elegance," a word used a number of times by women and men to refer to her integrity: once she gave her word, one could count on her to keep it. People remarked on the intense directness of her gaze, a quality that some found deeply moving, others discomforting. Odile Krakovitch, a feminist historian who started working at the Archives near the end of Édith Thomas's career, remembered her affectionately and chided me for describing her as unknown:

I haven't read her novels, but anyone who works in French women's history must contend with Édith Thomas's work. It's of fundamental importance. We liked each other. My family was in the Resistance and my father belonged to the Communist Party. Another link was our shared

Protestant background. She had a special relation to Protestant ethics, even though she wasn't a believer. Of course she had enemies at the Archives; they do her honor. She had trouble with right-wingers, misogynists, and submissive women. She enjoyed scaring people, but the people she really liked were those who weren't afraid of her. During the sixties my boss gave me a hard time because I wore a miniskirt in the public reading room. Édith was amused by it all and entirely on my side.[17]

According to Yvonne Lanhers, her closest friend at the Archives,

Édith could be gratingly ironic and even unjust, especially with people she considered reactionary. Her barbed comments created distance with many people but she was an incomparable friend, absolutely loyal and devoted. In religion she was an agnostic rather than an atheist, always seeking and questioning. Her desire to be a writer and to write well counted for her more than anything else. Paradoxically, although she was fundamentally unhappy and depressive, she was also bursting with energy.[18]

The cartons of papers in the Édith Thomas dossier showed that she had saved everything related to her professional and political life but nothing about her personal life.[19] Contrary to my initial assumption that her journalism had been restricted to articles about World War II Resistance, there were hundreds of articles, literary and cultural as well as political, written between 1935 and 1969, including two series of pieces from 1936 and 1938 about the Spanish Civil War and a number of articles written in the Soviet Union immediately after the war. In addition to press reviews and commentaries about her works and her political activities, her dossier contained dozens of short stories and poems, some published, some not; postwar lectures given not only in France but also in Germany, the Soviet Union, and Yugoslavia; her thesis at l'École des Chartes on Louis XI; notes for a book project on the history of flowers in the visual arts; and notes for all her biographical histories. There was also a series of plays, some of which were produced on the radio: *La Révolte des esclaves* (about Spartacus), *Les Pétroleuses, Sappho,* and *Prométhée*—a play she wrote in 1940 which shows surprising affinities with Sartre's 1943 play *Les Mouches* (*The Flies*).

The most intriguing discovery at the Archives nationales was a typed manuscript dated "1947–1949" and titled "L'Humanisme féminin."[20] This manuscript, a historical anthology of writings by French women of letters, is illuminating both as a document exactly contemporary with Simone de Beauvoir's *Le Deuxième Sexe* and as a reflection of the competing humanist claims made by Marxists and existentialists in the postwar period. The word *féminin* in her title is meant to highlight the discrepancy between the inclusive, universal ideal of humanism and the historical reality that has excluded women. Although the word might suggest an analogy with *écriture féminine* and theories of feminine difference in the 1970s, Édith Thomas's meaning is much closer to Beauvoir's feminist and egalitarian assumptions. The manuscript is contained in a folder with a puzzling notation in what appears to be Thomas's handwriting: "published by the Éditions Hier et Aujourd'hui." But the manuscript was not published. The press Hier et Aujourd'hui was linked to the Communist Party. When Thomas publicly resigned from the Party in December 1949, generating considerable controversy, Hier et Aujourd'hui withdrew its offer of publication.

After reading the mass of documents at the Archives nationales, I still knew little about Édith Thomas beyond her public activities and her publications. Although most of her novels seemed to be autobiographical, I was all too aware of the elusiveness of any reliable method of inferring a life from fictional representations. The oral testimony of people Thomas had known at the Archives was revealing but insufficient. As I was questioning the feasibility of my biographical project, I decided to write a few letters to people whose names had caught my attention. One of them was Dominique Aury, who had written a moving obituary for Édith Thomas. Her name was familiar to me as the editor, with Jean Paulhan, of an anthology of Resistance writings, *La Patrie se fait tous les jours* (The homeland is created day by day) and as an editor for Gallimard, the most prestigious of the traditional French publishing houses. Since she described Thomas's funeral as including only family and close friends, I assumed that Aury had to be among them. When I wrote to request an interview, she accepted immediately, welcoming the opportunity to speak about her friend.

During our first conversation, in an office at Gallimard, Dominique Aury recalled that she had met Édith Thomas through Jean Paulhan, then a mutual friend, just after the liberation of Paris in 1944. A petite, charming, and austerely beautiful woman, Dominique Aury seemed as oblique and enigmatic as I imagined Édith Thomas to be direct and forthright. When I asked her my first general question about Édith, her initial response, preceded and followed by a long pause, was "She liked cats." Looking at the eighty-three-year-old woman sitting across from me, I suddenly saw Claude, the woman in her thirties described in Édith Thomas's last novel, *Le Jeu d'échecs:* "the unusually high forehead," "clear eyes which seemed to take in all the light," "an abstract, rather spiritual face whose ambiguity attracted me."[21] Dominique Aury, I realized, was the model for the woman with whom Thomas's fictional protagonist falls in love. Almost in passing Aury said, "We had a brief love affair, she and I." Their romantic relationship lasted just under a year, ending when Aury became the lover of Jean Paulhan, the longtime éminence grise of French letters.

After Dominique Aury became Paulhan's companion in 1947, she continued

to see Édith Thomas and, she told me, telephoned her "every day of her life until her death" for the next twenty-three years. The regular contact between them
became particularly difficult after Paulhan, who had been with the Resistance
from its beginnings, published his *Lettre aux directeurs de la Résistance* (1951), a
controversial polemic against the purge of collaborators that took place after the
war. Like many fellow *résistants*, Thomas interpreted Paulhan's book as an attack on the Resistance. Her complex literary and political relationship with
Paulhan, reflected in a correspondence that goes back to 1939, had begun many
years before either of them knew Dominique Aury. In the controversy generated
by Paulhan's *Lettre*, he and Thomas stopped speaking, their adversarial positions complicated further by the triangular relationship with Aury. Paulhan demanded that Dominique end all communication with Édith, which she refused
to do. Édith Thomas and Jean Paulhan were not reconciled until 1967, a year before his death.

I soon learned what had been an open secret in Paris for some time: Dominique Aury was the author of the controversial erotic novel *Histoire d'O*
(1954), which she wrote under the pseudonym Pauline Réage.[22] Jean Paulhan,
whom many believed to be the author of *O*, was the man for whom Dominique
Aury wrote her story.[23] So open was the secret that President de Gaulle alluded
to it in public. In the 1960s Dominique Aury accompanied Paulhan to a reception for literati hosted by de Gaulle at the Elysée Palace. On the receiving line,
after she was introduced to him, he remarked: "It is said that you are the author
of *Story of O*." She neither confirmed nor denied the rumor, just smiled, her
standard response on such occasions.[24]

In the summer of 1991, Dominique Aury began talking to me about her novel,
taking it for granted that I knew she had written it. I discovered the surprising
presence of Édith Thomas in *Story of O*, as well as Aury's reciprocal presence in
much of Thomas's writing. In Dominique's description of what Édith represented for her, she said: "I had a deep respect for her, more than for myself. Of
course you need some respect for yourself in order to live. But I respected her
much more than myself. Édith was the noblest woman I ever met, in heart and
mind; she had a need for truth and authenticity that was fundamental. And a
rare generosity, except when politics was involved. She could be severe, glacial,
intransigent." With an affectionate smile, she added: "Thank God, she also had
a wonderful sense of humor."

As I was turning the interview tape during my first conversation with Dominique Aury, she leaned over the arm of her chair and handed me a large shopping bag I had not noticed before. It was filled with Édith Thomas's unpublished
papers: her eight notebooks of diaries; the fictional diary of Costedet; articles
written for the underground press; a number of poems; her typewritten politi-

cal memoir; and her handwritten personal memoir "À mon frère," in the form of a long letter written to her brother after his death in 1967. A biographer needs to find the shape and texture of her narrative within the constraints imposed by available evidence. This sudden windfall of new autobiographical material completely reconfigured my project by opening Thomas's life and adding unexpected dimensions to her writing.

When Dominique Aury handed me these documents, she explained that Édith Thomas's family had wanted her to have them, especially the diaries, since much of the material was too private to be given to the Archives. The papers were a loan, to be kept as long as I thought they could be useful.[25] A few weeks earlier, I had received a letter from Daniel Thomas, Édith's nephew and the legal heir of her estate, informing me that it was he who had given me permission to consult her dossier. After an exchange of letters, Daniel and his wife Andrée graciously invited me to spend a weekend with them at their home in St. Marcellin, in the lower Alps near Grenoble. As we were making arrangements for the visit, and after I succeeded in deciphering, with considerable difficulty, part of the first notebook, I wrote to tell them how moved I was by Édith's diaries. They immediately responded by telephone, with perplexity and dismay: "What diaries? We have never seen any diaries." It was not an easy moment. When I told Dominique Aury what had happened, she forgot or ignored what she had initially said: "The diaries were given to me, not to them," she declared. And sometime later: "I am not familiar with Édith's will. But she wanted me to have the diaries."

According to Daniel and Andrée Thomas, who have always been completely reliable in their information, it was Dominique Aury who initially sorted through Édith's papers after her death. She explained to the family that she had kept a few personal papers for herself, without specifying what they were, and sent on to them the letters she had found from well-known figures, including a long letter from Albert Camus and a letter from de Gaulle about the poem by Thomas written in 1943 that he had read in his speech from Algiers on the intellectual Resistance. When I spoke with Édith's friend and colleague Yvonne Lanhers, who had classified Édith's papers for the Archives, she also knew nothing about the existence of diaries or the other documents in Dominique's shopping bag.

It is probable that after Édith's sudden death in December 1970 of viral hepatitis, Dominique Aury went through Édith's papers in her apartment. Daniel and Andrée Thomas had recently suffered a family trauma and were unable to attend Édith's funeral. Dominique seems to have been the only person who knew about the diaries, in which she figured prominently, particularly between 1946 and 1947, the year of their love affair. Édith may have wanted her to have

Édith Thomas reading François La Colère (Louis Aragon), circa 1945.
Gift of Dominique Aury to the author.

them, or Dominique may have wanted to keep the diaries to protect Édith's privacy and her own. As far as the other, less private documents are concerned, in particular Édith's satiric diary and her political memoir, Dominique Aury might have had vague intentions of publishing them. Two decades after Édith's death, the gesture of giving these papers on loan to someone she knew for only an hour suggests both trust and impulsiveness. She seemed grateful that someone was going to work on the writings of the friend she loved and admired. "You would have liked her," she said, and gave me her favorite photo of Édith, which figures on this page.

From 1990 to 1995, I met with Dominique Aury two or three times each year to talk about Édith and her. Until the age of eighty-seven she worked part-time at her office at Gallimard, and we would lunch together at her favorite local Chinese restaurant. In 1996 she was too ill to see me but asked me to visit her on my next trip to Paris at the family home in Boissise-le-Bertrand, near Fontainebleau, a house that had been given to her by Jean Paulhan. When I saw her for the last time, in the summer of 1997, her son Philippe d'Argila and his wife were taking care of her. She hardly recognized me but lit up when I spoke of Édith; she wanted me physically close, as if Édith had been returned to her. Dominique Aury died during the night of April 26, 1998, at the age of ninety.

During one of our first conversations, I asked her if she and Édith had written to each other. After a brief hesitation, she replied that there were just a few postcards of no interest. However, when I met with Philippe d'Argila the summer after her death, he arrived at the café with two packets of letters. They contained letters addressed not to Dominique but to Édith: one packet, with forty-five letters, from Jean Paulhan; the other, with seventy-eight letters, from Dominique—both of which she must have taken from Édith's apartment, along with all the other papers, after her friend died. Forty-three of the forty-five letters from Paulhan to Édith Thomas, on literary, political, and occasionally personal questions, are dated from 1942 to 1952, the year they bitterly quarreled. The last two letters are dated December 1967, after their reconciliation.

Dominique's first letter to Édith, dated October 1946, is a passionate declaration of love. The others, while they no longer show the romantic intensity of the first one, begin "Mon petit chéri" and confirm the abiding tenderness that characterized their relationship over the years. Written from 1946 to 1970, the letters correspond to those times when either Édith or Dominique was away from Paris and not reachable by telephone, their favored mode of communication when they could not see each other. Except for Dominique's initial declaration of love, her letters give the impression of having been written rapidly, as if she were trying to continue the conversations with Édith she would have preferred. In one letter, she alludes to a photo of her friend in the *Figaro littéraire* that day: "not bad, but I prefer the one I stole from you," probably the photo she gave me. Initially, Philippe d'Argila found no letters from Édith to Dominique. During a subsequent visit to Paris he invited me to Boissise to explore for myself the many cartons of Dominique's correspondence. There I eventually identified a number of letters from Édith, most of them undated and without envelopes, scattered in various unlikely places.[26]

Among Édith Thomas's papers at the Archives nationales there is a curious single page, undated, a statement divided into three parts in which she examines the question of her name and her pseudonyms. The page, which she has typed, is not addressed to anyone in particular and has no apparent context. Its subtext, however, can be read as an argument about identity she had with Dominique Aury, who was attracted to pseudonyms in part as an expression of the multiple selves she felt she inhabited. "If you believe," Pauline Réage writes elsewhere, "as hundreds of millions of men do, that we live several lives, why not also believe that in each of our lives we are the meeting place for many souls?"[27] In contrast, Thomas insistently declares her single identity. She asserts that when she first started to write she thought of taking a pseudonym, since Édith Thomas was such a common name. But she decided against it, because she wanted to take full political responsibility for what she wrote and what she did. She specifies and explains the several names she took on in her writings for the Resistance—Auxois, Anne, Jean Le Guern, Brigitte—to demonstrate her conclusion: her pseudonyms were imposed on her from the outside for tactical reasons and never had any psychological implications in her life. A single name, in Thomas's argument, opposed to a plurality of names, becomes the sign of a single identity, whose authenticity is implied by what she refuses, "a kind of mask."[28]

The most remarkable aspect of Édith Thomas's statement is her need to make it. She often seemed to want to view her life through a narrative lens, as if she could confer the retrospective coherence of a story on the messiness of experience, magically conflating the living of life with the telling of it. In many of her works she returns to the theme of a quest for coherence in her life, by which she means consistency between her thoughts and her actions. Coherence, which she sometimes calls logic, reveals itself as the ethical counterpart of her psychological craving for wholeness. In the section "Claude" of Le Jeu d'échecs, she makes a clearly autobiographical allusion to the contrast between herself and Dominique Aury with respect to the need for coherence. Reflecting on her search for "an accord between what I believe, what I do, what I am," the narrator adds: "It seemed to me that Claude [Dominique] was led more by her instinct whereas I was led by what I call logic, which is perhaps just a pretentious word to disguise another instinct. In any case there was in me an effort at coherence that I did not find in Claude."[29]

We can follow a common autobiographical thread in Thomas's major biographical histories through her choice of subjects, figures whose lives she sees as passionate struggles to live in accordance with what they believed. That fidelity to their conscience brings together individuals as apparently diverse as Joan of Arc, Pauline Roland, Louis-Nathaniel Rossel, and Louise Michel. The quest for coherence continued to be one of Thomas's privileged values even as it became more paradoxical, most strikingly in the way she reinterpreted her own political choices through those of Rossel. During the Franco-Prussian War, Rossel was an officer in the French army. After France's defeat, he joined the Paris Commune and fought against the French military forces. He made that choice of action, like his initial choice, in the name of patriotism. Édith Thomas joined the Communist Party during the war and then resigned from it in 1949, in fidelity to the cause of social justice.

Thomas's belief in her own ethical coherence is called into question by the contradictions underlying *Le Témoin compromis*, as its title suggests. The story she tells of her itinerary from the 1930s to her resignation from the Communist Party in 1949 is filtered through conflicting accusations of betrayal, each with its own complexities, from the Party on the one hand and, on the other, from Jean Paulhan, who was deeply anticommunist. Paulhan was her friend and her adversary, her sometime literary mentor, and the lover of Dominique Aury. Whereas Thomas's relation to communism surfaces as a dominant theme of her memoir, the self-doubts raised by her quarrel with Paulhan remain for the most part submerged.

The writings of Édith Thomas testify both to her constant effort to be ethically of one piece and the ultimate impossibility of that oneness. A comparison of her writing in different genres about the same subject highlights the changes she made when memory came into play. The diary she kept for almost twenty years calls into question her belief in the possibility of a coherent life and a coherent identity. In its immediacy the diary does not favor an impulse to synthesize experience. Unlike the memoir, which constructs and justifies choices retrospectively as narrative, the diary notebooks consist for the most part of fragmentary and discontinuous entries. From 1931 to 1963 she wrote in her diary about matters both intimate and later historic, in the rawness of the moment. The diaries, in the context of Thomas's other autobiographical writings, confirm and complicate Dominique Aury's vividly divided image of what she found touching in her friend: Édith, she said, had "the naiveté of a young girl," but also "the fierceness of a great exiled lord."

Many people who knew her well, those who admired her and those who did not, described her as *entière*, an adjective with no exact equivalent in English but which can be translated as stubborn and uncompromising. The word also suggests a passion to be whole, of one piece. From the wealth of writings she left behind, with all their inconsistencies and contradictions, Édith Thomas emerges as *entière* in that sense, a singular witness and engaged participant in the convulsions of mid-twentieth-century France, struggling to find a way to live commensurate with her ardor for meaning.

1

A DAUGHTER OF THE REPUBLIC

The marriage in 1905 of Georges Thomas and Fernande Annoni was highly unconventional by the standards of the time. A well-bred girl was supposed to marry while she was still young and ignorant of the world, in contrast to her husband, who married only after he had completed his education and secured his social position, ensuring a gap of age and experience that would reinforce his authority over his wife. Against these norms of bourgeois society, Fernande at twenty-eight was not only "old" to be a bride, but three years older than her "young" husband who, moreover, was far from established in his profession. It was considered a humiliation for the family if a middle-class woman worked outside the home; according to a popular novel published in 1900, "le travail de la femme la déclasse" (working lowers a woman's social class).[1] When Fernande and Georges met, she was working as a schoolteacher, both because she needed to support herself and because she enjoyed the independence it provided, although she chose to stop working after she married. As a young girl she had wanted to be a doctor, but a medical career involved long and costly study and she was obliged to earn a living early in her life. For Georges's wealthy family, Fernande's age, her lack of fortune, and her position as a workingwoman made the match a misalliance. Adding to their consternation, Fernande seemed to be in fragile health; she had "no flesh on her" according to Georges's mother, who was convinced she was soon going to die. Although in the early years of her marriage she spent long periods resting on a chaise longue and may have had tuberculosis of the kidneys, she recovered and in fact lived to the age of eighty-two, surviving her husband by seventeen years.

The marriage of Georges and Fernande was built on mutual respect as well

Family photo, September 1910. *In front:* Édith and her mother, Fernande.
Standing in back, left to right: the housekeeper, Marie-Anne Cabon;
Édith's father, Georges; his sister, Berthe Deiss. Courtesy of Daniel Thomas.

as love. During their engagement, Georges wrote to his fiancée: "We don't always have the same opinions but I am grateful to you for having any. So many
young girls have none at all." Although Georges, steeped in the patriotic traditions of his family, was more conservative than his wife, his position was that of
a *libéral* in both its French meanings: a belief in laissez-faire economics but also
in a politics based on free expression. Like Fernande, Georges was committed to
French republican values of tolerance and individual rights. In spite of his opposition to socialism, he had great personal admiration for the socialist leader
Jean Jaurès. Édith Thomas and her brother, Gérard, were brought up, she writes,

"in a climate of great liberalism: the respect for other opinions, a concern for veracity. All of that was never expressed but taken for granted."

Like most of the French population, both Georges and Fernande were born Catholic. However, since they did not practice their religion, they decided on a civil wedding. "I do not think of myself as an iconoclast," Georges wrote his bride-to-be, "but I do not want people to oblige me to bow before idols." Their refusal to be married in the Church, a scandal in 1905, cost Georges Thomas his job as preceptor in a Catholic school.

Georges's commitment to French patriotic traditions, inherited from his family, was intensified by his military service as an officer in the Great War. A reserve officer after the war with a degree in agronomic engineering, he worked as a middle-level official in the Ministry of Agriculture, where he served as principal inspector for product control, a position well suited to the moral and intellectual rectitude that characterized both his rebellion and his sense of discipline. He was assigned to monitor claims for foods and fabrics, to ensure that they accurately represented the products' actual contents. Meticulous in his investigations, he did not hesitate to apply strict sanctions against anyone who failed to observe the law, even if the culprit happened to have connections in the administration or in influential political circles. Such disinterested behavior did not endear him to his superiors, nor did it help him climb the career ladder.[2]

The Great War, which broke out when Édith was five years old, deeply marked her childhood. In the Manichean climate of the time, the world was divided into allies who were good and their enemies who were bad. She remembered reading children's books in which the little Serbs were "nice" and the little Bulgarians "naughty." Writing to her father at the front, she wanted to know if it was all right for her and her brother to play with a little Swiss boy and a little Swedish girl who were "neutral." Her father didn't seem to understand the question and answered that if they liked the little Swiss boy and the little Swedish girl, there really was no reason not to play with them. In her memoir (1952) she notes: "France was pure and spotless, Germany was charged with every crime. I got rid of my most beautiful doll because it bore on its neck its label of origin, made in Germany."[3] Her performance of patriotism during the Great War almost exactly parallels that of another little middle-class French girl, Simone de Beauvoir, a year younger than Édith, who recalls in *Memoirs of a Dutiful Daughter:* "I embraced with passionate devotion the cause of the righteous. . . . I had already given proof of an exemplary patriotism by stomping on a celluloid doll 'made in Germany' which belonged by the way to my sister."[4]

Édith always felt distant from her father. After he returned from military service he seemed withdrawn and unable to relate to his children, absent even when he was there. In the 1930s when she discovered politics and the Communist

Party, her father symbolized for her the nationalist, right-wing values against which she was rebelling. That perception began to change as she let go of political stereotypes and could perceive her father's positive qualities. In August 1939, a time when she found herself financially dependent on him, she wrote in her diary: "Who could know from the outside, under his petit-bourgeois appearance and his old worn clothes, the immense generosity of my father, his total absence of vanity, the depth of his affection, his absolute devotion. Needing nothing material for himself beyond metro and bus fares but signing checks for you for thousands of francs without batting an eye, and then forgetting about it."[5] In 1940, the opposition of both her parents to Pétain's armistice with Nazi Germany was as immediate and unambiguous as her own. After Georges's death in 1942, her feeling that her father did not understand her shifted: she regretted that she had not understood him. Remorsefully she remembered a letter about some military question, which she had refused to type for him. She was antimilitarist at the time and rejected the veteran mentality she saw in her father. Her ambivalence is expressed in the inscription she wrote in her father's copy of her second novel, published in 1934: "To my father, from a daughter whose words are harsher than her thoughts. With affection, Édith."[6] Looking back on her family's values, she credits her father with having instilled in her the importance of the freedom to choose and to take responsibility for her choices.[7]

Whereas distance marked her relationship with her father, Édith always felt close to her mother. Thinking about Fernande as a young woman, she imagined her as a left-wing intellectual who subscribed to the literary *Cahiers de la quinzaine* and followed the lectures of the avant-garde director Jacques Copeau at the Vieux Colombier theater. Édith was an adored child, born after the death of a son who had strangled on the umbilical cord. Two years later her brother, Gérard, was born. They grew up in Montrouge, a comfortable suburb southwest of Paris, connected to the city by train and streetcar lines even then. The family lived in a two-story stone house surrounded by a walled garden, similar to many homes in the town today. Édith attended elementary school in the first and only school for girls that had just been built in Montrouge in 1910, the École Rabelais.

Édith's little brother became her closest childhood playmate and accomplice. A specific incident stood out in her memory. During the Great War, when their father came home from the front, he decided that it was time for the children to have their first theatrical experience. The play he chose for them was Corneille's seventeenth-century Roman tragedy, *Horace,* in which the warrior hero's exclusive devotion to the glory of Rome leads him to murder his sister, who has dared to blaspheme against Rome and her brother's patriotism. When Fernande objected that the children were much too young to understand *Horace,* Georges responded that they just had to read it before they saw it. Édith, who must have

Édith, eight years old, and her brother Gérard, age six, 1917.
Courtesy of Daniel Thomas.

been about seven years old, didn't read very well; five-year-old Gérard didn't read at all. She remembered the two of them sitting in their little wicker chairs, "me reading *Horace* and you listening to my groans and shaking your brown curls." Their mother's good sense finally won the day and the family went to see *Sleeping Beauty* instead. But for brother and sister *Horace* became part of their secret language: "It's like *Horace,* we would say to each other, and burst out laughing."

Growing up, Gérard was gentle and patient while Édith was rebellious, especially when aunts and uncles imposed rules on her that she did not understand or accept. As very young children, however, it was Édith who tended to be the serious, well-behaved child, "well brought up" as French tradition demanded. Gérard was the more difficult, and subject to fits of temper. One day when he had been particularly obstreperous, their mother told them that rather than have such naughty children, she was going to retire to a convent, and she proceeded to walk out to the garden, dressed in a brown bathrobe. The threat was not very credible, but Édith was terrified, already envisioning her mother in the robes of a nun. It was one of the few times Édith remembered being angry with her brother.

The family of Fernande Annoni had immigrated to France from Italy in the mid-nineteenth century. In 1870 they bought a house in Sainte-Aulde, a village on the Marne River surrounded by farmland rich in wheat, potatoes, corn, beets, and sunflowers. Fernande's childhood home became the house where the Thomas family spent summers throughout Édith's childhood and to which she continued to return during her adult life as well, a place of refuge and permanence. Although they grew up in Montrouge, Édith's written memories of her early years in "À mon frère" focus on vacations in Sainte-Aulde, a world of beauty and carefree country pleasures that brother and sister enjoyed together. She recalls nostalgically the games of cops and robbers—both of them always wanting to be robbers—chasing each other in the big garden on the side of the hill. There were fishing expeditions and swims, "avoiding the tall grasses which slithered between our legs like lizards," explorations of the river in their boat, bicycle trips and horseback riding, long walks in the woods where their father taught them about flowers and mushrooms. Playing in the gentle landscape, they often wished it would present more surprises, "opening the door to adventures we imagined beyond the hills. But beyond the hills there were still only fields and calm forests." Édith remembers her great-uncles: Uncle Fish, "because he went fishing" and Uncle Horse, "because he taught us horseback riding." Her Uncle Fish with his striped sweaters always looked as if he were coming out of an impressionist painting of the Seine. Uncle Horse in his leggings looked as if he were coming back from a ride in the forest. Her aunt would go off with her easel and a parasol to paint in the fields. Except for a few occasional companions from the village, usually too young or too old, brother and sister were the only children among the adults.

The other member of the household was Marie-Anne Cabon, who had become part of the family as a young single mother and Édith's wet nurse. At that time in France, it was still not uncommon even for middle-class families to have live-in help; such assistance was particularly important for Fernande since her health was often precarious. Marie-Anne lived her entire adult life with Édith's family. After the death of Georges in 1942, Fernande moved to the house at Sainte-Aulde, where she and Marie-Anne continued to live together until Marie-Anne died of emphysema in 1951. Born in Brittany, Marie-Anne is described by Thomas in terms that evoke cherished associations with that region in the French imagination: "silent and fierce and faithful, the kind of person who once she gives her loyalty never takes it back. I found in her sea-green eyes, which darkened sometimes like the sea in the wind, a world of passion and secret violence." Marie-Anne's love for the family, and the life she led within it, came to symbolize for Édith the equality of human beings: "I found my housekeeper quite superior to many people I know who might have considered her inferior because of her situation." Thanks to Marie-Anne, Édith decided, with more than a little sentimentality, she never had the feeling of belonging to a "class."[8]

Neither Édith nor Gérard was baptized. Their parents were not, however, anticlerical. They assumed that their children, when they were old enough to make such a choice, would embrace whatever religion, if any, suited them. Although both parents were nonbelievers, Édith's aunt practiced a Catholicism that was "part paganism and part bourgeois conformity."[9] During vacations, with her parents' approval, she accompanied her aunt to Mass, where Édith learned the Lord's Prayer and Hail Mary. When she went to bed, she regularly recited the prayers her aunt had taught her.

Listening to her mother and her aunt discuss religion, she could not decide who was right. The conflicting religious beliefs in the family became a source of confusion and anxiety. She remembered lying in the grass at the age of ten, looking at the sky and waiting for some manifestation from God, reasoning that if someone desired so much to believe in Him, He would send proof of His existence. She tried to fill her being with silence, and waited. When she opened her eyes again, nothing had changed; there was no revelation. She still saw the clouds in the summer sky, heard the sound of the grasshoppers, and felt the grass making her back itch. Perhaps her wish did not count as a prayer, she decided, or perhaps God did not listen to little girls of ten. She would try again when she was older.

After elementary school at the École Rabelais, Thomas attended the Lycée Victor Duruy in Paris, named after the minister of public education (1863–70) during the Second Empire whose efforts led to a movement that extended public secondary school education to girls. In contrast to the elementary schools, the official system of girls' high schools that came into being in 1880 was neither free nor obligatory. Its curriculum, less demanding than what was mandated for boys, led only to a certificate of secondary studies rather than to the nationally administered baccalaureate degree, the passport for higher education in France. The Catholic Church saw even this modest reform as an act of war against religion and a dangerous subversion of women's place in society.

The Lycée Victor Duruy opened its doors as a secular high school for girls in 1912, less than a decade before Édith received her certificate of elementary secondary studies there in 1920 when she was eleven years old. The school was housed on the boulevard des Invalides in the elegant buildings of the Ladies of the Sacred Heart, an educational community of nuns that had been obliged to close down after legislation in 1904 prohibited religious teaching orders. When the state acquired the property, including a spacious park, one part of the domain became the Rodin Museum and the other the Lycée Duruy. Beginning in 1918, it came to be known well beyond its district and even abroad as one of the best lycées for girls in France.[10] After the Great War and its catastrophic slaughter of French sons, many families, concerned that their daughters would remain unmarried, wanted assurance that at least they would be able to find employment and support themselves. The absence of young men also created a need for qualified women. To prepare girls for the baccalaureate and university entrance, Latin was introduced into their schools and classes in philosophy were strengthened.[11]

During the year in which she began her lycée studies in philosophy, at the age of sixteen, Édith Thomas resolved to become a Protestant. The decision was her first affirmation of independence both from her family and from her schooling, although she also claimed a remote Protestant ancestry, going back to the generation of her Alsatian great-grandparents on her father's side. When she spoke to her father about her plan, he characteristically made no objection, and in fact took her himself to the local Protestant minister. As a new Protestant, she was baptized, received communion, and began going to church services more or less regularly, activities she hoped would inspire a religious rebirth—which did not happen. Thinking about God as a hypothesis, she decided she was closer to believing that God existed rather than not, a weighing of possibilities that was far from the mystical passion she wanted to feel.

She identified strongly, however, with the dissident, protesting aspect of French Protestantism, embodied in the outlawed French Huguenots who endured persecution from the sixteenth century to the French Revolution for defending the primacy of individual conscience and resisting the oppressive authority of the Catholic Church. She was also attracted to the idea of interpreting the meanings of sacred texts by herself. She decided to reread the Bible, which she had already read in part, in its entirety this time. The idea of belonging to a minority appealed to her as well. In a Protestant country, she writes, she might very well have chosen to be a Catholic.[12]

It was only in 1924, a few months after Édith Thomas had completed her certificate of secondary studies, that a law was passed by the Ministry of Education instituting the same curriculum in public secondary schools for girls as for boys. After three years of study beyond the certificate, Édith Thomas received her baccalaureate diploma with honors in Latin, modern languages, and philosophy. Comments from her teachers at the Lycée Victor Duruy describe her as a serious student with an excellent mind, "full of the best kind of curiosity," who "deserves to succeed."[13] The baccalaureate examinations were given to boys and girls together. Writing many decades later to her nephew, she notes that in the examination room "an idiot named Thomas kicked my chair and said to me, 'Women belong at home.'" With obvious satisfaction she adds, "The said Thomas flunked his exam. I scored highest in my section."[14]

In November 1927, having completed a year of preparation at the Collège Sévigné, Édith Thomas began a three-year program of study at the École des Chartes, which is housed in the Faculty of Letters at the Sorbonne, in the heart of the Latin Quarter. The school was created to form an elite of young scholars trained in interpreting the manuscripts of French history, in particular the Middle Ages. With the successful defense of her thesis, "The Relations of Louis XI with Savoie," she was awarded the degree of *archiviste-paléographe,* a diploma whose name indicates the importance in French culture given to the task of deciphering historical handwritten documents. Her training at the school was to be invaluable for her future work as a historian, from her study of Joan of Arc to her biographies of nineteenth-century women, although at the time she did not seem to be aware of any special vocation to be either a *chartiste* or a historian. Nevertheless, much later, along with her frequent criticism of the world of archives and archivists as "dull and dusty," she occasionally conveyed its special excitement: "From my chartist studies I've kept a kind of inner thrill when I face a handwritten document, as if I expected each time to see emerging from it the most secret miracle of a live being."[15] And elsewhere: "It happens in fortunate moments that one actually feels the shock of history, a little like a believer feels the shock of God, or an artist the illumination of his art. And then, as it does for the believer or the artist, the feeling fades. And one falls again into the ordinariness of the everyday."[16] When the parents of Thomas's autobiographical narrator in *Le Champ libre* ask her why she wants to continue her studies, she answers that she wants to earn a living. However, the desire for financial independence is only one aspect of a desire she finds much harder to define. In earning a living she is seeking a way to earn her life, a hope that work will be able to confer worth and meaning to life in the world.

A diploma from the École des Chartes, a school that was relatively accessible to the small minority of women pursuing higher education at the time, would enable Édith to find work as a researcher and archivist. In contrast to other schools of higher learning in France, about half the students admitted to the École des Chartes were women, but the official explanation for their presence is difficult to reconcile with the school's claim to be a scientific institution whose aim was to teach the historical method. A brochure published by the school's director in 1927, the year Édith began her studies, conveys the assumptions and expectations of the time about educated women who worked in the world:

Since 1906, women have been admitted to the school and actively compete with men, as they do elsewhere. Whatever opinion one might have about the role of woman in society, and even if one regrets that she does not remain in the place assigned to her by nature, one cannot deny the aptitude of women for scientific study. Nor should one be surprised that they turn to the École des Chartes; for if their situation is such that they are obliged to work and earn a living, the functions of an archivist or a librarian are among those in which there is less mingling with the external world and which therefore is more appropriate for them and even, to a certain extent, reconcilable with the role of mother and housewife.

To justify this transgression of woman's natural vocation as wife and mother, the director of the École des Chartes finds it necessary to insist on the unworldliness of her future profession, which will therefore not pose an obstacle to the fulfillment of a feminine destiny should her fortune—in both senses of the word—improve. He further assumes that if a woman works, it is because she is has to work, either because her family has insufficient dowry to ensure an appropriate marriage or because there is insufficient income within the marriage. Since women do well at the École, he needs to find an explanation in accord with his idea of woman's nature: "Young girls in the École are classed in the first ranks. It is generally granted that they have better memory than men, and less initiative, which would explain their success in examinations."[17] In a newspaper interview with the man who was director of the school in 1934, shortly after Édith had completed her studies, he cites the advantage of "feminine qualities" for archival work, which does not prevent him from warning female applicants for admission that the best professional positions, given the economic crisis, will be offered to men. Fortunately, he adds, many women at the École des Chartes have hobbies.[18]

Édith soon discovered that philology and paleography, the daily bread of learning at the École des Chartes, did not excite her. Most of her fellow students were royalists, and the young women tended to be "budding nuns."[19] There was one bright exception, however. At the Collège Sévigné, the preparatory school for the École des Chartes, she met a spirited young woman who shared her rebellion against the confining ethos that dominated the thinking of most of her classmates. The two women studied for examinations together and were in the same graduating class, becoming soul mates and best friends. When Madeleine Guillon told her that she came from a Protestant family, Édith confided proudly that she too was Protestant.

Some years later, in February 1932, in a single ecstatic entry in her diary addressed directly to "mon amie," she explains that she has not yet spoken of her friend because she writes in her diary only when she is unhappy, and her friend, who remains unnamed, brings her a form of joy. Her writing has the earnestness of a shy adolescent's description of a first romance, although Édith carefully names this new emotion friendship rather than love—"No one is dearer to me than you are, since I do not know love"—and describes her "recognition" of Madeleine not as a sudden revelation but as a process that has taken place timidly and gradually, "inch by inch," with sometimes one and sometimes the other moving closer.[20] The ardor of Édith's description of her friendship with Madeleine is reminiscent of Simone de Beauvoir's passionate feelings for Zaza, although Édith was seventeen, several years older than Simone, when she made her discovery. It was expected that the emotional lives of young girls of the bourgeoisie in the early part of the century would be contained within the family unit. For Édith, both dutiful and rebellious like her contemporary Simone, the first encounter with strong feeling outside the prescribed bonds of family love had the exciting taste of something new, love as a free choice.

In metaphorical language Édith alludes to obstacles between her and Madeleine, which she insists strengthen their relationship: "Our friendship is not built on sand or on a gentle, even soil. We had to tear out the thorns which slowed our movement toward each other." In the single diary entry about Madeleine, Édith does not say what that uneven soil, or the thorns, might be. Some of the thorns may have come from Édith's prickly candor and—the same virtue and the same fault—her lack of tact. The two young women shared a passion for literature, and books were a favorite topic of conversation. Often but not always they shared the same tastes. As a woman in her eighties, long after Édith's death, Madeleine still remembered telling Édith that her favorite novelist was Victor Hugo and hearing Édith respond scornfully that his novels were "for concierges."[21] In the diary however, any suggestion of conflict between them is subordinated to Édith's exalted platonic ideal. All other friends she has known have been merely shadows, she tells her diary, dim reflections of what she and Madeleine have together. The intensity of their intimacy seemed to be a sign that it would endure.

2

ILLNESS AND PHANTOM LOVERS

Édith Thomas's first diary notebook, from 1931 to 1934, is a testimony of despair. Alternating between grief and rage, self-pity and self-flagellation, she struggles with an ordeal she does not narrate or even name. Dates have been branded into her brain: "January 23, 1930–October 1, 1931 and that flaming month of June when my downfall began." Although there is no evidence to determine with certainty exactly what those dates represent, we know that throughout her studies at the École des Chartes she felt constant pain in her knee and was haunted by the fear of becoming a cripple. Eventually the pain was diagnosed as tuberculosis of the bone, a disease that caused intense suffering for a number of years. It left her with a limp and a permanent sense of being physically and psychically maimed. Shortly after receiving her degree from the École des Chartes in March 1931, she was confined to bed for a period that lengthened from days to months to over a year. The pain flamed into a crisis that June, the date of what she calls her *déchéance*, her downfall. She was twenty-two years old. Her first diary entry, which follows two pages that have been ripped out, mourns the girlhood she has lost and the svelte, graceful woman she will never become: "You cannot be one of them. Turn to the wall."[1] She tries to fortify herself with the words of philosophers but finds no consolation for the loss of health, strength, and agility.

Contrasting her situation with that of the tuberculosis patients in Thomas Mann's *Magic Mountain* who can still lead at least a semblance of real life, she notes that "we," patients who suffer from tuberculosis of the bone, are deprived of space as well as time, reduced to a spatial notion "that oysters or clams might have, limited to the exact dimensions of our body, with the tiny prolongation constituted by the circle we can trace with our arm."[2] She invokes "Leysin-Berck,

Leysin-Berck" and then: "The pendulum oscillates slowly in my head, pressing down a little harder each time." Leysin, the sanatorium in the Swiss Alps, and Berck, the sanatorium in the north of France which specialized in treating tuberculosis of the bone, merge into a single image of agony and terror bearing down on her: "The hammer falls heavier each time, each time digging the nail in deeper."[3]

In fact, Édith did not stay at either sanatorium; the invocation of Leysin-Berck functions as a propitiatory incantation to ensure that she will not be sent away.[4] Traumatized physically and emotionally, she projects her terror onto "Leysin-Berck," one hyphenated word, one place. Her brother, Gérard, had stayed at Leysin a few years earlier when he was suffering from pulmonary tuberculosis. She may have visited him there and been horrified by the condition of patients with tuberculosis of the bone. The name Leysin became conflated with her nightmarish imagination of what Berck might be like. Treatment for tuberculosis did not always require a stay at the sanatorium, since a cure was not possible in any case. For families who could afford it, the strict conditions of hygiene and diet at a sanatorium could be replicated at home, under the supervision of an experienced doctor.[5] The Thomas family had both the financial means and the will to care for Édith at their house in Montrouge.

In her diary months later, still confined to bed, Édith turns her distress into an elegy for the young life she can no longer live. Looking at a lush bouquet of bright yellow narcissus flowers in her bedroom, she sees them saying, "No, no" with their yellow heads, rebelling against being cut off from the sun and the dew on their petals while the spring air enters through the open window. She asks them about her fate: "Narcissus, narcissus, will I rise again and return to the countryside, as alert and young as I was before?" "Will the one I love hold me naked in his arms?" "Will I run everywhere, all over the world, with my beloved?" "Will we stretch out our brown bodies in the sun?" "Will we tumble down the hill of lavender and rosemary, holding hands till we reach the sea?" With each question the flowers shake their heads, "No, no." And then she asks her final question: "Will I still bend over books and lose my life with each page, in a dust that has no name?" And this time the narcissus flowers do not reply.[6]

In other entries her despair becomes self-flagellation, as if by beating herself as she has been beaten she can take control of her ordeal. She writes her epitaph: "She was good for nothing," followed by "not even to" and a list of things, ordinary or extraordinary, that she has decided she will never be able to do: live like everyone else, hold a child or a husband in her arms, cook, clean house, write novels, and—an image that recurs in her work as a metaphor of physical grace—become a champion skier.[7]

Does suffering have a meaning? Writing in neat, outline form, like the good student she always was, she constructs her two possible answers: either suffering has its place in the universe, in an order established by God; or everything is disorder and chaos. If the first answer is correct, then she can either accept this law that cannot be understood, adore the mystery, and pray, or rebel against an incomprehensible God. But there is no conclusion that brings her alternatives together. Either way, whether or not the universe has a meaning, she finds no help for the question of what to do with her life. She tries to console herself with remembered words in English from Byron's *Manfred*, which she does not identify: "Old man, it is not so difficult to be dead." However, she is not an old man, and suicide seems more inviting than the prospect of accommodating herself to the limits and restrictions of her infirmity, which she equates with a reduced, mediocre life. She refuses to be one of the helpless people, the "horizontals" of Berck or Leysin. Nor can she accept limping her way through life.

Throughout this first notebook, the ragged edges of torn pages that appear intermittently mark a recurring decision to end her life, those moments when she feels death already inside her and the effort of living more than she can manage. At other moments, resisting that impulse, she finds in the act of writing her last and only hope, one day at a time. Recalling the first pages she wrote and tore up that summer of 1931 "in the paroxysm of my despair," she is determined to continue to write and to keep everything she has written, to "dig this suffering to the bottom, if by chance it has a bottom."[8]

Although Édith was cared for by loving parents, her long intimacy with pain and despair left her with a sense of utter aloneness. *La Mort de Marie* (1934), which takes that experience of desolation to its extreme of abandonment and death, won the prize for the best first novel of the year. The book's epigraph comes from Pascal, whose *Pensées*, written under the impact of his conversion to the most severe form of Christianity, became intimately threatening during her long ordeal: "Your principal maladies are pride which takes you away from God and concupiscence which attaches you to the world." Some critics of the novel were shocked by what they saw as its blasphemy, but the book is also deeply religious in its spiritual hunger.

Marie, a young woman of twenty-two who works for a lawyer in Paris, finds herself ill and is told by the doctor that she needs a month of complete rest. Since both her parents are dead, she takes refuge with her paternal grandmother, who lives in a small town and whom she has never met. The character of Madame Chanteau is clearly modeled on Édith Thomas's grandmother, whose son dared to marry against his mother's will. Madame Chanteau receives her granddaughter only out of obligation, with repugnance, seeing in her the daughter-in-law she has tenaciously detested. When Marie, feeling increasingly feverish, is diagnosed with pulmonary tuberculosis, her grandmother abandons her to the perfunctory care of the maid and no longer makes even the gesture of visiting her room. The pious old woman trembles in fear of omnipresent invisible germs and resents the intruder whom she cannot send away because people would talk. Moving between Marie and Madame Chanteau, the novel constructs two worlds and two levels of reality, each sealed from the other.

Upstairs, the young girl struggles with the end of a life she has barely lived. Battling the walls of pain and solitude that close in on her, she desperately seeks an opening to "physical life" and "freedom." She tries to believe in her soul but grieves for her body and the sexual ecstasy she has never known. Religious and erotic yearnings merge, inseparable. Echoing her diary, Édith evokes remembered physical joys, the enchantment of discovering flowers in the Alpine mountainside, bathing in ice-cold water, dancing in someone's arms and feeling her legs entwined with those of her partner. In a hallucination that seems to come from Édith's terrified fantasies of the sanatorium at Berck, Marie sees ghosts entering through the closed windows and door, phantoms of those who have been brutally disfigured by their illness. As her lungs bleed and the suffering in her body becomes intolerable, Marie's revolt is increasingly bitter. She cannot accept that she must die when she has lived so little. Her passion leaves no place for Christian resignation. When the local priest comes to visit, she refuses to see him, telling the maid she would rather believe that God does not exist than think Him an idiot. The next day, Marie is dead.

In the second part of the novel, Madame Chanteau is haunted by a strange remorse and the need to domesticate her granddaughter's death by bringing Marie into the family pantheon. Madame Chanteau's growing obsession is described in counterpoint to the town gossip about her odd behavior. In a vain attempt to recreate through a cult of memory the granddaughter she had no desire to understand while she was alive, she looks for people who have noticed Marie and have something to say about her. Outsiders are rare in the village, and Marie, she thinks to herself, was "someone people didn't know."[9] Her words echo the favorite phrase of the aunt of Marcel Proust's narrator, Tante Léonie, who is at the center of village life in Combray. In *La Mort de Marie* the name "Léonie" is given to the maid, a decidedly less sympathetic character. We are far from the charmed circle of Proust's childhood world and closer to the fallen world of François Mauriac's darkest novels, with no hope of grace. Madame Chanteau embarks on the unheard-of project of leaving her hometown and going to Paris to find out who her granddaughter really was. She learns nothing. Marie in death seems to take revenge, turning away and concealing herself. At the end, Madame Chanteau returns to her life of hypocrisy and denial.

In spite of its despairing subject, *La Mort de Marie* can be interpreted as an act of at least partial recovery and transcendence. When Marie falls ill with pulmonary tuberculosis, her rage, misery, and revolt echo the emotions of her creator. While Marie can only suffer and finally die, Édith Thomas, after the worst phase of her own illness had subsided, was able to write about Marie's fate and give it artistic form. It is striking, however, that even in this deeply pessimistic novel, as in her optimistic novel *Le Refus* (1936), her protagonist suffers from pulmonary tuberculosis rather than tuberculosis of the bone, allowing Thomas to avoid the traumatic physical and psychological aftermath of her own illness.

Thomas made no allusion in her diary to *La Mort de Marie*, either its conception or its elaboration, until it was accepted for publication. The active creation involved in fictional expression, however autobiographical, inhabits a different psychic space from the self-expression of the diary, which reproduces the conditions of day-to-day existence. "The diarist," writes Béatrice Didier, "does not have an active form of writing: he does not undertake a constructed, organized work; he allows himself to live and is content to allow this deposit, this sediment of successive hours, to accumulate."[10] In contrast, as a novelist, Édith Thomas brings forth an alternative world, in a framework of time she has invented, inhabited by the characters and situations of her creation.

La Mort de Marie is dedicated to Édith's best friend, Madeleine Guillon. Madeleine had spoken of Édith's manuscript to her employer at the Bibliothèque des archives, Georges Girard, who knew the president of the jury for the *Revue hebdomadaire*, the conservative journal that would be deciding on books to be considered for the annual prize of best first novel. Girard, who had lost his wife to tuberculosis, was deeply moved by the book. The jury included several well-known writers, among them Jean Giraudoux, François Mauriac, André Maurois, and Julien Green. They divided their choice between two manuscripts, the first novel of Raymond Oussilane, a brother of Mauriac (who abstained from voting), and *La Mort de Marie*. Ignoring one of the stipulations of its award, *La Revue hebdomadaire* decided not to serialize Édith Thomas's novel, out of fear of offending its respectable readers. Their decision echoes the response of the Librairie Plon, to whom she had sent her manuscript for publication on the strength of the prize. Plon rejected it for the same reason that *La Revue hebdomadaire* refused to serialize it: "Unfortunately, we are obliged to consider our clientele, and it is quite certain they would be rather seriously shocked by the entire first part of *La Mort de Marie*."[11] The novel was taken up by Éditions Gallimard, along with *L'Homme criminel,* her non-autobiographical second novel, less accomplished and less successful, which was published shortly thereafter.

In spite of the prize, Édith took to heart the few negative reviews she received, noting in her diary: "Where does one go to find self-confidence? In what country?"[12] An interviewer at the time found her "unpretentious, tiny, slender, modest, alarmed at being the target of journalists and photographers."[13] In her memoir she describes herself as stiff, on the defensive, unable to feel that the prize was worth the suffering she went through to write her book. Among the novel's mostly favorable reviews, Ramon Fernandez praised the novel as "remarkable in its atmosphere and the inner life of its characters," finding in Édith Thomas "a born novelist."[14] Another reviewer, Robert Brasillach, a literary critic for the right-wing *Action française,* writes condescendingly of *La Mort de Marie* and *L'Homme criminel:* "They correspond rather well to the idea one might have of a first novel and particularly a woman's novel. What we know is that they certainly don't succeed, and are no less certainly likable."[15] Whatever criticism one might have of the two novels, it is difficult to see how either one could fit into the stereotype of "a woman's novel." In her memoir, Thomas alludes to her "right-wing" prize and the "support" of literary critics of *Action française,* although the article by Brasillach hardly qualifies as support. She subsequently resolved to situate herself on the "extreme left," a move that took novelistic form two years later with the publication of *Le Refus.*[16]

Édith Thomas may have contracted tuberculosis from her brother Gérard, who experienced an early infection when he was eight years old. The onset of tuberculosis was frequently known to occur in childhood as an infection that appeared to be minor and remained undetected. It was generally much more contagious in children than in adults but could stay dormant for a number of years. Gérard's illness, which began on July 14, 1919, the date of the victory celebration after the end of the Great War, seemed unremarkable: pleurisy, mild fever, and a cough, successfully treated by rest and a stay in the Swiss mountains. After completing his studies at the Lycée Buffon, he was ready for the intensely competitive examinations that would pave the way for a diplomatic career. During the preparatory year of 1927, he was diagnosed with pulmonary tuberculosis. Abruptly he had to interrupt his studies and forego the grueling competition for entry into the École Normale Supérieure, where his closest friends were headed. After a stay at the sanatorium at Leysin, he returned to the family home in Montrouge and changed his career plans, deciding to pursue a less strenuous law degree that would still enable him to become a member of the bar.

Gérard seemed to have recovered when Édith became stricken with tuberculosis of the bone in 1931. Madeleine came regularly to the house in Montrouge to see her, and Gérard would drive her home in the family car. Gérard and Madeleine had first met some years earlier after she and Édith had become close friends. At the time, Madeleine was eighteen and Gérard "a kid of fifteen." Madeleine remembered that Édith, seeing her beloved brother and her most intimate friend getting to know and like each other, began to fantasize marriage between them. It seemed like a perfect arrangement to have Madeleine part of the family, a way for the three of them to be permanently together. Without Édith's awareness, Madeleine fell deeply in love with Gérard, who reciprocated her feelings. Engaged in 1933, they planned to marry a year later, but two days before their wedding, Gérard started spitting blood and felt it would be wrong to go through with the marriage. Madeleine would not hear of it and dragged him to the local minister, who tried to convince him to change his mind. Gérard decided to leave the final word to Madeleine's mother, to see whether she would still approve in spite of the state of his health. When they arrived at her home, she was having problems with the circulation in her leg—and did not open the door. Madeleine's reaction to the incident: "We narrowly escaped catastrophe."[17] Gérard Thomas and Madeleine Guillon were married in July 1934.

Not surprisingly, the idealized attachment among the three of them did not last, although one of Gérard's closest friends was struck by their extraordinary affinities: "We are three heads under the same hat," one of the three told him (he does not remember which).[18] But the two women's friendship had become far more ambivalent. Madeleine remembered an incident just after the engagement when Gérard canceled plans the two of them had made, refusing to give an explanation. Furious, she considered breaking the engagement. Many years later he revealed that he had promised to drive his sister, in despair about her knee, to see a faith healer. Édith, too embarrassed to let Madeleine see her having recourse to magical thinking, in flagrant contradiction to her sense of herself as an intellectual, had asked Gérard not to give away her secret to his fiancée. The incident makes clear that she trusted her brother, but not Madeleine, with the knowledge of her most carefully guarded vulnerabilities.

In Madeleine's telling, Édith's fantasy of their getting married meant she would keep her brother and her best friend always close to her, strengthening her ties to each one and theirs to her. However, when the marriage became a reality, it led to a bond within the couple far stronger than Édith had anticipated. Édith's imperious need to be loved left no emotional space for the new situation in which she found herself. What had been a strong connection of kinship between Madeleine and Édith almost broke when they became legally kin. In spite of the intense feeling recorded in the diary entry about her *amie* three years earlier, Édith's jealousy was directed entirely at Madeleine, as if she were the other woman who wanted to take away her beloved Gérard. The mutual distrust between the two women created a painful emotional triangle that continued over the years. Although Édith remained close to her brother and would often visit him and his wife, she never recovered the intimacy of her earlier relationship with Madeleine.

Édith, Gérard, and Madeleine, 1934.
Courtesy of Daniel Thomas.

The narrative of their three-way relationship finds no place in Édith's diaries. However, she does record, in the 1930s and to a lesser extent in the years that followed, her ambivalent infatuation with various men in turn, playing out the contradictory impulses between autonomy and obsessive love that dominated her emotional life. A diary entry of passionate intensity is usually undercut by a subsequent entry, the next week or even the next day. None of these four or five relationships, which tend to blur into each other, became sexual, although most of them seem to have been lived in her social life as something like friendship. Each phantom lover, described with little specifying detail even as he is crystallized into the obscure object of her desire, seems not quite real. The single exception is Stefan, the militant journalist she met in 1938, who became an emblem of impossible love. He too, however, was most real in the extraordinary power he exerted on her imagination.

Thomas's diaries sometimes incorporate a letter to the phantom lover with whom she was romantically obsessed at the moment. The letters are addressed to a shifting "you," their identity indicated only by initials if at all. She follows or precedes her declaration of passion with a preparation for failure, her self-deprecating analysis of all the reasons why the man in question will not reciprocate her feelings. It becomes apparent that the letters most often are not drafts of actual letters, but rather solitary exercises of expression and exorcism that are intended to be read only by herself. "I don't know if you will respond," she writes in one letter; "it's unlikely since I'm not going to send you this epistle."[19] In *Le Jeu d'échecs,* she was able to transpose the idea of the imaginary letter into an effective esthetic device. Her novel takes the form of a long letter to Stevan, a character based in part on Stefan, her phantom lover before and during the war years.

The issue of whether or not to send a letter to her phantom lover of the moment continued even after Édith's affair with Dominique, and made its way into one of the tales in *Eve and the Others.* In "Joseph and Mrs. Putiphar," the wife of Putiphar, a professor of differential calculus, finds herself in love with Joseph, his young disciple who has come to lodge with them. She is all too aware that she is thirty-five years old, old enough to be his mother. The story is based on Thomas's infatuation with a historian friend when she was thirty-nine years old—and he was all of five years younger. In her diary account as well as in the story, she finally decides to write him a letter declaring her feelings, fully convinced that he will find her ridiculous. Joseph says nothing and they continue as before, enacting an emblematically autobiographical scene.

Édith Thomas's diaries convey the impression that the alien role of the feminine became an issue only after her illness—after the fall—although her sense of self before her illness remains unfocused. She offers an alternative understanding in *Le Jeu d'échecs,* in which the narrator, Aude, sees her awakening to femininity as a "crack" in her identity and dates that self-division to early and uncertain beginnings, perhaps in childhood, perhaps in adolescence. In her imaginary letter to Stevan, Aude explains: "I've never known how to play the role expected of a woman. There's always been something distorted and I don't know from when I should date the crack." The crack of which she speaks, thematized in Thomas's novel, is played out in her diaries, where the self-consciousness of an intellectual, who asserts control by her ability to observe what she feels, is difficult to distinguish from the self-consciousness of an adolescent (although she is in her twenties), whose watching self paralyzes her ability to respond spontaneously.

In the novel, she recounts two anecdotes that are autobiographically credible both in their congruence with what we know about Édith and in the way their indelible imprint on her memory belies their apparent insignificance. The narrator remembers a day in childhood when a friend of her parents said to her, "You are going to be a naval officer"—at a time, of course, when such a career was impossible for a woman. In adolescence she remembers one of her cousins, a hospital intern, saying to her, "Why don't you go to medical school?" When she says to him, "I thought you were horrified by women doctors," he replies, "But I forget when I talk to you that you're a woman." She does not know whether she is supposed to be flattered by that remark and tells him so. He laughs: "Take it as you like," he says. In hindsight she concludes that she never accepted being a woman, or rather, that she always resisted the idea of womanhood expected of her.[20]

In her diary, Édith's first evocation of a phantom lover, while she was still bedridden, is not only a completely invented creation but a comic one as well. Musing on the vagaries of names and dates, she gives this creature a name she dislikes, Philippe, and brings him into existence on Bastille Day, 1932. She imagines Philippe "stronger in skiing than in brains," a description radically at odds with the real phantom lovers who succeed him. Convalescing a year later, she still dreams of a stud of a lover who would overwhelm her: "He will take me in his arms, hold me tight until it hurts, until I could die of it. I will be no more than his thing, his drink and his nourishment." Her fantasy exaltation is subverted by the comic evocation that immediately precedes it, a reversal of familiar male stereotypes of the mindless female: "I don't want a myopic intellectual but a big, idiot male with gleaming skin who talks only of horses, dogs, and cars."[21]

Usually, however, her diaries paint a more complicated picture, showing her repeated struggles with a cultural norm of femininity she could neither accept nor dismiss. She seems to have had little awareness of her body as sexual until she became ill and convinced that she was not desirable. After that trauma, when she began to see herself as an object of male judgment, her verdict on herself was always damning. She would make a list of all the possible ways her phantom lover might respond to her, most of them versions of direct or indirect rejection that proved to be self-fulfilling.

The few explicit allusions to one of Édith's early phantom loves point to a particularly poor choice, a friend of her brother whom I will call Monsieur C., who had little use for intellectual women. In my interview with him two decades after she died, he described her as "breathtakingly clumsy in her behavior with men for whom she had romantic feelings. Out of pride, she never wanted nor was able to resort to the usual techniques of flirtatiousness. Instead of trying to flatter masculine vanity, she gave the impression of wanting to dominate the man who inspired her feelings of affection by impressing on him her intelligence and her strong personality. Her femininity was always subordinated to her pride. She didn't understand the strategy of seducing by a certain submissiveness."[22]

Édith was aware of the persona she projected and its contradiction with the painful vulnerability she tried to hide: "Cold, haughty, and proud, who can believe in this plea for tenderness?" In relation to another phantom lover, she writes in her diary: "I wish he would read my books and know that I'm not a bluestocking but a little girl frantic with the desire for completeness [*plénitude*]."[23] In *Sept-Sorts* (Seven-Fates), her study of the mediocre, monotonous life of a French village, she projects those longings onto her protagonist, the only vibrant character in the novel. Lucie, who works with her mother in the local bakery, delivering bread in her truck, is spirited and independent. But her desire for a full life becomes embodied in René, a young man in the village whose presence she comes to depend on, wanting "the weakness of loving him."[24] He finally rejects her for a woman whose dowry is more substantial.

Although Édith curses her pride, she also relies on it as her best protection, her armor. There are occasional moments when she tries to play the game, spending days at a time preoccupied with clothes, makeup, and hairdressers. Even as she tries on the scripted feminine role, she rails against men and what she is doing to please them: "It's a question of making oneself the most stupid and vain object possible. Shining eyes and a hollow brain, a mouth ready to smile at empty thoughts—but which give them the illusion of being superior." She wants to let go of the stiffness, the insolence, the absence of spontaneity that men reproach in her but at the same time does not want to abandon herself to what she calls "the softness of women" (*la mollesse des femmes*). Desperately she tries to invent a "kind of virility that would not exclude a certain gentleness" but remains stuck in an uncomfortable tension in which she finds herself both too assertive and too withholding.[25]

That struggle is mirrored in the cultural contradiction imposed on women between intellect and the desire for passion. In a review of Édith Thomas's autobiographical novel *Le Champ libre*, a critic writes: "An extravagant intellectualism and excessive pedantry invade this arrogant little creature who would be no worse than anyone else if she were willing to remember for a moment that love bears a very distant relation to metaphysics. A young female student who thinks about Kant and Spinoza and speaks about individuality and her courses when a boy wants to kiss her will most probably be disappointed in life."[26] Édith Thomas's situation, as an intellectual and a woman alone, left her vulnerable to that kind of misogyny, in spite of the friendship and admiration of a number of men as well as women. Whatever one's criticism of Jean-Paul Sartre in relation to Simone de Beauvoir, it is also true that his respect for her intellect served as a shield against the devastating impact of such judgments.

The dynamics of pride and vulnerability, along with the play of presence and absence, were complicated further by confusions of sentiment and desire. After confiding a secret passion to her diary, she would question the next day whether what she feels has anything to do with love, this conflict between "the intellectual pride of what I am and the desire of my body, between an ascetic singularity that is killing me and my sexual curiosity. I don't want to need anyone and no one needs tenderness and caresses more than I do."[27] She defines her singularity in relation to an ascetic autonomy she wants not only to project but also to embody, against the emotional and sexual desires that remind her of her vulnerability.

She also vacillates between wanting only true love and wanting to play the masculine role in the ritual of courtship. Although she yearns for love, "the great encounter between two beings who are equal and who love each other tenderly, in soul, heart, and body"; at other moments, waiting for her phantom lover to make his move, she fantasizes a masculine role in which she would say: "I'd like to go out with you from time to time in the evening. Would you like that? Or more directly: I've never had a lover. Would you like to be the first?" At least, she decides, such assertiveness would lead to mere "physical gymnastics" and she would not suffer. In the intimacy of her diary, the self in distress provokes an ironic alter ego that mocks her feelings. Brutally she proclaims: "O young—or old— maids. An unsatisfied genital organ is indeed a cumbersome piece of furniture!"[28]

Édith was always aware that her love of the moment, in one form or another, "is perhaps only the ghost created by my reveries." A poem she writes in her diary metaphorically distills that reflection:

L'homme de lune est venu chez moi.
Un peu de sang est resté sur le drap
. . . .

O homme de lune, mon amant
cristal où se mirent les rêves
que j'appelle de ton nom.

[The moon man came to see me
A little blood remained on the sheet
. . . .

O moon man, my lover
crystal which mirrors the dreams
that I call by your name.][29]

In different incarnations there is always one man, one fantasy love. Thinking obsessively about G., she knows that her infatuation depends on his not being there, so she can invent him. At moments, she steps back from the Sturm und Drang, determined to get some distance on herself. Angry to be suffering for a man she probably does not even like, she wonders: "Are these stupid little stories going to begin again? Mad pages? Finely wrought despair? *Merde.*"[30]

Toward the end of her first diary notebook, invoking the God in whom she cannot believe, Édith gives voice to a quest that will remain constant: "If I have to live always torn between my man's brain, my woman's body, and my old person's knee, at least let it be that my life is not completely sterile and that one day, finally, there will be harmony. Amen."[31]

3

"TO REDISCOVER A REASON TO LIVE"

On February 6, 1934, the *service de presse* took place at Gallimard for Édith Thomas's first two novels, *La Mort de Marie* and *L'Homme criminel*. In a ritual that is still customary at major French publishing houses, the author is given a generous number of books to sign, which are then sent to review journalists and other public personalities as well as to friends.

Another event on that same date marked a turning point in French history. During the evening of February 6, a number of extreme right-wing leagues which had been proliferating and growing stronger since the beginning of the decade—Action Française, the Camelots du Roi, Croix de Feu, and the Jeunesses Patriotes were among the most important groups—summoned their militant followers to a demonstration at the place de la Concorde. They converged in front of the Chamber of Deputies, which they saw as a symbol of the corruption and ineffectiveness of the current parliamentary regime and of democracy in general. At the end of a night of clashes between demonstrators and police, fifteen people were killed and two thousand wounded. Historians now interpret the riots as a violent protest against the status quo rather than an organized movement to take power. But for the left, a year after Hitler had been elected chancellor of the German Reich, it was a wake-up call to the threat of fascism taking over in France. Left-wing parties and organizations began to join ranks, temporarily overcoming the divisions that weakened them. Their efforts to mobilize for a program of united action to oppose fascism culminated in the election of the Popular Front government in May 1936.

At the Thomas family home in Montrouge, Gérard's closest friends from his lycée years, Jean Luc, Julien Kravtchenko, and Jacques Soustelle, often came to visit and engaged in passionate discussions of politics, in which Édith was often included. The three friends attended the prestigious École Normale Supérieure, where Gérard had hoped, until his bout with tuberculosis, to be a student with them. Their talk was of revolution; like so many other intellectuals on the left, they found the idea of merely reforming the regime hopelessly inadequate. The Third Republic's parliamentary government, mired in corruption and escalating scandals, seemed unable to control the worsening economic crisis and unwilling to change unjust institutions.

Among the *normalien* group at the Thomas home, the most brilliant was Jacques Soustelle, who had begun his advanced studies at the age of seventeen and received his *agrégation* in philosophy at the age of twenty.[1] In 1934 his article in the journal *Spartacus,* directly inspired by the riots of February, became a point of reference. It was titled "General rehearsal for fascism. To those who say: 'Fascism is not possible in France.'" At the time, Soustelle was a Marxist close to the Communist Party. In the leftist spirit of those years, he was also fiercely antimilitarist. His eloquence and intense commitment exerted a strong influence on Édith. Julien Kravtchenko remembered Soustelle saying to them: "If you are young, intelligent, and generous, you can only be a revolutionary."[2]

In her memoir Édith records the convergence of private and public urgencies that had led her first to writing and then to communism. She had written *La Mort de Marie* under the pressure of despair, seeking release by recreating her own suffering in a novel about loneliness and death. The revolt against God had left her with a need to move beyond her singular experience to a collective social vision she could believe in: "Because I rebelled against my own destiny, I took the side of those who rebelled against their destiny. Instead of retiring into my shell, incessantly brooding on my own reasons to despair, I could join the suffering of others. I needed to rediscover a reason to live on earth, without any imaginary compensation in an afterlife. That could only be with other people. But how would I find them?"[3] The rhetoric of her rebellion, however self-dramatizing, highlights her need for a narrative of meaning beyond the solitary self, which she found for many years, however ambivalently, in communism. As a child, her only image of communism had been the poster of a hairy Bolshevik with a knife between his teeth. But in her memoir she also recalls her instinctive hostility to the pervasive right-wing Catholic ethos of the Action Française at the École des Chartes, her sense even then of being alone and different. Struck down by illness, searching for a way out of the prison of self, she could not have failed to be impressed by the messianic dimension as well as the brilliance of the discussions among the *normalien* comrades visiting her brother in Montrouge.

After the February riots in 1934, an increasing number of French intellectuals turned to communism as the best hope in their antifascist struggle, either joining the Party or supporting its policies as fellow travelers, *compagnons de route.* The attraction of communism in France was based in large part on the perception that the theory and practice of Leninist Bolshevism was entirely compatible with a national tradition that considered revolutionary violence in the name of social justice a sacred obligation. That tradition was born with the nation itself, in the French Revolution of 1789, and continued to manifest itself through the uprisings of 1848 and the Paris Commune of 1871. The French Communist Party, founded in 1920, developed out of diverse militant workers' movements of the nineteenth and early twentieth centuries. From the beginning it was a legal party, and by 1936 it had achieved significant power in the Chamber of Deputies, receiving almost 15 percent of the votes cast. Against the Socialists, whom they considered a party of compromise, the Communists presented themselves as the only truly revolutionary force fighting for the working class in particular and the disadvantaged in general. Many leftist intellectuals embraced communism in spite of their unease with the realities of Stalinism and the Soviet Union. For idealists especially, the promise of a brighter future, *les lendemains qui chantent,* proved stronger than observable realities.[4]

Through her leftist friends, Édith became intrigued by the Association des écrivains et artistes révolutionnaires (AEAR), a group founded in 1932 by Paul Vaillant-Couturier, then editor of the Communist Party daily newspaper *L'Humanité,* and Louis Aragon, the celebrated French poet, formerly a surrealist, who was already on his way to anointing himself spokesman for writers in the Party. Vaillant-Couturier and Aragon had also become directors of the Association's monthly journal *Commune,* which included many prominent writers of the time, among them André Gide, on its editorial committee. Édith's friend Jean Luc suggested that she be introduced to Aragon and arranged a meeting for the three of them at the Closerie des Lilas near the Luxembourg gardens. Looking back in 1952 at that encounter, Thomas describes her first impression of Aragon: "I watched Aragon eat his croissants. His sharp little white teeth, which were tearing them to shreds, made me think of a wolf, or a fox, some carnivorous animal. I had to make an effort to talk to him, he seemed so foreign to me. No, now that he had finished eating his croissants, he didn't remind me of a fox. A snake, rather. Not at all a cat or a dog, for example, with which one could have a comfortable relationship."[5] Her memory of that impression is surely shaped retrospectively by her later judgment of him. In her diary a couple of years after that first meeting, she still included Aragon among a short list of mentors, all of them politically committed male writers who, she felt, could "save" her.

When Aragon asked her to write an article for *Commune,* assuring her that the AEAR had embarked on a policy of openness toward "bourgeois" writers, she replied that she was not sure she was capable of writing the article he wanted from her. Instead, she wrote to the editors, questioning whether the AEAR should accept her as a member, a letter that appeared as the lead entry of the May 1934 issue, along with Vaillant-Couturier's response in the affirmative.

Her letter begins with a shift from "I" to "they," an attempt to see herself and the class to which she belongs from a militant's point of view. Situating herself among those writers or artists who are bourgeois by birth and who profit from all the advantages of capitalist society, she affirms that the only motives powerful enough to make them emerge from their social apathy are "sentimental" in nature: the desire not to be on the side of those who strive to keep their wealth by fighting those who are hungry. Like all those on the left in 1934, they still consider themselves pacifists, convinced that "the capitalist regime can lead only to war." She admits that they don't know Marxism very well and they abhor "churches, labels, and sacred texts," feeling attached above all to "the right to be mistaken and to contradict themselves." In those conditions, she asks, since "a revolutionary association is not an enterprise for personal salvation, can it admit them without becoming rotten?"

Vaillant-Couturier begins his response by reassuring her: "Without any doubt, comrade, you can join the AEAR," and he indulgently concedes that this "sentimentalism" is not so bad, that in fact "it is the most usual path for a bourgeois intellectual on the way toward socialism." He promises that she will find in Marxism "not a church or a label" but a scientific method and a dialectical vision she still partially lacks, which will lead her to "the true path of struggle—without compromise—for socialist civilization, the way of Marxism-Leninism."[6]

Although Thomas notes in her memoir that if she finds the letter she will include it in her narrative as a "supporting document," this published exchange is not part of Le Témoin compromis; nor is it included in the extensive dossier of articles she kept, now housed at the Archives nationales. It is possible that she simply lost the letter. However, one can imagine that reading her letter in 1952, after her break with the Party, she felt embarrassed by the tone of what she had written, its mixture of provocation and the desire to be accepted nevertheless, which did not readily fit into the political narrative she had constructed of her relationship with the Communist Party. Her letter to Vaillant-Couturier evokes a rebellious and confused daughter determined to stand up to her stern father while still hoping to please him. Their exchange of letters is certainly not a dialogue between equals.

On January 1, 1934, Édith Thomas confided in her diary: "I think I am a revolutionary"—her first allusion, on any level, to politics. She did not return to the subject until four months later, just about the time the letter to Commune

Édith Thomas, 1934. Courtesy of Daniel Thomas.

was published. Not surprisingly, the ambivalence revealed in her diary is far more candid than what she was able to say in her public statement. On May 1, the day that marks Labor Day in France as it does in most other countries, she seems to have participated for the first time in a Party demonstration at the Renault auto factory, distributing tracts to workers. Noting that her "three companions play the game, sincerely, faithfully," she wonders about her own role: "I'm not yet at the point of making propaganda for a promised land that—I feel it clearly—will destroy me. And yet, I cannot be against it, I'd like to be for it. I'm ashamed not to be for it more. Marx . . . Engels . . . Lenin . . . Stalin . . . the Party . . . I collide with their hardness, their narrowness, their lack of critical thinking."[7]

A month later, she was asked to participate in a public meeting of the AEAR organized around the theme "For whom do you write?" The literary critic Ramon Fernandez, vacillating at the time in his political allegiance, was in charge of rallying speakers who were not members, chosen from all points of the political spectrum. In Édith Thomas's presentation, transcribed in full in her memoir, she first examines the question's agenda, seeing it as a means for the AEAR to count those who are with them and those who are against them. Using herself as an example, she sets out to blur that line of demarcation, explaining that when she started to write, it was out of "biological necessity." When she began her first novel, she had no idea whether it would be published, but had to write because she could not do otherwise. Beyond what she calls her "graphomania," she writes for those who are likely to read her, in other words, individuals of the bourgeoisie, who tend to think of themselves as individuals rather than as a class. During the time she is writing, she affirms, the only reality that counts is the thread that leads her characters as well as herself in unpredictable directions, without any other conscious intention. She finds herself, therefore, far removed from the possibility of making propaganda for any cause, whatever it might be.

From her personal writing practice, she argues that *la littérature à thèse* "misunderstands the essential process of esthetic creation, limiting it to an a priori reasoning" which the novel then "simply develops and sustains by examples." Recognizing the luxury implied by this individualist way of thinking, she points out as a paradox that it is precisely the individualism of her bourgeois background that leads her to question its values and its consequences. Her personal argument is a general one as well. She insists on the essential role of bourgeois writers, who could be sympathetic to the goals of revolutionary struggle if they were not "bludgeoned" with Marxist-Leninist propaganda. France's long tradition of critical thinking, she asserts, must be brought to bear on the self-questioning of the bourgeoisie.

Following Édith Thomas's talk, Pierre Drieu la Rochelle gave a presentation, and then Aragon. Drieu, who had returned from a week in Berlin in 1933 impressed by Hitler's "socialism," was about to publish *Fascist Socialism* with Gallimard. After Drieu's speech, Aragon responded to his remarks in a tirade of contempt, soon joined in by most of the others in the room. In spite of herself, Thomas found her sympathies going to the underdog, Drieu, "who had faced his adversaries alone," and not to Aragon and the others "who crushed him so easily." In the overheated room, with Drieu's adversaries booing and venting their rage, she felt displaced: "We were not yet on the barricades. It seemed to me that intellectual battle should be accompanied by a little more elegance."[8] The diary of another woman attending that meeting, Maria Van Rysselberghe, the friend of André Gide known as *la petite dame,* echoes Thomas's reaction: "Suddenly," she writes, "as if carried away by his advantage, Aragon became so rude, so basely insulting, that one wanted to take Drieu's side."[9]

Édith Thomas's real political awakening happened that September when she decided to take what was supposed to be a tourist trip to Algeria. She responded to the seductive beauty of Algiers, the forests of Kabylia, the ruins of Tlemcen, the oases of Biskra. What made the most forceful impression on her, however, was the visceral discovery of colonial exploitation. France had ruled Algeria as part of its own territory since 1830 on the basis of a politics of assimilation, which in itself was based on a profound misunderstanding that continued throughout the history of French Algeria. The metropolitan French understood assimilation to mean that the Arabs of Algeria should be part of French civilization, although there was little grasp of the contradictions involved in such a formula. For the French and the naturalized Europeans (the *pieds noirs*) who lived in Algeria as French citizens, the policy of assimilation meant only a recognition of their own rights. The few attempts by various French governments at modest reforms of colonial injustice were abandoned after violent opposition on the part of *pied noir* pressure groups who refused any change. As a result, Muslims continued to be French subjects but not French citizens. By the mid-1930s, no more than 2,500 Muslims had succeeded in becoming French citizens; most of the indigenous populations lived in conditions of dismal poverty and oppression.[10]

In the village of Amouchas, the mistress of a farm pointed out to Édith Thomas "her" Kabyle women squatting in a hovel, weaving blankets in gray, beige, white, and brown: "Look at them, they make these crude designs, they live like animals," she said, as if the women had chosen the miserable conditions she imposed on them. Thomas writes of colonists with similar attitudes: "In their own country these people would be despised—rightfully—as vulgar and vain petits bourgeois. Here they think they're at the top of the scale of status and civilization and have nothing but contempt for the others." At the post office, a Frenchman shoved his way to the front of the line where Arabs had been waiting, taking it for granted it was his right to do so. The everyday spectacle of injustice overwhelmed Thomas with shame. At Bougie (Bejaïa), she saw a monument for the Great War and began a list in her diary of the Arabic names it inscribed: Belkacem and Mohamed and Mebarek and countless others who "died for France."[11]

Yet it was right after her return from Algeria that she submitted her resignation to the AEAR, fully aware of the apparently "crazy" contradiction between her deepening anticolonialist and anticapitalist convictions and her decision to leave the revolutionary organization she had joined only a few months earlier. As she put it much later, she saw only a distant relationship between the abuse hurled at Drieu and the exploitation of indigenous Algerians. Her letter of resignation shows much greater confidence than her initial letter asking to join. She explains that she has found it impossible and, moreover, of no importance, even from a revolutionary point of view, to adhere to an orthodoxy. With evident pleasure in her provocation she concludes: "You will certainly judge as I do that it is useless to encumber the AEAR with an element that is so resolutely anarchic and petit bourgeois, whatever my sympathy for your cause."[12]

Between 1934 and 1936 Édith Thomas's diary spells out her vacillations between belief and radical skepticism toward both the Communist Party and Marxist theory. Sometimes she writes like a true believer, finding in communism her own salvation and that of humankind, a discovery elaborated in a number of earnest, sentimental poems as well as in prose. At other times, Marxism is just "a theory like any other" that happens to be seductive to intellectuals. Even then, she prefers to stand with the Marxists simply because in a struggle where her own privileges are at stake, she would rather be on the other side. Although she did not become a member of the Party during the 1930s, emotionally she joined and quit and joined again countless times.

After the riots of 1934, socialists and communists tentatively began to converge in their common opposition to fascism. On Bastille Day 1935 there was a massive demonstration at which members of all the leftist and centrist parties—Communists, Socialists, and liberals—agreed on common action to defend democracy and "give bread to the workers, work to the youth, and peace to the world." Elections during the week of April 26 to May 3, 1936, consecrated the victory of the Popular Front, headed by the Socialist Leon Blum. Although the Communists refused Blum's offer to participate in the government, they offered him conditional support. Within the first three months of the Popular Front, legislation was passed for two-week paid vacations, a forty-hour workweek, and compulsory collective bargaining for labor disputes.

During that brief, hopeful period, Édith Thomas began a new career in journalism, contributing articles to the major progressive journals of the time, including *Commune, Regards,* and *Europe.* In November 1935 she became part of the team that inaugurated *Vendredi,* a weekly political and literary journal named after Daniel Defoe's "good savage" Friday, with echoes of Rousseau as well. The journal, which had a remarkable success in its first year, brought together all the tendencies of the Popular Front and in particular many leftists like Thomas who were not members of the Communist Party. Among Thomas's investigatory articles for *Vendredi* was a series about the exploitative conditions of women in factories and other low-paying jobs, especially the jobs available to working mothers. In those articles social protest merged with what we would now call a feminist critique.

By 1936 Thomas had made the leap of faith and considered herself a fellow traveler, convinced that whatever her reservations about Party methods, the communist struggle was the only effective way to create a human future. She records her passage to that faith in an extended and eloquent diary entry in May, an intensely personal account that she also sees as representing the collective change of her generation. Her diary entry was published just over a year later as an article titled "Passage" in *Europe,* with almost no modifications. "We suffered from living in closed rooms," she writes. "We knocked our heads in vain against the wall, sometimes as a game, sometimes in despair. . . . And then, abruptly, through some rift—but the rift is different for each one of us—the external

world invaded. It broke the walls. It shattered the windows. . . . We found ourselves stunned, as if we had fallen from another planet. Into the midst of other
people. . . . We had nothing to offer except our good will, our immense will that
life should belong to everyone."[13] For Thomas, writing in the year of victory for
the Popular Front, that will was part of a historical continuum, the affirmation
of human dignity that had been embodied by different groups in different historical periods: by early Christians, by believers in the Reformation, by the revolutionaries of 1793.[14]

Thomas completed her fourth novel in the glow of belief. Once she began *Le
Refus*, the most political of her novels, she briefly decided that keeping a diary
had become superfluous: "The act of writing finds its goal and reward in itself. . . . Is that the criterion for 'vocation'? It doesn't matter. I recognize the approach of a form of joy." And a few months later: "I'm putting this notebook
aside. Brigitte [the protagonist] is my justification; she lives for me."[15] In *Le Refus* Thomas returns to her years of illness, the source of *La Mort de Marie*, but
from a completely different perspective. The narrative begins with Brigitte
Chevance on the train returning home from the sanatorium at Leysin with her
health restored, in wonderment at being alive and present in the world after living for so long in the proximity of death. At the age of twenty, Brigitte must figure out what to do with the life she has unexpectedly been given anew.

The novel narrates Brigitte's progressive refusal of her bourgeois milieu: family, friends, and the man she is expected to marry. Returning to her wealthy family in the provinces, she finds herself suffocating in the comedy of bourgeois
rituals that make up their daily existence. Her future life of respectable marriage
and maternity has already been traced for her. Since she has a substantial dowry,
she will make a good match and claim her rightful place in the social hierarchy,
just like her mother. The easy acceptance of bourgeois hypocrisy by Anna, who
had been her best friend before her illness, has cooled their friendship beyond
recognition. Beginning her university studies in Paris, Brigitte meets Pierre, a
magistrate as smug as he is successful, and eventually turns down his proposal
of marriage. Her loneliness makes her all the more determined to find a way to
reach out to others, to create an "authentic" life that will not shame her. At the
end of the novel, she goes to a Communist meeting and finds a new beginning:
moved by the Internationale, sung by workers who call her "comrade," she hopes
that she can be part of their effort to create a more human world for all.

In spite of Édith Thomas's criticism of the thesis novel less than two years
earlier, the structure of *Le Refus* places it in that tradition. Describing her own
writing to the Association of Revolutionary Artists and Writers, she had told
them she was far removed from the possibility of making propaganda for any
cause. In *Le Refus*, however, she does exactly that, most likely against her inten-

tions. An authorized voice gives us the proper interpretation of characters and events. Nowhere in the novel does Thomas dramatize, either through Brigitte's reflections or her relation to others, her own doubts and ambivalence. Not surprisingly, Brigitte's refusal of her bourgeois surroundings is more convincing than her discovery of the right path.

The Russian literary theorist Mikhail Bakhtin would call Thomas's novel "monological" rather than "dialogical." Bakhtin describes the monological novel as one in which ideas are either affirmed or discredited, with no middle ground. Readers are expected to identify completely with the protagonist as he progresses from ignorance to knowledge of a correct system of values.[16] All the characters in the book besides Brigitte are ciphers, objects of her perception rather than complex subjects in their own right, a strategy that is successful only in the intermittent passages where Thomas satirizes the bourgeois milieu she knows so well. At the end Brigitte is on the threshold of finding her true self by becoming a member of the group that will save her. Even Communist and leftist critics of the novel, while generally sympathetic, criticized the decisive revelation of the ending as not very plausible.

It is possible, however, to read *Le Refus* differently. Its originality for a novel of the thirties, in spite of its serious flaws, is that its hero is a woman. *Le Refus* appeared just a few months after the *succès de scandale* of another novel about young women, *Young Girls* by Henry de Montherlant, who was considered one of France's major writers. An epistolary novel for the most part, its title refers to a number of young and not-so-young women who have fallen hopelessly in love with a famous writer. They outdo one another in protesting that they are nothing without his love, seeing in him a god, the one being who can give them life. But the great man only rarely deigns to answer their letters. When he does, it is to let them know that he has no feelings for them and finds their adoration tiresome.

Juxtaposing the two novels, a few of Édith Thomas's friendly critics saw in Brigitte Chevance the first portrait of a new kind of young woman, far more representative of her time than Montherlant's "whimpering, submissive Andrée Hacquebaut."[17] Thomas was sufficiently disturbed by Montherlant's novel to write him a personal letter. In his response to her he declares, not altogether convincingly: "No one rejoices more than I do that a young woman is being born who 'has conquered her autonomy.'" His task, he lets her know, is to bring alive through art the "psychological nonexistence" of *les jeunes filles,* a state "which is and will remain for a long time that of many young girls of the French bourgeoisie."[18] In that context, Thomas's representation of Brigitte's rebellion is a refreshing alternative to the vapid creatures who inhabit Montherlant's universe. In the progression of its narrative, *Le Refus* offers a radical departure from the love or marriage plot that was supposed to characterize novels by or about women.

Among the articles that Thomas wrote for *Commune* was a review of Montherlant's novel *Demon of Good,* his sequel to *Young Girls.* Writing in her diary about the novel, she finds in Montherlant's representations of women an awful but effective antidote to her own recurring obsessions with men: "I am reading *Demon of Good,*" she writes, "and it's good therapy."[19] A little exposure to Montherlant's misogynist portraits functioned, at least temporarily, as effective shock treatment. Thomas's review of the novel was her only article of the 1930s that she wrote explicitly from her position as an intellectual woman. The beginning of Thomas's critique points to a tacit interdiction in the discourse of the 1930s and 1940s: "I do not like to judge a book as a 'woman,'" she writes. "I'm not very concerned, generally speaking, about that distinction."[20] Her defensiveness points to the social text of the time, which tended to represent the intellectual woman as an oxymoron. Even more than the writer, the vocation of intellectual in France constituted a sacrosanct cultural domain, reserved for masculine intelligence.[21] If a woman wanted to be taken seriously as an intellectual, she had to impersonate a man or at least accept a certain idea of human values as male. The capacity for thought and even moral imagination was defined as masculine. Thus Paul Nizan proclaims in his review of *Le Refus,* "Nothing is more difficult for women than to be interested in others more than in themselves" before praising Thomas's "virile curiosity about unfamiliar lives."[22] In that context "virile" takes on the meaning of one of its dictionary definitions in French as well as in English: "having the moral characteristics generally attributed more specially to man: active, energetic, courageous, etc."

Almost in spite of herself, Thomas was provoked by Montherlant's misogyny to claim the legitimacy of a woman's different sexual perspective: "It is an obligation of calm lucidity to try to distinguish in oneself what is specifically 'feminine,' in other words, biological and eternal, from what is acquired through education, the prejudices of one's milieu, and the proprieties and corresponding improprieties that they determine. The new woman, even more than the new man, is yet to be created. She is already being born: a woman who works, who is involved in life without a mediator, who constructs herself on her own, who has conquered her autonomy."[23] Thomas felt the need to convince her reader that her remarks, although written by a woman about women, showed calm but also lucidity, a privileged value in the French tradition. Her awareness of woman as a social construct and her sense that a new woman was being born announce major themes of *The Second Sex.*

Since Thomas's work as a journalist was not sufficient to earn a living, she obtained a job at the Bibliothèque nationale, although she found herself frustrated by what she calls the work of "intellectual laborer" demanded of librarians and archivists. "I like historical research," she writes in her memoir, "but only on the condition of being able to work out the results, bringing together the material, but also constructing the house." The constraints of her job at the Bibliothèque nationale became particularly unacceptable after the outbreak of civil war in Spain in July 1936: "If I had been a man, I would have joined the Spanish republicans. But I was a woman, and I limped, how could I be useful?"[24] She talked to Aragon, who was one of the editors at *Vendredi,* about her desire to go to Spain. A few weeks later, he proposed that she accompany a truck that French writers were contributing to the Loyalist cause. Determined to get to Spain, whatever the consequences for her position at the Bibliothèque nationale, she approached the library's intimidating administrator, Julien Cain, and requested his authorization for a highly unorthodox leave of absence. In the polarized climate of the time, Cain turned out to be an ally and granted her request, on the double condition that she not let her colleagues know where she was headed and that she report to him what was going on in Spain after her return. She invented a respectable pretext for taking a leave—the estate of a sick cousin in the provinces needed looking after—and left for Barcelona in November 1936.

4

FELLOW TRAVELING AND ITS DISCONTENTS

During the few weeks that Édith Thomas spent in Barcelona in 1936, her articles focused less on the civil war than on the social revolution that was taking place in spite of the war. She talked to anarchist professors and unionized workers, defrocked nuns who had become nurses, and young girls in uniform who were leaving for the front. As a special envoy working for the French press, she saw her primary task as mobilizing support in France for the antifascist struggle. Quoting the words of a poster in Barcelona that asks the passerby, What have you done for victory? she asks the French public: What are we doing for victory?[1] Although she saw indications everywhere of the divergent formations on the Loyalist side—Stalinists, Trotskyists, anarchists, socialists—her articles do not register the competing ideologies and power struggles which would soon become deadly. In the fervor and hope of those early months, she defined the conflict in Spain as a struggle between two forces, those of the revolution and those of fascism.[2]

In France, the outbreak of civil war in Spain provoked a crisis for the Popular Front government, already in serious trouble economically and politically. Although Blum had immediately promised to send planes and ammunition to the legitimately elected government, close in spirit to his own, that aid was discontinued as early as August when France and Great Britain, along with twenty-seven other nations, signed a nonintervention pact. It became clear almost immediately that Germany and Italy were continuing their aid to Franco—and that the Soviet Union was continuing aid to the Loyalists—in spite of the pact they had signed. Blum nevertheless did not change his decision, which he had made in great personal anguish. His policy was a response to the divisions within his own government, intense pressure from Britain that demanded abstention, and his fears of provoking a European war.[3] For Édith Thomas as for many others on the left, her opposition to the policy of nonintervention marked the end of the pacifism that had defined leftist thinking since 1914.

Early in 1937, Aragon founded *Ce Soir*, a Communist newspaper launched as the afternoon counterpart to the mass circulation *L'Humanité*, and offered Thomas a position as one of its regular reporters. She accepted with alacrity and during the next eighteen months wrote a wide range of political and human interest articles. In March 1937, exactly one year before Austria was occupied by German troops and made part of the Reich, she was sent to Vienna, where she found a city overwhelmed by poverty, unemployment, and fear. Under Chancellor Schussnigg's dictatorship, ruled by the police and the church, rumors abounded of a putsch by Hitler—or a restoration of the monarchy.[4] Shortly after Édith Thomas's return from Vienna, Paul Nizan wrote in his review article of *Le Refus* that she had "just been revealed as one of the best journalists of her generation."[5]

Thomas's assignments in Paris included a series about the Marais, the fourth arrondissement in the center of Paris on the right bank. Today one of the most fashionable districts of the city, it was then one of its worst slums, with the highest population density in Paris. It also had one of the highest mortality rates of any district, along with the thirteenth arrondissement in the south and the twentieth in the north, the two other poorest neighborhoods in the city. Families in the Marais lived in crumbling rat-infested buildings with rotting hallways and courtyards so narrow that no ray of sunlight could reach the muddy ground. The tiny, dark rooms that smelled of urine were breeding grounds for tuberculosis. In those conditions, Thomas writes, illness was almost better than health; children at least had the hope of being sent to a sanatorium where they could be cared for and adequately fed. She describes the entire Marais in those years as an "immense desert of stone" with only the Tour St. Jacques and the place des Vosges showing a few patches of green. In the seventeenth century, when the buildings of the Marais were constructed, there were no good and bad neighborhoods: "From top to bottom a house was the image of society." People of different classes lived in the same building but not on the same floor. The first floor above the entrance, with its large windows, was reserved for the rich; the second floor was for artisans and the higher floors for journeymen workers. That system, however, no longer corresponded to social reality: "The rich have fled to the western sections of Paris, leaving old buildings that are neglected, since they shelter only people about whom society cares less than it does for the dusty antiques of the Carnavalet Museum."[6]

The most unexpected series of articles by Thomas in *Ce Soir* is "L'Envers des variétés" (Variety shows from the inside), based on her conversations with performers from a traveling show in Montmartre. She talks with a fire-eater, a clown, a wild animal trainer, a tightrope walker, a trapeze artist, and a "serpent woman," fascinated by their otherness. Her response to the fire-eater, a lost and homesick African immigrant who propositions her, gives voice to the anticolonialism that crystallized during her trip to Algeria in 1934: "I have always been partial to people of color. In their relationship with whites, the 'natives' are, for me, always right and the whites always wrong. Here, after all, the black man of the rue Fontaine is only what white men and white women have made of him. Their mission, as everyone knows, is called civilization." The serpent woman's performance inspires awe: "Her body coiled and uncoiled, twisted, bent, and stretched into shapes that seem impossible for a human being. As if she had no femur, no tibia, no vertebrae."[7] Édith Thomas, whose body has been an intimate adversary, is mesmerized by the agility that allows this young girl to transform herself into a being that seems to have no physical limits, as if she could transcend human materiality.

Avidly following events in Spain, Thomas was eager to be at the Spanish front but found herself thwarted by the decision at *Ce Soir* that she did not have the physical strength to be a war correspondent. In April 1938 she was finally given an assignment in the Pyrenees, on the frontier between Spain and France where refugees were fleeing Franco's troops. Her dispatches are remarkably upbeat, as the headlines convey. On April 13 she writes an article from Luchon, "With Refugees Confident in the Final Victory," describing the solidarity between two peoples, the generosity of French workers and villagers who are doing whatever they can to help, and the courage of the refugees, in spite of their suffering and exhaustion.[8] On April 16, the headline is a quote from a Lieutenant-Colonel Garcia, whom she meets on the passes of the Val d'Aran: "'The population has regained confidence; it knows we will defend it.'" Inspired by his determination, she defies those who announce "that everything is over, whereas the resistance is ready."[9]

However, in another article written in April, just before her return to Paris, she sounded a prophetic note. With other sympathizers and militants of the Loyalist cause, she listened to a speech by a worker from Tarbes who argued that the destiny of France was linked to Spain, and that France's security depended on giving arms to the Spanish popular front. The French, he says, need to learn from the Spanish example to prepare their defense more effectively, to understand that pacifism will not bring peace. Thomas looked at the old peasants sitting in the room and wondered: "Will they too soon be fleeing on the roads, heading to the north of France as it is attacked from all sides?"[10] Two years later, millions of French people would be fleeing on the roads, heading south rather than north, as France was invaded not by Franco's Spain but by the Germans.

Returning to Paris, she found that hostilities and rivalries at *Ce Soir,* present from the beginning, had intensified, along with her personal sense of isolation. Thomas would always be ambivalent about political journalism. On the one hand, she thought of journalistic writing as an effective forum to discuss major social movements and issues of the day; on the other, she despised what she saw as the corruption and cynicism of many in the profession. On July 1, a few months after her return from the Pyrenees, Thomas records in her diary that Aragon called her into his office. He lectured her at length about her political attitude, her excessive need for justifications, and her recalcitrance to "political realities" which he did not define. He reproached her for not believing in his sincerity and told her that he wanted respect from her, "more than you know." All of this served as a prelude to informing her that the newspaper was having financial difficulties and she was fired.[11]

Although the diaries record her sense of failure, loneliness, and despair after Aragon's action, she was able to get herself hired that same day on a temporary basis by Agence Espagne, the Spanish Loyalists' press agency in France. At the end of July she left for Barcelona as a special envoy for Agence Espagne and the leftist magazine *Regards.* In spite of mounting evidence that the Nationalists were winning the war, her articles still tried to be resolutely optimistic. She quotes a woman after one of the bombings of Barcelona, as people were racing to shelters: "Do they think they'll discourage us with that? The effect is just the opposite." A few kilometers from the front, before a major offensive, she encountered French volunteers from the International Brigades. One of them told her: "I've been here for twenty-two months. Don't think I volunteered because I was out of work. That's been said a lot and for most of us it's false. I was a deliveryman and I quit my job at vacation time, without saying, of course, where I was going. I came out of solidarity with the Spanish people and because I could no longer bear to be anywhere else."[12] Thomas describes the everyday heroism of ordinary women in Barcelona, the attitude they've adopted of waiting for "mañana" when the war will be over and won, when their sons will be home from the front, when they will be able to eat and to resume their lives. These women, she notes, have been won over by the Loyalists, who have helped them as mothers, helped their children with schools and day care and hospitals: "That is why," she writes, "they are unshakable in their new hope and new faith in the victory of the Republic."[13]

In her memoir, however, looking back on that time in Catalonia, she records her dismay at the changes that took place between her first trip to Barcelona in 1936 and the second one twenty months later, where she found a climate of disarray, famine, and fear. While she was there in 1938, André Malraux and his film production crew were making the film *Man's Hope*, based on his novel of that title: "But hope was shrinking for them, for us," she comments. She defends the positive emphasis of her articles at the time, which she saw as war communiqués: "Since I was on the side of [the Loyalists], I had to support the desperate wager of their hope."[14]

Exhausted by the distress of the situation in Spain and her personal situation as well, she went to the mountains for a while to recuperate. When she returned to Paris it was just before Chamberlain and Daladier signed the Munich Pact with Hitler on September 30, 1938, accepting his demands. In her diary she writes: "The great torment has passed—at what price? and for how long? And what measures will follow of reaction and mindlessness?"[15]

A few months earlier the man who was to become Édith's emblematic phantom lover appeared in her diary, a man who remained in her imagination and appeared in her writings until the end of her life. At the outset, the familiar pattern played itself out. When he showed sexual interest, her first impulse was to reject him because he did not love her; when he then became distant, she decided she was in love and pursued him, which made him flee. Nevertheless, feelings of genuine respect and affection developed between them, along with her growing fascination with what she saw as his enigmatic personality. A theater critic for the Communist press, Stefan was of Polish descent and a "Judeo-Marxist," as she puts it, someone she admired intellectually and with whom she shared political values. When Aragon fired her from *Ce Soir*, it was Stefan who intervened for her and helped her to obtain assignments with the Agence Espagne and the journal *Regards*. Divorced, the father of two children, he seemed to her solidly anchored in the world, as she was not.

In May 1939 she wrote in her diary a long letter to Stefan that most probably she never sent. Declaring her love, she accepts that they should not get married, since such a commitment would involve their families, a mistake for both of them. The experiment she has in mind would be transitory: "I would not want you to feel tied down, since I am an old little girl."[16] She is now thirty years of age, and her feelings for Stefan awaken a new desire. Although they have never slept together, although she is still a virgin, she wants to have his child. The desire for a child, for whom she alone would be responsible, was to haunt her throughout the 1940s.

A week later, having coughed for several days, she had an X ray taken. The diagnosis was a form of pulmonary tuberculosis. Unlike her first illness that caused terrible physical suffering, what she now felt was fatigue and some discomfort. In contrast to the desperate rebellion that marked her ordeal of tuberculosis of the bone when she was twenty-two, she reacted this time with melancholy resignation. There was hardly even surprise, as if her body had been on reprieve and she was waiting for another illness. "It's so easy to devour melancholy," she writes, "with Koch's bacillus,"[17] an allusion to the discovery by the German microbiologist whose name became attached to the disease. Depressed both by her personal failures and by the somber political situation, especially the defeat of republican Spain, she felt as if illness had come as a negative solution from the outside, relieving her of the need to choose a life.

Nor did she panic this time at the prospect of a sanatorium. She spent the summer months of 1939 at the sanatorium at Assy in the French Alps, where she was given the available treatment of the time, a pneumothorax (collapse therapy), which consisted of injecting sterilized air into the pleural cavity between the lung and the chest wall, thus collapsing the lung to maintain it immobile and at rest for as long as possible. The medical discipline imposed by her illness was coupled with a personal discipline of reading and writing, creating a "quasi monastic" life. Although she claimed to accept the judgment of specialists that there was no particular psychology of tuberculosis, she notes the affinities she sees among many tubercular artists, in particular Watteau, Chopin, and Katherine Mansfield, "a kind of detachment from the real, a gaze turned to an elusive beyond." By contrast, it seems impossible to her that Balzac, Victor Hugo, or Tolstoy could have written their "powerful and massive" works if they had suffered from tuberculosis.[18]

In one of Édith Thomas's best short stories, "Promenade au Villaret," a woman tries to penetrate the mystery of another woman who has committed suicide just after being pronounced cured of her illness. A diary the woman has left behind reflects on the role biology plays in defining her deepest needs, an interpretation that seems less eccentric today than it did to Thomas at the time: "Most people," the diary narrator writes, "don't need a system or a justification. That's the only thing that really separates me from them. . . . It's doubtless just a glandular question that only the biologists will perhaps resolve effectively someday. But how could they resolve it? It doesn't matter; we're not there yet."[19] In Thomas's own diary as well, she notes the biological aspect of what she feels, stating her conclusion, as she so often does in the diary, in its most extreme terms: "I realize more and more each day how much everything in me is physical, only physical, how much my thoughts, which are only the rather vague expression of feelings, are directly determined by the state of my organs and my knee, by the temperature and the look of the sky. Physiology and meteorology, that's what sums me up." Some years later she offers a biological reading for the cycles of passion she repeatedly goes through: "All that, I think, depends on my period (to be examined: the psychology of love varies according to the time of month)."[20] She did not, however, return to the question.

To restore her strength of will while she was in the sanatorium, Thomas wrote a chronicle which she called "Letters to Ariane or Of the Good Use of Illness," in the form of a two-week diary addressed to her alter ego, Ariane, the mythical figure whose thread she will follow to find a way out of the labyrinth. Her chronicle gives expression to the rationalist faith on which she tried to construct her life and to which she always returned. Lucidity must be the starting point: "There is no problem that cannot be reduced to clear and distinct givens and thereby diminished. There is no situation that cannot at least be looked at directly. You see, I think psychoanalysis, that bastard child of confession, is a method that should be applied only by oneself. No ghost can survive in the bright light of noon."

Notwithstanding the Cartesian rationality of those statements, less rational impulses did not disappear from the chronicle. Thinking desperately one night about Stefan, Édith left her bed in the sanatorium and went outside to lie down under the moon. At least "I didn't die of cold." Her agitation, she decides, is also a symptom of illness, as much as fever or coughing. She adds: "I am ill and he is well, and the act of love between us seems to me as forbidden as if one of us had changed sex"[21]—an ironic analogy when one considers her passionate love affair some years later with Dominique Aury. During the time she was in the sanatorium, Stefan wrote her a number of affectionate, caring letters.

On August 24, 1939, alone and ill at Assy, Thomas received with disbelief the news of the Nazi-Soviet nonaggression pact, which had just been signed. Private anxieties were pushed aside as she tried, day after day, to "see clearly." She read the newspapers feverishly—quite literally, since she found herself running a fever for several days. In the Communist press, Paul Nizan, foreign affairs editor for *Ce Soir,* and Gabriel Péri, foreign affairs editor for *L'Humanité,* remained silent, an eloquent expression of their dissent.[22] Aragon took on the task of justifying the pact to the masses, explaining that it was the triumph of the Soviet will for peace. "For this playboy of the eastern world," she writes later in her memoir, "nothing was easier than to prove it is daylight in the middle of the night."[23]

Until then, Thomas had managed to rationalize all the doubts about the Soviet Union that continued to assail her—the Moscow trials, André Gide's critical account of Soviet life in his *Return from the USSR,* Trotsky's denunciation of Stalin—although her doubts had been sufficiently strong to prevent her from becoming a Party member. Most of her friends were in the Party and she didn't mind people thinking she was a member as well. After 1935, she saw in communism the only effective guarantee against fascism, as all her political writings make clear. That these two systems, which she had considered polar opposites, should suddenly be in collusion seemed an impossible madness.

Thomas's despair was made worse by her complete isolation; the only communist at Assy was the sanatorium dishwasher. Each diary entry records another analysis and another failure to comprehend the incomprehensible: "I'm trying to see clearly." "I'm absolutely sick, trying to understand." "I'm knocking my head against the wall."[24] In order for her refusal of the pact not to remain "platonic," she wrote letters to the editors of the two pro-Communist journals to which she contributed—Pierre Unik, editor of *Regards,* and Jacques Decour, of *Commune*—asking them not to publish her articles.[25]

Along with these letters and her own notations in the diaries, she also transcribes the letters she wrote to Stefan and to another Communist mentor. In their lengthy responses that she kept in her diary notebook, Stefan's in a more personal voice, they both elaborated a similar rationale, not very different from Aragon's position. Their reasoning was that any Soviet act must be considered not in itself but dialectically. From that perspective the nonaggression pact delivered a tough blow to Hitlerism. It isolated the Reich from Spain, Japan, and Italy, thereby breaking the anti-Komintern pact; moreover, by preventing an immediate overt aggression against the Soviet Union without giving anything in exchange, the pact was, in the Party's official phrase, "a contribution to peace." In order to isolate Hitler, preserve the security of the USSR, and save the peace, only one means was available, whatever its risks, the announcement of a nonaggression pact. Stefan concludes his letter by assuring her that he is sympathetic to her scruples and her anguish.[26]

In spite of her love and admiration for Stefan, and her respect for the other Communist figures to whom she wrote and who sent letters of explanation in response, Édith Thomas remained stubbornly unconvinced. It seemed clear to her that even if the catastrophe of war was inevitable, the pact was hastening its outbreak: "It is as if [the USSR] has voluntarily moved forward the hands of the clock for each man who *will be killed.*" Although she was not prepared to let go of the communist cause in which she put her faith in a more human future, she could not accept the Party rationale for Stalin's act.

Breaking through the convoluted reasoning that justified the pact, she protests: "No, no, and no. The means affect the end. What will this *end* be when duplicity, crime, and bad faith are used to achieve it? It is because I believe in the human truth of [the revolutionary] cause that I think the shameful privilege of such means should be left to others—those who defend an indefensible cause. I believe there is still a basic value that needs to be preserved: good faith. Like washing, or brushing your teeth." Repeatedly Thomas insists that her opposition is not based on ethical considerations, since for Marxism the only

ethics is what serves the proletariat: "Only later, and on the basis of other economic relationships, will a human ethics be possible."[27] The defensive tone of
her protest discloses the heart of her political thinking. Duly reciting the orthodox Communist position, she cannot hide her fundamental need for a "human ethics," revealed inadvertently, as if it were a secret vice.

On September 2, a week after the signing of the pact, "a contribution to
peace," Germany invaded Poland; on September 3, Great Britain and France declared war against the Reich. In the first weeks following the declaration of war,
twenty-one of the seventy-two Communist deputies in the National Assembly
broke with their party. During the next months, until the beginning of May, Europe lived through the eerie period, neither war nor peace, that came to be
known as the phony war. In October Édith moved from the sanatorium in the
Alps of Assy to Arcachon, a coastal town near Bordeaux in the southwest of
France where she lived in a villa with her brother, Gérard, who was suffering
from tuberculosis of the vertebrae and had been separated from his wife and
children because of the danger of contagion. As people waited for the cataclysm
of war they knew would come, everything seemed immobile, suspended in time.
At the end of April, Édith took the train to Paris to consult her doctor there. He
advised her to have rib resection surgery, since the initial pneumothorax had
not sufficiently collapsed her lung and the lesion persisted. Arriving in Paris, she
felt the ghost of war in the absence of young men, most of whom had been
drafted. She walked along deserted avenues in the evening and heard her steps
"resonate as they do in empty rooms, in which it seems that no one will ever live
again."[28] Street lamps gave off a blue haze, barely enough to find one's way, a
veiled light that would become familiar during the occupation years.

On May 10, 1940, a massive German force invaded the neutral countries of
Holland, Belgium, and Luxembourg, which the German government had declared inviolable. Édith Thomas, glued to her radio, quotes in her diary the
words of Hitler: "Soldiers of the Western front, the hour has come. The struggle that began today will decide the fate of the German nation for the next thousand years. Do your duty, and the German people will accompany you with their
blessings." By May 13, German panzer divisions were breaking through the supposedly impenetrable Ardennes forest and moving toward Dunkirk with stu-
pefying force and speed.

Édith Thomas's operation was postponed indefinitely because of "external
events," and the doctor advised her to leave Paris. On May 23 there was still a
train that could take her to Arcachon. She found herself in the midst of masses
of people who had already begun to flee the Germans. They were coming from
northern France, Belgium, and Normandy, carrying with them whatever was
most precious or indispensable: bundles of all shapes, blankets, a bird in a cage,

a cat on a leash. Sometimes nothing. Many left under German machine gun fire, with no time to take any belongings.

In June the exodus from Paris began, a contagious panic that grew to massive proportions once it became known that even the government had fled the capital. Over two million French people, mostly old men, women, and children, left the Paris region between June 10 and June 14 heading south or west on foot, on bicycles, in improvised vehicles of all kinds, frantically trying to reach some place that would be inaccessible to the advancing Germans. On June 11, Édith Thomas's only entry in her diary is a quote from the Apocalypse: "And I looked, and behold a pale horse: and his name that sat on him was Death, and Hell followed with him. And power was given unto them over the fourth part of the earth, to kill with sword, and with hunger, and with death, and with the beasts of the earth." On June 14 the Germans invaded Paris, now deserted by its population, and paraded on the Champs Elysées.[29]

During the week that followed, many of Thomas's notations in her diary read like news bulletins, headlines of the defeat as she hears it happening on the radio, sometimes hour by hour, with all the confusion such immediacy entails. On June 16 in the morning, trying to make sense of divergent messages that have been communicated to the French in the last two days, she wonders if their aim is to prepare French opinion for the continuation of war. By the end of the day she writes: "We know nothing." Pétain appears in her diary for the first time on June 17 when she notes that he will replace Paul Reynaud as head of the government. Her brief summary of Pétain's speech, "the voice of an old man breaking with emotion," points to the "negotiations"—what could still be interpreted as such—that have begun during the night. Famously, he offered France "the gift of my person to ease its misfortunes" before declaring: "It is with a heavy heart that I tell you we must cease fighting." He adds that he has spoken with "the adversary" to ask "if he is ready to seek with us, between soldiers, after the struggle and with honor, the means of ending hostilities." Pétain's words that day (which she does not record) allowed the last brief hope, however irrational, for an armistice short of capitulation. For Édith Thomas, the illusion of an honorable peace was brief. In the evening, at half past eight, she writes: "British radio claims, according to neutral informers, that Germany will demand capitulation." At half past nine: "We would refuse." On June 18, "the Germans are in Orleans, La Charité-sur-Loire, Dijon, and are pushing toward the Jura Mountains."

Although, like most of France, she did not hear de Gaulle's call to resistance on June 18, she records the next day that "the government has recalled General de Gaulle, who yesterday evening gave a speech on British radio inviting the army and the air force to join him." On June 21 she reports the meeting between

Hitler and the French armistice delegation in the forest of Compiègne at Rethondes in a train car, the exact place where Germany had been obliged to accept its defeat on November 8, 1918. Taking his revenge, Hitler demanded French expiation for the harshness of the Treaty of Versailles after the war of 1914–18, and blamed Britain and France for having started the present war. The armistice agreement presented to the French delegation was in fact a diktat of Hitler's. By ten in the evening of June 23, the day after the signing, any lingering ambiguities were dispelled and Thomas writes: "British radio gives us the conditions for armistice: capitulation. One would like to know the definition of 'honor' for our generals. De Gaulle is in England forming a committee charged with representing the interests of France."

She concludes this notebook on June 24: "The End. The Beginning."[30]

5

DIARY OF RESISTANCE,
DIARY OF COLLABORATION

Armistice conditions were very harsh. War prisoners, two million men, would be taken to Germany as political hostages. France agreed to pay a huge daily indemnity for the costs of German occupation. Germans who had taken refuge in France were to be surrendered to the Reich on demand. The provinces of Alsace and Lorraine were annexed to Germany and the rest of the country was divided into two zones, three-fifths occupied, two-fifths unoccupied, separated by a line of demarcation. Germans would occupy the northern regions of France, running from Tours to the border near Geneva, as well as the entire Atlantic seaboard. In the south, the so-called free zone would have a so-called French government located in Vichy.

In contrast to the great majority of the French, who were relieved or resigned to an armistice ending the war even though it meant defeat by Nazi Germany, Édith Thomas's immediate response in her diary was opposition, in entries that combine local anecdote with the prophetic tones of a Cassandra warning her compatriots of what lies ahead. On June 25, 1940, the day the signed armistice took effect, Thomas writes: "They are going to teach us now to hate everything we loved and were right to love. They are going to teach us now that reason is wrong and madness and despair are the greatest wisdom. People are ready to believe it and will believe it." The next day: "At the bookstore, at the pharmacy, people are very pleased. 'This time there will be order, you'll see.'" She comments: "The order they deserve: cemeteries and concentration camps; the moral order of the dead."[1]

The historian Philippe Burrin emphasizes the choice that was forced on everyone in France during the occupation years: "The occupation put the whole

of French society to the test. It gave rise to contrary reactions and to unclear, uncertain and ambivalent attitudes. Nobody was dispensed from making a choice."
Most French people chose neither resistance nor active collaboration but what
he calls "accommodation," an elastic concept that included various forms of
passivity, adaptation, and compromise.[2] At the time of the armistice, Thomas's
mother, father, brother, and sister-in-law found themselves together in Arcachon. In spite of their divergent politics, ranging from her father's conservative
positions to her own extreme leftist stance, family members discovered they
were of one mind in choosing resistance to Pétain's acceptance of defeat by Nazi
Germany, an attitude shared by only a small minority in 1940. As early as August, Édith Thomas asks herself: "What can one *do*?"[3]

The signing of the armistice enabled the Pétain government to put in place
its project for a national revolution that would restore "eternal France." Marshal
Pétain's New Order exalted the return to a mythical golden age before the French
Republic, before the French Revolution. It defined itself as a revolution from
above in which the authoritarian rules of hierarchy and obedience to the leader
would prevail against the dangerous egalitarian illusions of the republic. France
would return to the values of discipline, hard work, and sacrifice for the community, repenting for the decadent individualism that was responsible for its
defeat. The truth of the land and rural life would triumph over the degenerate
vices of the city.

On October 20, 1940, Thomas began to write a fictional diary, *Le Journal intime de Monsieur Célestin Costedet*. Her satiric journal was initially inspired by
Pétain's creation of a national day for collecting beechnuts, which scarcity had
made into a source for oil.[4] In her own diary she writes a page of breathless en-
comium to the youth of France, burning to devote itself to the marshal, and
notes: "Only irony can save us from dictatorship and avenge us." A week later,
she thinks approvingly about her brother Gérard's idea that she begin the diary
of a "bourgeois pétainien," recording his daily routine, his self-satisfied commentaries, and the local gossip he hears—a collection of what she calls "all the
idiocies of the day." Use the tone, she tells herself, of the national day of beechnuts; "we'll see what comes of it."[5]

That entry during the night of October 28, 1940, seems to be the only allusion, in her personal diary or elsewhere, to the fictional journal. At the time, she
was still convalescing in Arcachon, and the kind of literary resistance in which
she could participate had not yet found its voice. Irony served as a private way
to resist the pervasive mystification that was transforming individual consciousness as well as collective life in the name of the New Order. The initial date
inscribed in Costedet's fictional diary goes back to October 18, which allowed

her to note the reaction of her antihero to the antisemitic measures of the following day.

Édith Thomas was undaunted by the challenge of making her narrator different from herself in every respect: a zealous Pétainist with real power and therefore, inevitably, a man. Célestin Costedet, veteran of the Great War, member of the Legion of Honor, family man, and owner of the department store Ladies' Paradise,[6] lives in an unnamed southwestern coastal city of occupied France near Bordeaux, clearly based on Arcachon. He has become a leader of the community thanks to his upward marriage to Marie-Louise Dutheil, daughter of the owner of Ladies' Paradise, where he was first an employee. His admiration for his wife's superior social status only reinforces his misogyny and his need to demonstrate the authority conferred on him by his patriarchal role. When their bewildered adolescent son Patrice misbehaves, Costedet exerts his authority by ordering him to copy one hundred times the sentences of the father, whom we can read interchangeably as Costedet or Pétain, on the values of discipline, obedience, and hierarchy.

Costedet peremptorily fires the other member of the household, the maid, after her unemployed husband indignantly rejects Costedet's suggestion that he find work in Germany. She is replaced by a new maid who has the double advantage of being the niece of the local tripes butcher, which means their meals will improve, and of being young and buxom as well. In accordance with official morality, Costedet exalts Marriage and the Family, which does not prevent him from trying to sleep with Bernadette. His furtive and ultimately successful attempts fall within a familiar tradition of French domestic comedy, subverted by its somber political context.

The boundaries between public and private are further collapsed in Costedet's jealousy of the charismatic Dr. Cagire, whose contempt for Pétain as a pathetic old monarchist and fiery praise for the youthful dynamism of what he calls the "real revolutionaries" in Paris exert a magnetic attraction on Marie-Louise. The Pétainist Costedet and the fascist Cagire embody two currents of right-wing ideas in Vichy as they are defined by the historian Stanley Hoffmann: on the one hand, the pursuit of "a kind of pseudo-Latin mirage, a vision of a static, classical society governed by the values of order and hierarchy that characterized the great periods of Western civilization—the *Pax Romana* and the Middle Ages"; on the other, "a pseudo-Nordic mirage of a dynamic, romantic society, extolling the values of heroism and struggle, blood and earth, inscrutable forces and revolutionary masses."[7] Célestin fervently admires the Middle Ages and is proud of his medieval ancestors, the great "builders of cathedrals," whose virtue was to believe and obey. Like his ancestors, he takes satisfaction in following the orders of his leader—directives that Édith Thomas finds readily in local newspapers and on the official radio.

In moments of moral uplift, Costedet's representations of Pétain evoke the sentimentalized images of the time. The marshal, he notes, has gone to visit "his people" in Toulouse and Montauban and has distributed money to the poor. Costedet's creative genealogy of France begins with Saint Genevieve, lingers in the Middle Ages, embraces Louis XIV through Louis XVI, ignores the French Revolution and the 150 years that follow, and arrives at the continuation and culmination of this teleology of glory in the person of Marshal Philippe Pétain:

> Like Saint Genevieve watching over Paris, like good king Dagobert or the valiant Charlemagne who separated the good clerics from the bad and placed them without consideration of their birth at his right or at his left, according to their merit, like Saint Louis who dispensed justice under an oak tree, like Philippe le Bel who chased the Knights Templar and the Jews from the kingdom, like Joan of Arc who ousted the English from France—since the English, the Jews, and the masons were already conspiring against us—like the great Louis XIV, like Louis XV the beloved, like Louis XVI, our holy martyred king, Marshal Philippe Pétain continues the history of France and its grandeur.[8]

Costedet understands that the new revolution of Pétain, unlike that of 1789, comes from above. It is "hierarchical and largely social," a phrase taken directly by Thomas from Pétain's description of the domestic politics of his regime. Noting Pétain's decision that secretaries of state, high-ranking functionaries, and dignitaries will henceforth be directly responsible to him, Costedet compares this system to that of the Middle Ages, when the vassal took an oath of loyalty to his suzerain: "The power of the suzerain came only from God, just like that of the marshal."[9]

In contrast to the solitary voice of her own journal, Thomas's fictional diary includes an extensive cast of thirty-three characters. Costedet's shifting relationships with friends, associates, and adversaries, often presented as transcribed conversations, reflect his community's divergent responses to the effects of France's defeat. Thomas's own voice emerges most clearly through a short, bald commercial agent, Monsieur Davy-Burnaud, whom Costedet has not seen since 1930. Davy-Burnaud, who is seventy years old, explains that he has had to begin working again, since his son is a prisoner in Germany and his grandchildren have no one to support them. The ensuing argument between the two men over the rhetoric of reconstruction and the virtues of Travail, Famille, Patrie, the trinity of values that replaced the Liberté, Égalité, Fraternité of the republic, soon becomes an argument about the true glory of France, reproducing an ongoing conflict over representations of French history that became particularly acute during the occupation years. When Costedet extols Pétain as the inheritor of the eternal France of Joan of Arc and Louis XIV, Davy-Burnaud counters in the name of the critical, libertarian legacy of Montaigne, Descartes, and the enlightenment Encyclopedists.

Their dispute echoes, in a different register, a speech Thomas imagined herself giving to the National Assembly, just before the vote that gave Pétain full powers to draw up a new constitution for what would become the French State. She wonders whether there will be one man courageous enough to vote in opposition to the dissolution of the French Republic. Two days later, on July 10, 1940, eighty deputies voted no, still a small minority in a parliament of 672 representatives. Thomas uses her diary for what she would have liked to say:

> Gentlemen, this is doubtless the last time in France that an opinion contrary to yours can still be expressed. After today silence will fall like a tombstone on what used to be France. I mean by that what France was for the world: the country of Montaigne, of Descartes, the country of Voltaire and the Revolution. . . . Liberty no longer exists. With a contemptuous smile we are burying today even its memory. For years now there has been an effort to make us believe that since equality does not exist in nature, it was puerile to want to make it govern in law and thereby try to assure that social iniquities would not be added to the inequalities of nature. We humbly repent believing all that. We now know that justice means the law of the most powerful, and that the brotherhood inscribed on our public monuments is only a hollow word, since it postulated equality. . . . The homeland has been invaded. . . . Each person, gentlemen, will tell the story in his own way. I will stay with the evidence of facts—facts that any Frenchman of the other France, without a newspaper, with only the information that you are willing to provide, but with his Cartesian good sense, can clearly and distinctly discern. . . . You can prepare to accomplish with impunity this resurrection of servitude, this apology for the stupidity you call the recovery of spiritual and moral values, because the enemy has taken over on our soil. . . . For you to triumph here, you needed Hitler's Germany to be victorious, leaving France as nothing but a pile of corpses and ruins.[10]

Costedet and those who think as he does are inevitably victorious in this struggle over definitions, since they now have the power to impose their idea of the "true France." "This time," he tells Davy-Burnaud, "for the first time, we are among Frenchmen, and those who do not understand will be excluded from the national community."[11] Taking his revenge in the name of duty, Costedet writes a menacing letter to all Davy-Burnaud's associates to inform them of the latter's unacceptable criticism of Pétain and the New Order, letting them know he expects them to take "appropriate" measures and will make his own decisions accordingly.

The notion of a diary, particularly one not intended for publication, usually implies a record of private life. In Thomas's personal and fictional diaries, however, the boundaries between public and private are blurred. Since she wrote Costedet's diary at the same time as her own, both journals depend on the same historical present. The most intriguing intersections between Thomas's diary and that of her fictional collaborator occur in entries of specific public events and attitudes. Some are registered in one diary and not the other; some are recorded in both. In either case, a parallel reading of the two diaries creates a complex dynamic of reflections in which silences are often as revealing as what is said.

From the beginning of the occupation, Thomas records her dismay and despair at the antisemitic measures being enacted. Her first shock of antisemitism on display took place when she checked the bus schedule at the local information center and saw stamped on the poster: "Our enemy is the ———. Our enemy is the ———." Someone has tried to erase the last word. Finally she deciphers it: "Our enemy is the *Jew*." Her reaction is revealing: "Where are we?"[12] In spite of everything she knows, her immediate response is a reflex of disbelief that this could be happening in France.

On October 3, 1940, the first Jewish Statute was promulgated by Vichy, before any demand had been made by the Germans. It defined who was Jewish in the eyes of the French State in order to exclude Jews from most positions of public service as well as professions influencing public opinion—the press, radio, cinema, theater. Thomas writes: "Maybe there will be something that can be done. Live for that. And only that."[13] On October 18 a German ordinance required all Jewish enterprises in the occupied zone to be registered and placed under trusteeship. In her entry for that date she notes simply: "Law against the Jews: one does not feel proud to be a goy."[14]

Thomas's single sentence on October 18 collides with the two pages Costedet devotes to the same measure. His enthusiastic "Finally, a law against the Jews!" generates all the stereotypes of the time, which would become increasingly murderous: Enough half-breeds, Jews are cowards, France for the French. Costedet's exclamations are embedded in a narrative in which he imagines with delight the distress of the Jews he knows, starting with his business competitor Crémieux, a name chosen by Thomas to evoke the Jewish legislator Adolphe Crémieux, whose decree in 1870 enfranchised the Jews of Algeria and gave them citizenship. Costedet also thinks with pleasure of his old Jewish classmate Ernest Lévi, who always acted as if he knew everything, had read everything, and then pretended he was Catholic when Costedet and his buddies beat him up. Now, Costedet exults, Lévi can no longer use intrigue to win out over good Frenchmen.[15] Some weeks later Costedet gets up in the middle of the night to record his amazement at having been able to live fifty years of his life without knowing he was an Aryan, and a good Aryan. Costedet's diary is the only place where Thomas uses the word Aryan without putting it in quotations to highlight its illegitimacy. Since Costedet is in himself a parody, his words provide their own ironic distance. During the early period of Vichy France, from 1940 to 1941, Thomas found in the rhetoric of her first-person narrator an indispensable vehicle to voice not only her moral outrage but also her sense of insult to the Cartesian rationality that she considered part of her national heritage.

A comparison of the discourse of collaboration in the two diaries is equally illuminating. After meeting with Hitler at Montoire in the occupied zone on October 24, 1940, Pétain announced their agreement to the French people: "With honor and to maintain French unity, a unity of ten centuries, in the framework of constructive activity for the new European order, I am embarking today on the path of collaboration." When Costedet describes local incidents against the occupying forces, he worries that the Germans will stop believing in France's desire for collaboration. Thomas's own analysis of the politics of collaboration takes place on two levels. Listening to speeches by Hitler shortly after Pétain's message, she notes that there is not a word in them about collaboration, that Hitler completely ignores the Vichy government and what she calls its servile attempt to apply national socialist methods to France. "France," she writes, "simply does not exist any more."[16] Her analysis is in accord with the future judgment of historians that collaboration was not a German demand, but a proposal that came from the French, and that Hitler rejected.[17]

In the language used to describe the New Order of collaboration, Thomas finds a confirmation of France's discursive and cultural annihilation. Concepts that defined desires of the French left during the previous decade—Europe, revolution, socialism—have been redefined and taken over by a policy described by Thomas in 1940 as "the Europe of Attila or of the Holy German Empire; the revolution of 1815; a socialism whose aim is to enslave the individual."[18] The conflict of definitions between the two diaries takes place within each diary as well. Costedet struggles to understand that revolution, which he always thought was bad, is now good, since it is a revolution from above. Thomas struggles to rethink some negative terms in her Marxist lexicon, specifically "bourgeois freedom" and "individualism," which have now become negative terms in the Pétainist lexicon as well.

An entry in Costedet's journal on October 19 shows that tracts supporting de

Gaulle have already been circulating in the occupied zone. Costedet notes that he has found in his mail an envelope containing tracts from the "sinister" General de Gaulle and comments that de Gaulle "feigns" to be antisemitic and anticommunist while at the same time condemning Germany and the government of Pétain. Costedet's entry includes a direct quotation from the tract that praises de Gaulle's "greatness, the spirit of sacrifice and determination that drives him" and attacks the "iniquity" of those who call him a traitor, thereby "bring[ing] dishonor only on themselves."[19] The direct quotation suggests that Thomas or one of her friends must have received the tract in the mail. Costedet's horror that someone would send him such a tract is intensified by his panic that the maid will report him to the Kommandantur, and by his rage at being implicated in a "conspiracy" in which he is not even able to denounce anyone.

In Thomas's personal diary the few allusions to de Gaulle are brief mentions without commentary, although in one entry the subtext provides its own commentary of her support for unified resistance against the occupiers, beyond factional differences between Gaullists and leftists within the Resistance. On November 11 a student demonstration took place in Paris with students carrying signs that read simply "Vive le général." Writing from Arcachon, she records the event a few days after it occurred. The general being celebrated is left unnamed in her diary as he was in the demonstration. But she takes note of the big poles that the students carried on their shoulder; in French the term is "*de grandes gaules.*"[20]

During this period when she was writing in two journals, Thomas showed her ambivalence toward the Communists and the Soviet Union. She records her unease about their intentions, noting that without the USSR the cause will be desperate "for a thousand years," followed by a question she leaves unanswered: "And with it?"[21] In February 1941, four months before the invasion of the Soviet Union by Hitler's armies, she writes that the USSR has put itself on a war footing (a false rumor), and wonders against whom. In Costedet's journal, although the word "revolution" appears often—both the good kind of revolution and the bad—there are no direct allusions to the Soviet Union or the Communist Party. Since the USSR was effectively neutralized by the Nazi-Soviet pact, it became briefly irrelevant as a target for Pétainist propaganda and was hardly mentioned in *La Petite Gironde,* the regional collaborationist newspaper to which Thomas refers frequently in both journals.

The opposed voices of resistance and collaboration find their most striking symmetry in evocations by Thomas and Costedet of a local parade of German troops, an entry dated April 26, 1941, in both diaries. Costedet watches the spectacle of these troops in a delirium of admiration, punctuated with exclamation points. Thomas describes the same parade in her own diary in a language that is both metaphorical and visually precise, conveying her horror without the need for any commentary. Her rendering of opposed emotional reactions to the image of men metamorphosed into an inhuman, all-powerful entity goes far in explaining the choices of those who resisted and those who actively collaborated with the forces of the Reich.

When Thomas saw the first German soldiers of the occupation entering Arcachon, on June 29, 1940, she described her dominant feeling as hatred. The next day she watched them with their machine guns pointing to the sky, on motorcycles, in cars, and in trucks, "green and gray, like huge insects with a hard, chitinous shell."[22] Not surprisingly, her response to Nazi actions was in direct opposition to that of Costedet. However, the portrayal of individual German soldiers in the two diaries is diverse, often more sympathetic in Thomas's journal than in the fictional diary. When Costedet records local stories of brutality by German officers, against their own soldiers as well as against the French, he most often approves, in the name of the higher interest of collaboration or out of admiration for the Germans' superior power. In response to his wife's occasional distress, he reproaches her for criticizing officers of the army of the country with which the French are collaborating, an army which is protecting them from "perfidious" England, the "traitorous" ex-general de Gaulle, and "real" revolution, the one that would take everything away from them.

In her own diary, Thomas recounts a number of anecdotes that humanize individual German soldiers. In February 1941, from the window of the villa in Arcachon where she was convalescing, she looked at the house across the courtyard that had been occupied by Germans who departed for maneuvers in Royan, where many were killed in bombings by the Royal Air Force: "There was Hans, there was Ludwig, there was Ernst or Heinrich, the one who played with a little dog, the one who whistled at the window when he brushed his clothes, the one who threw bread over the gate for my neighbor's chickens." Even German officers are sometimes represented as bewildered and vulnerable, victims as well as victimizers. She presents a series of anecdotes she has heard about the occupiers that she calls "distant and unverifiable" but in which she finds a sympathetic "human resonance"—very different, she notes, from the chauvinistic stories of "the other war," the Great War of 1914, when all Germans were demonized.

In one anecdote, a German officer follows a woman and her small children in the street. In response to her fear, he tells her that he is following her children, and asks permission to embrace them, which she grants. A few minutes later, she hears a shot ring out; the officer has killed himself. Under the heading "Refusal to obey?" Thomas records several accounts by women who have had rooms in their homes requisitioned by Germans. An officer breaks down sobbing after he learns that his son has been shot for refusing to obey orders. Another is in drunken despair after following a command to execute thirty of his men who had dared to rebel. As late as March 1941, she asks what now seems an astonishing question: "Do these stories indicate insubordination in an army which from the outside looks like a perfectly regulated machine?"[23] Like many others on the French left during this early period of the occupation, Édith Thomas had not yet abandoned hope that there could be a resistance by ordinary German soldiers and even officers against their Nazi masters.

Since she no longer had access to the public forum of journalism to voice her political opinions, the two diaries served as her writing link to the external world, taking over as the primary outlet of expression for what she saw happening around her. In Costedet's fictional narrative, multiple voices are dramatized through his reporting of conversations with and about a number of other characters. Multiple voices in a different sense emerge from Thomas's own diary as well. Her solitary voice fragments into a complex polyphony of political analyses, observations of the local scene, anecdotes she has heard, political and personal poems, doubts about herself as a writer and a woman, reflections on her illness, notations about "Prometheus" and "Sappho" (two epic plays she was writing), and abundant quotations from her readings.

Always a voracious reader, she liked to cite passages that made a strong impression on her, positive or negative, taking special pleasure in quoting classical writers in whom she finds a critique of the ideology of the French State: Diderot, Proust, Flaubert, and even Racine. Transcribing with a few changes an extended monologue from Racine's biblical tragedy *Esther,* she wonders if anyone would have the courage to perform it in occupied Paris and imagines the role of the villain Haman played as Pierre Laval, Pétain's hated minister of state. She filters all her reading through the lens of the occupation: from works on history, philosophy, and politics to the writings of contemporary literary icons like Colette and Gide, both of whom disappoint her. She copies in its entirety a haunting poem by Aragon with the comment "Much will be forgiven Aragon for having written and published his 'Santa Espina' now."[24] For readers in 1941 who understood its allusions, the poem evoked a song that was well known to Republicans fighting against fascist Spain, linking the emotion of their struggle to the French Resistance.

In the collaborationist newspaper *La Gerbe,* Jean Cocteau addressed a plea to young writers, asking them to defend the territories of "l'Esprit." Thomas responded—in her diary—with a long letter in which she contrasts France's rationalist Cartesian heritage with the irrational belief in Pétain demanded by the Vichy regime. As she puts it, "To the *cogito ergo sum* of Descartes, which was rather satisfying to one's intelligence, what is preferred now is *credo quia absurdum*" (I believe because it is absurd). In its original context, the latter credo was a formulation by the early Christian Tertullian about the irrationality of true religious faith. Thomas decides it is pointless to send her letter since it cannot be published; she concludes the entry on December 7, 1940 with a note to herself: "See in the spring what can be done. Act wittingly—but act."[25]

Intimate experiences were shaped by the public realities of the occupation. When symptoms of what could be a recurrence of tuberculosis appear, she wonders if she will have the courage to live; but she feels imprisoned whether she is well or ill. She describes her resection surgery that was performed in a nearby clinic; the treatment involved excising segments of the ribs in order to immobilize the lung. Before each part of the procedure she tells herself that whatever happens, whatever the pain, she will not cry out, "the only elegance that remains to me, my head under a towel."[26] Her desire to forget and remember her obsessive love for Stefan is complicated by his being a Polish Jew, intensifying her anguish and creating a need to transform him into an embodiment of the wandering Jew.

Thomas decided to bring Costedet's diary to a close on May 2, 1941, after the death of his mother-in-law, who leaves her daughter and son-in-law a considerable estate. With that inheritance and the huge profits he has made in black market transactions, he will sell Ladies' Paradise and become a gentleman farmer, as will his son after him. They will start a family dynasty as leaders of the New Order, since Pétain has proclaimed the nobility of the land. One of the explanations for this rather abrupt ending is circumstantial; Édith Thomas provisionally left Arcachon at the beginning of May to return to Paris. But one can also suppose that she had exhausted the cathartic function of her satire and wanted to be done with this Pétainist diary. In the spring of 1941, when neither the Soviet Union nor the United States had yet entered the war against the Nazis, an Allied victory was difficult to imagine. The only credible dénouement for her fictional diary, dictated by the real historical situation of the time, was the triumph of Célestin Costedet.

In September 1941 Édith and Gérard left Arcachon definitively. Gérard, who continued to suffer from spinal tuberculosis throughout the occupation years, went to reside with his mother's sister, who took care of him in Imgrandes, a village in the province of Touraine, while his wife and two children were obliged to live apart from him in the next village, two kilometers away, to avoid the risk of contagion. Édith returned to Paris, sufficiently recovered, according to her doctor, to resume normal life, so long as she continued periodically to have artificial pneumothorax (collapse therapy).

Although she questioned what "a normal life" could possibly mean when her country was occupied, she felt that she could no longer permit herself to use illness as a refuge or an alibi. After having been obliged for two years to depend on the financial assistance of her father, she first needed to confront the urgent question of how to earn a living. She went to see Jean Paulhan, who suggested she could earn money by writing either for the *Nouvelle Revue française,* the most prominent French literary journal between the wars, or for *Comoedia,* a theatrical journal. Paulhan himself had resigned from the *NRF* in 1940 and its direction had been assumed by Drieu la Rochelle, "the house fascist," as Herbert Lottman puts it.[27] For Édith Thomas, the *NRF* was out of the question; as for *Comoedia,* after reading one issue, she was determined not to publish anything for the official press, however innocuous it might seem.

As a graduate of the École des Chartes and still in need of some way to support herself, she registered as an "unemployed intellectual" (*chômeur intellectuel*). An official category of the period, it was designed to provide work for people trained in specific public sectors, including archives, libraries, museums, and laboratories.[28] In her diary Thomas comments bitterly on the appropriateness of that title to describe her situation, "Intellectual, certainly, doubly and triply, alas! And unemployed as a consequence, since these times deny and scorn any work of the intelligence. Moreover, it is in the name of what is least precious to me—my title of *archiviste-paléographe*—that I could be co-opted by that world: poets and writers need only keep quiet."[29]

Shortly after returning to Paris and beginning her work at the Archives nationales, she renewed acquaintance with someone she had known for a long time in the library world whom I will call "Renaud," the name by which she sometimes refers to him in the diary and the one she will give the character based on him in her novel published in 1945, *Le Champ libre* (Free and clear). In contrast to Stefan and her other phantom lovers, Renaud was Catholic, "bourgeois," and concerned mostly about the financial hardships of the time. Nevertheless, his admiration and his romantic interest in her made her determined that it was time to get rid of "the sclerosis of virginity." With no illusion that this was or would be the great love she had dreamed of, she approached the situation as a belated initiation to femininity. After their first sexual encounter she writes in her diary, "Last night R. made me a woman: more pain than pleasure. But at least the 'inferiority complex' is destroyed. Perhaps pleasure will come after knowledge, and from that knowledge." Although she initially saw Renaud as a womanizer à la Montherlant, she soon realized that she had been entirely mistaken. With humor and self-mockery she writes, "What complexes! Freud's entire arsenal would not be enough to throw light on them. Here I have the proof that Catholic education is the most pernicious there is. Unless [Renaud] has been sent to me by divine Providence to manifest the existence of His Imma-

nent Justice. With my ethical and sublime scruples, I poisoned the life of two excellent fellows [Georges and Stefan] who saw in love no more than what I am
putting into it now. And I meet in turn a man racked by moral and religious
taboos."[30] After a couple of months Renaud decided he could find happiness
only in marriage, and the relationship ended. She continued to feel a certain affection for him, for his qualities of sincerity and lack of pretense, and because
he was her first lover.

In order to work in a state job, or even to travel from one zone to the other,
individuals were required to swear under oath that they were neither Jewish nor
freemasons. Simone de Beauvoir, as a professor of philosophy at the Lycée
Camille Sée, has been much criticized for signing such a statement. In *Une si
douce Occupation* (Such an easy occupation), a polemic against both Jean-Paul
Sartre and Simone de Beauvoir, Gilbert Joseph claims that her oath was "equivalent to committing an unworthy act and joining the mass of consenting French
people whose cowardice she otherwise scathingly attacks."[31] In contrast to Simone de Beauvoir, Édith Thomas made her acts conform to her thoughts during the harshest years of the occupation, even when it meant risking her life. In
this instance, however, the response of Thomas to the same situation calls into
question Joseph's purist argument, which ignores the day-to-day realities of occupied France. At least twice, for work and for travel authorization, when she
was obliged to declare that her father and her mother were Catholic and that she
herself was neither Jewish nor a freemason, she did so with unconflicted cynicism. Applying for a pass to the unoccupied zone, she had to swear she was
"Aryan" and the employee said to her: "Swear on anything you want but not on
my head. I don't want to die from all the false oaths that are made every day in
this room." Another employee, examining her application, remarked: "You say
you want to visit your aunt. A very distantly related aunt, I'm sure. Don't protest.
If that cons them one more time, I'd be only too pleased."[32]

The edict of May 29, 1942, which obliged Jews who resided in the occupied
zone to wear the yellow star, was the first antisemitic measure imposed by the
Germans without the cooperation of Vichy officials, who had warned that it
would create sympathy for the Jews and widespread disgust. The imposition of
the yellow star marked the first clear change in public opinion during the occupation. Previously, anti-Jewish legislation could be ignored by most of the
French public. Now, the forcible marking of Jews made persecution real and visible in everyday life. Édith Thomas recorded the edict in her diary on June 6
when she saw two little girls coming out of school on the rue des Archives: the
yellow star had been "sewn carefully on the girls' aprons, at the place of the
heart." She imagines the mother's tears of rage and despair as she sews the star
on her daughters' clothing. And Thomas experiences "a sudden shock, as if I

didn't understand, as if I didn't believe, in spite of everything, that this infamous possibility was going to become real."[33]

The scene of the two girls on the rue des Archives inspired Thomas's short story "L'Étoile jaune" (The yellow star), which she wrote in 1942 or early 1943, although it was not published until after the war. Thomas puts herself in the place of a mother, Thérèse Lévy, who is sewing the star on her eight-year-old daughter's coat. The yellow star is described as "an evil talisman from the depth of the ages, like a curse never extinguished, which fell on them implacably from generation to generation." Thérèse knows that this ignominious emblem has been imposed on Jews in Germany, but in France, "chez nous," she thought that could not happen. Yet she is well aware that France has already taken measures against the Jews and sent them to concentration camps. After Thérèse was fired from her job at the Bibliothèque de l'Arsenal, a bookstore owner felt sorry for her and found work she could do in his attic, where her presence cannot "contaminate the 'Aryans'" who come into the store. And now, the official newspapers gleefully welcome these symbols that allow people to know immediately who is Jewish.[34]

Thomas's fictional Thérèse is completely French, not only culturally but in her family history as well. Tracing her genealogy, Thomas provides brief reminders of the enlightened aspects of French Jewish history. Thérèse's family has lived in France for centuries, going back to the Lévy who was a doctor in the court of Francis I. From the sixteenth century, Thérèse can follow the Lévy family's male line from father to son, all of them doctors. On her mother's side, her known family history goes back to the French Revolution, which gave Jews human and civil rights "after centuries of ostracism, contempt, and persecution." The father of Thérèse lost a leg in the war of 1914–18. Her husband was killed during the war in 1940.

Thérèse is a counterpoint to the foreign and cosmopolitan Jewishness represented in Édith Thomas's imagination by Stefan, whom she describes somewhat exotically in her diary: "I can't stop thinking about you . . . , this Jew without a country, from every country: Poland, Switzerland, Russia, Germany, France, and now, faithful to your wandering destiny, perhaps England. This classless Jew from every class: bourgeois, intellectual, and artistic, in the revolution that opposes and denies them all. This Jew of every culture and every language." Early in the war she had written: "I love him because he is who he is—with his heavy bull-like shoulders, his curious Mongol face, his foreignness: the background of Polish Jews and tsars, of artists, bankers, ghettos."[35]

The Jews in Édith Thomas's milieu, French or foreign, had been completely assimilated into French culture. On that level Thomas's cosmopolitan Stefan, a wandering Jew, an intellectual and a communist, is no different from her fictional character. Thérèse tries to understand what in her is "Jewish" and finds herself perplexed. For generations, her family has not practiced Judaism as a religion. She wonders how she can explain Jewishness to her daughter when she herself cannot define it, although she realizes that many Jews who recently arrived in France from countries where they had been persecuted—as they were now being persecuted in France—still "narrowly practiced their ancient religion." Her description reflects the terms in which secular, assimilated Jews, whether French or foreign, tended to differentiate themselves from orthodox Jews. In the Enlightenment spirit common to so many French progressives, Jewish or not, Thomas minimizes the specificity of Jewish identity, ascribing to Thérèse the feeling that "she suffered more as a Frenchwoman than as a Jewess to see the spirit of France crushed and destroyed, the France that proudly and generously claimed to legislate for Man."[36]

As a French historian, Thomas was well aware of the history of the Jews in France, which in her reading made their persecution during the occupation all the more awful and difficult to comprehend. In the early years of the French Revolution, France became the first European country to emancipate and integrate its Jews into the republic as French citizens. In the nineteenth century and up to the Second World War, Jews played a major role in French social and cultural life, far beyond their numbers. In spite of crises like the Dreyfus affair, it seemed to Thomas that French society was moving beyond the historical problem of antisemitism. In her diary she wonders how long it will take to reestablish the truth "that there is no Jewish question, that this is one of the false problems invented by these times to avoid posing and resolving the others."[37] The phrase "Jewish question" is a clear reference to the Institute for the Study of Jewish Questions, sponsored by the Germans, and the General Commission for Jewish Questions, created in March 1941 and charged with the execution of a French anti-Jewish program. In May 1942 its commissioner, Xavier Vallat, deemed too soft, was replaced by Darquier de Pellepoix, who oversaw the atrocities that followed.

On June 24 Thomas returned in her diary to the wearing of the yellow star in order to reflect on its meaning from another perspective:

> It proves to us that the Jewish race does not exist. Only one out of ten Jews has the classic physiognomy that one usually attributes to them and that can be found just as easily and even more so in Spaniards or Arabs. The others are racially assimilated to the people among whom they have lived. . . . Faces in all shapes, every eye color and hair color, noses of every type; every height. Jews, therefore, are not *a* race. A religion? Not that either. How many are converted, or nonpracticing? How many are there

who obey the Law of Moses? So what remains? A certain kind of mind [*esprit*]? But "Aryans" like me have a Jewish mind (rationalism, internationalism, Marxism, etc.), whereas many Jews are not concerned about those issues or react differently, for instance the pro-fascist Jew before the war.[38]

She repeats the conclusion of her earlier diary entry that the Jewish question is one more imposture of the times.

Thomas's brief argument against a Jewish essence is strikingly suggestive of arguments that will be elaborated and complicated in Jean-Paul Sartre's portrait of the Jew in his *Réflexions sur la question juive*, first published in 1946. Among the contradictory stereotypes of Jews, Thomas gives as an example the rationalist, internationalist, Marxist mentality that happens to characterize her own way of thinking. Sartre in his argument chooses the opposed and equally murderous stereotype, that of Jews who dominate the financial world, "without taking into account," he writes, "that their apparent autonomy within the nation comes from the fact that they were originally forced into these trades by being forbidden all others. Thus it is no exaggeration to say that it is the Christians who have *created* the Jew."[39] In her June 6 diary entry on the yellow star, Édith Thomas writes: "Throughout history, the unity of a dispersed people was artificially maintained from the outside, through contempt, isolation, and persecution. They have never been allowed fully to merge. It is the goys who have created the Jewish mind." For Édith Thomas as for Sartre, and almost in the same terms, the Jew is not a race, a religion, or an *esprit*. He is defined entirely from the outside as a creation of the antisemitic other, Christian or goy. When Sartre—and Édith Thomas—write that the antisemite has created the Jew, their meaning is the idea of the Jew as a problem. In that context, Sartre makes an analogy with a comment of Richard Wright's: "There is no Negro problem in the United States; there is only a White problem."[40] Édith Thomas's reasoning is entirely compatible with that of Sartre in their common refusal of a Jewish essence, the basis of antisemitic ideology.

After the armistice between France and Germany in June 1940, Édith Thomas's diary became the only place where she could express her opinions on issues more or less freely. However, once she began to be directly involved in Resistance activities, beginning in the summer of 1942, she wrote in her diary at increasingly infrequent intervals. There was less time and more she could not say, since she would be risking not only her own life if she were arrested, but the lives of others as well.

6

WRITING UNDERGROUND

Édith Thomas felt grateful for her position at the Archives, although her pneumothorax was considered a health handicap, which made her officially ineligible for a tenured appointment, should such a position become available. The pay she received as an "unemployed intellectual" provided just enough to live on. But she found in the Archives during those years a haven and a refuge. From the window of her attic office she looked out on the garden and heard blackbirds and pigeons; in the spring she saw the trees turning green. Most important, her work involved nothing that could serve in the construction of Nazi Europe. The Archives turned out to be an ideal place to "write poems, conspire, and hide tracts."[1] It was a good hiding place for other forbidden material as well. After a rendezvous that hadn't worked out during which she was supposed to pass on some printing plans for *Les Lettres françaises,* she hid them in the back of a neglected closet. Many years after the war a young man who worked in the Archives doing errands came to her office door holding the dusty blueprints with evident distaste: "Mademoiselle, these must belong to you."[2]

Like so many Communist and leftist intellectuals of her generation, she discovered how much she loved her country only after it was invaded. Until then, as an internationalist and a Marxist, she was not conscious of any particular solidarity with France, which appeared most often in her writings of the 1930s to show the injustices of capitalism. With the German occupation, she awakened to a visceral love of France that she felt first of all as a physical attachment to the places she knew intimately, especially Sainte-Aulde and its surroundings. It is surely not a coincidence that the neighboring towns she evokes in this context are Chateau-Thierry, the birthplace of La Fontaine, and La Ferté-Milon, the birthplace of Racine. The sight of German soldiers with their boots and helmets and guns taking over her home village of Sainte-Aulde, trampling on her rose garden, was intolerable. She felt the same repulsion when she watched them marching through the deserted streets of Paris, "like monstrous insects,"[3] and when she saw the swastika on the Nazi flag at the place de la Concorde, also described in insect imagery as "a huge spider, glutted with blood."[4]

During the winter of 1941, Thomas tried to no avail to engage in some form of resistance. Most of the people she had known and worked with before the war were dispersed. Some were prisoners in Germany and others were refugees in the southern zone or exiles somewhere else; they had disappeared without leaving any trace. When she talked about entering the Resistance with comrades who remained in Paris, she was told nothing or given vague responses to the effect that she could be more helpful outside the underground movement. She was given a few tasks: raising money for families of people who had been deported and writing a few clandestine articles, although she had no idea if they would appear. These typed articles, which she kept, are attributed to "René Luynes," a name she seems to have taken either from a village in Touraine near the family home or from the rue Luynes in Paris, a street near the Gallimard publishing house.

One of her early pieces, inspired by the German-imposed censorship, is called "Forbidden Literature." In September 1940, the Syndicate of French Publishers submitted to the demand of the Propagandastaffel that they agree to "self-censorship." Previously published books judged undesirable would no longer be available in bookstores. The long list of books that could not be sold, called the Otto list, was widely distributed. In successively more restrictive versions it included, among other interdictions, all books by Jews and any book that could be construed as either anti-Nazi or anti-German. Vichy made its own contributions to what Thomas calls "the abundance of fruits deemed poisonous from now on": "The pink and blue nonsense which reigns in the little kingdom of Vichy has condemned *Tartuffe* as immoral, something we've forgotten since the seventeenth century." Vichy could not have chosen a more perfect commentary on its policies than its condemnation of Molière's classic satire of hypocrisy. Going through the list of all that has been forbidden, Thomas finds the only satisfying response in the mocking voice of Beaumarchais's Figaro: "Provided that I do not write about the government, or about religion, or politics, or morals, or those in power, or public bodies, or the Opera, or the other state theaters, or about anybody who is active in anything, I can print whatever I want with perfect freedom, under the supervision of two or three censors."[5]

Censorship laws, severely restricting information that could be released and themes that could be developed, were reinforced by a series of regulations pertaining to the material production and distribution of undesirable publications. As early as October 1940 an ordinance from the Paris police prefecture forbade manufacturers and wholesale merchants from selling duplicating machines and paper that could be used to make circulars or mimeographed tracts without police authorization. As a result, machines, stencils, and paper had to be procured illegally, either at the exorbitant prices of the black market or through thefts from merchants or official administrative offices. Distribution was also a major problem. In addition to German laws against even receiving anti-German tracts without informing the local Kommandantur, a measure in September 1941 stipulated that persons who collaborated in distributing tracts, as well as persons who spread Communist ideas through the spoken or written word, would be arrested.

The first underground publication of the occupation was the journal *Pantagruel,* which appeared in October 1940 in linotype, two double sheets clearly and elegantly typed. Its editor, Raymond Deiss, a solitary man unaligned with any political party or movement, was a music publisher who worked from his home, which happened to be on the rue Rouget de Lisle, named for the composer of the French national anthem, the Marseillaise. Deiss pushed audacity to the point of sending *Pantagruel* to his neighbor, the Kommandant of Gross-Paris, who resided across the street in the Continental Hotel. He urged his compatriots: "Do not remain inert or indifferent. France has not been defeated." With two associates, Deiss printed and distributed sixteen issues of *Pantagruel* until October 1941, when he was arrested along with his two associates. None of them survived. Deiss was sent to prison in Cologne, Germany, and on August 24, 1943, he was decapitated with an axe. The modest aim of his journal had been "simply to preserve our thousand-year-old right to think for ourselves."[6] Raymond Deiss was the first cousin of Georges Thomas, Édith's father.

One of the people that Thomas had contacted during the winter of 1941–42 was Claude Morgan, a Communist militant she had known slightly before the war. Although they were on the same side in their way of thinking, he gave her the impression he was not involved in the Resistance. On a summer day in 1942, Morgan came to see her at the Archives, at the end of a labyrinth of poorly lit corridors above several flights of stairs, "an ideal place to conspire," as she puts it in her memoir. In the tone of self-deprecation she often assumed when she wrote of her work as an archivist, she asks rhetorically: "Who would believe that human beings who have chosen the dust of the past could still be interested enough in life to risk their own?"[7] Morgan told her of the death of Jacques Decour, whom the Germans had executed on May 30. Decour, a young novelist, professor of German literature and editor-in-chief of *Commune,* was one of the people to whom she had written after the Nazi-Soviet pact, asking that he send

back any work of hers he was planning to publish. She had met him a few times
and remembered his ironic smile and his subtle intelligence. Although he was
born into a wealthy bourgeois family, he decided to join the Communist Party.
Decour seemed to refute by his example the Marxist idea that class determines
consciousness. His death as a communist for the Resistance revived Thomas's
faith in communism as a living ideal.

With the help of Jean Paulhan, Decour had brought together a group of Resistance writers to found the Comité national des écrivains (CNE), whose members included both communists and noncommunists, and to prepare the
publication of an underground newspaper. After Decour's arrest, the printing
press and the articles that had been intended for the first issue fell into German
hands. The CNE ceased to exist. In September 1942 Morgan by himself put together what became the first issue of *Les Lettres françaises,* consisting of a few
sheets that had been reproduced on a mimeo machine after a second printing
press disappeared. The Communist Party gave him the assignment of reviving
the initial committee but he did not know who they were, except for Jean Paulhan, whom he had never met. Morgan urged Édith Thomas to go and see Paulhan, who could give her the names of the original members, which he did.
Beginning in September 1942, the underground *Lettres françaises* eventually became the most influential organ of intellectual Resistance during the occupation, appearing every month until the liberation.

Édith Thomas's most powerful contribution to *Les Lettres françaises* was the
editorial she wrote for the second issue in October 1942. That issue, too, was
hastily put together on a duplicating machine, since she and Morgan did not yet
have the resources or the network of comrades that would enable them to se-
cure a printing press. Thomas announced her subject in large, calligraphic letters: "Crier la vérité!" The article builds on repeated juxtapositions of what can
be talked about and what remains silent. It is pleasant, she writes, to evoke the
sweet melancholy of autumn, "its asters and its dahlias, and its leaves turning
russet on the beech trees" or the sound of the radio playing Debussy's *Pelléas
and Mélisande.* The truths of the war are kept silent, both the horrors "over
there" in the east, and "here" as well. Much of what she writes in the article was
initially recorded in her diary.

In "Crier la vérité!" she evokes "thousands and thousands of men in prison
or in camps," "their only drink two ladlefuls of dishwater a day, their only food
two hundred grams of bread," a reference to the horrendous conditions in the
concentration camp outside of Paris. Her diary entry on Christmas Day, 1941, is
more explicit. She names and describes the camp of Drancy, administered by
the French, where "Jews are dying of hunger." Bread is sold clandestinely in the
camp at a grotesquely inflated price; "it is the French police who apply that rate."

Les Lettres françaises

OCTOBRE 1942   N°2

Crier la vérité!

Est-ce déjà l'automne avec ses asters et ses dahlias, et ses feuilles roussies par pla ce s, sur les hêtres? Est-ce la mélancolie de l'automne sur l'asphalte tiède et les petites voitures des marchandes de quatre saisons pleines de fruits aussi beaux que des fruits de paix et si étonnants d'exister encore?

Là-bas, là-bas, à l'Est, des millions et des millions d'hommes dans le choc effroyable des tanks, dans le bruit- inhumain -qui a dépassé la zone où l'oreille humaine peut encore entendre- se jettent les uns sur les autres, en cet instant.

Une cloche sonne, ici et là. Et plus loin encore, se répondant d'un clocher à l'autre. Un pigeon roucoule sur les arbes du jardin. Midi. Qui pourrait parler de la douceur de l'air...

Ici. Ici. Des milliers et des milliers d'hommes sont en prison ou dans les camps. Sais tu qu'ils ont deux louches d'eau de vaisselle à boire par jour pour tout breuvage, et deux cents grammes de pain pour toute nourriture? Et qu'un homme d'un mètre soixante-quinze ne pesait plus que trente kilogs? Il est mort tout à l'heure.

Un appareil de T.S.F. vaguement joue PELEAS et MELISANDE. J'ai vu passer un train. En tête, un wagon contenait des gendarmes français et des soldats allemands. Puis, venaient des wagons à bestiaux plombés. Des bras maigres d'enfants se cramponnaient aux barreaux. Une main au dehors s'agitait comme une feuille dans la tempête. Quand le train a ralenti, des voix ont crié: "Maman". Et rien n'a répondu que le le grincement des essieux. Tu peux dire ensuite que l'art n'a pas de patrie. Tu peux dire ensuite que l'artiste doit savoir s'isoler dans sa tour d'ivoire, faire son métier, rien que son métier.

Notre métier? Pour en être digne, il faut dire la vérité. La vérité est totale ou n'est pas. La vérité: les étoiles sur les poitrines l'arrachement d s enfants aux mères, les hommes qu'on fusille chaque jour, la dégradation méthodique de tout un peuple- la vérité est interdite, la douceur de l'automne? C n'est pas la vérité. Elle est un mensonge si tu oses en parler en l'isolant de l'espoir qui te la laisse encore. Pire, elle est un rideau de fumée cachant la vérité, masquant le crime, protégeant le criminel! Elle est complicité.

-on
Or, que nous p rmet/désormais d'exprimer dans nos livres? Les écrivains allemands Suite page 2.....

D'UN FRONT A L'AUTRE

Il y a huit jours, HITLER hurla que Stalingrad serait pris. Mais Stalingrad tient toujours. Et la Caspienne est encore loin, et Bakou encore plus loin et les pas ses du Caucase ne sont pas franchies. Mais le sang allemand coule à flots par d'effroyables blessures. Miracle? Non. Conséquent ce/d'un peuple qui se bat comme seuls se battent des hommes conscients de défendre mieux que la vie: tout ce qui rend la vie digne d'être vécue. C'est bien pour cela que Stalingrad rappelle tant Valmy qu'un DEAT, obsédé par cette idée, tente piteusement de prouver que l'esprit de Valmy se trouve du côté des armées de KRUPP, ROE LING, GOERING & Cie!

Déjà l'hiver pointe. On est émerveillé devant l'intelligence de la stratégie soviétique qui est passée de la tactique du recul défensif à la bataille d'arrêt au moment précis où l'armée allemande se trou vait dans une position stratégique difficl le à tenir cet hiver.

C'est en effet un ordre du jour de STA LINE qui amenage les premiers jours de sep tembre que la phase des reculs était Suite page 2...

"Crier la vérité!" *Les Lettres françaises,* no. 2 (October 1942). Courtesy of Daniel Thomas.

With the kind of irony that informs her diary of Célestin Costedet, she adds, "Jewish capitalism, of course, can easily pay."[8]

Édith Thomas was one of the few writers to speak of the deportations, in that same early editorial of October 1942. She cries out what she had witnessed first-hand, a scene she had initially evoked in a brief, shocking diary entry on August 31, 1942: "I saw a freight train. In the cattle cars, there were children. Their hands passed through the bars. For the first time in my life I felt a *chill of horror* in my back."[9] It is likely that Édith Thomas saw the train as it went through one of the stations near Sainte-Aulde, which is about forty miles east of Paris on the Marne River. The trains were heading east to "an unknown destination," in the official phrase, from the camps near the Paris area: Drancy, Pithiviers, or Beaune-la-Rolande. More than six thousand children were deported to Auschwitz in 1942 alone. At the end of August of that year, children often made up most of the train.[10] In "Crier la vérité!" she writes:

> I saw a train go by. In the first car, there were French policemen and German soldiers. Then came cattle cars sealed with lead. Thin arms of children clutched onto the bars. A hand outside fluttered like a leaf in the storm. When the train slowed down, voices cried out: "Maman!" And the only reply was the grinding of the axles. . . .
>
> Our job? To be worthy of it, we must speak the truth. . . . The truth: the yellow star, children snatched from their mothers' arms, men shot every day, the methodical degradation of an entire people—the truth is forbidden. . . . If we want to remain worthy of our mission, there is only one possible way: to break the tomb of silence under which we are being suffocated and CRY OUT THE TRUTH![11]

Who are the intended readers of "Crier la vérité"? Édith Thomas is addressing her words, first of all, to other writers, to convey to them the urgency of voicing the truths that cannot be spoken in the official press. In 1945, Jean-Paul Sartre first announced his idea of *littérature engagée* in the presentation of his journal *Les Temps modernes*. "The 'committed' writer," he argues later in *What Is Literature?* "knows that words are action."[12] Already in 1942, Thomas's editorial for *Les Lettres françaises* put into practice the idea of the social responsibility of the writer that Sartre theorized after the war.

An undated article by Édith Thomas titled "Jews" seems to have been written after the summer of 1942. It is not clear whether this article, like others she signed René Luynes, was actually published by the underground press. She reports that increasingly brutal antisemitic measures have created some unexpected reactions. The previous night, a sudden clamor outside took her to her window, where she saw a car parked in front of a building down the street. Two forms were pushed into the car and she heard the cries of children piercing the darkness. The next morning she learned that the Gestapo had come to arrest a Jewish couple, leaving behind their children, two and five years old. The neighbors who took in these children belonged to the traditional right-wing bourgeoisie that for generations had been prejudiced against Jews. But that morning they said to her: "We will keep the children with us as long as necessary. We cannot be accomplices to such iniquity."[13]

Édith's father, Georges Thomas, died during the summer of 1942 after a brief illness. With the money from her inheritance, she was able to buy her own apartment at 15 rue Nicole, a quiet dead-end street on the left bank between the Luxembourg Gardens and the Val de Grâce church. From February 1943 until Paris was liberated in August 1944, meetings of the Resistance writers of the CNE in the occupied zone took place in Édith Thomas's apartment. Her building had an exceptional advantage from a Resistance point of view: the concierge lived in number 13 and could not watch the comings and goings in number 15, a particularly useful happenstance since the members of this clandestine movement were not very discreet. Looking out the window of her second floor apartment, Thomas would watch them arrive in little groups, walking unhurriedly, recognizable by that "*je ne sais quoi* that characterizes people of letters." When meetings were planned, she would receive phone calls that were supposed to be obscure but were so bizarre, she notes, that the most idiotic policeman could have figured out something was being covered up. She remembered walking one day near St. Germain des Prés and meeting two or three writers who said to her: "So, we're going to your place Thursday for a game of bridge?" The group was also remarkably imprudent. Although meetings of more than five people were strictly forbidden, Thomas recalled one meeting attended by twenty-two people, with fifteen bicycles parked in the entranceway.

The idea of a national committee of Resistance writers had been initiated by the Communist Party, which Thomas joined in the fall of 1942. In spite of its Communist origins, the group from the beginning was remarkably diverse, comprising poets, novelists, essayists, and journalists from divergent political, religious, and philosophical points of view, united only in their opposition to Vichy and the German occupation. There were communists, socialists, and Gaullists; Christians, agnostics, and atheists. The better-known writers in Thomas's apartment included Jean Paulhan, François Mauriac, Raymond Queneau, Paul Eluard, Jean Lescure, Jean Guéhenno, Albert Camus, and Jean-Paul Sartre, as well as the Dominican priest Father Maydieu. Thomas was the only woman at these meetings. She describes her role as if it were restricted to providing a meeting place and making sure that her guests were comfortable: "After I had managed to find enough chairs (which sometimes gave me a lot of trouble; the youngest sat on the floor), I remained silent in my corner." Anxiously on the alert, she felt responsible for the safety of everyone there and fearful that the Gestapo could surprise them at any moment.[14]

Since the most elementary caution required that she not take notes, she later was able to reconstruct only in general terms what they talked about: the forthcoming issue of *Les Lettres françaises,* the next volume of the Éditions de Minuit, news about the war, proposals for action suggested by Claude Morgan to the group. The fact that these suggestions came from the Communist Party did not create a problem. It was a time of reconciliation, of bringing together "celui qui croyait au ciel" and "celui qui n'y croyait pas" (the believer and the nonbeliever), as Aragon put it in one of his best-known Resistance poems.[15] Christians put aside their anticommunism and communists their anticlericalism.

According to the testimony of Claude Morgan, Édith Thomas was the linchpin of the CNE. In addition to contributing a number of poems and articles to *Les Lettres françaises,* she, more than anyone else, made the necessary connections among people and kept the group together.[16] Aside from serving as headquarters of the CNE, her apartment became the location for a number of delicate meetings between leaders, both communist and noncommunist, of the National Council of the Resistance. For instance, there were frequent meetings between Jacques Debû-Bridel, a Gaullist and representative of the Republican Federation, and Pierre Villon, a Communist and head of the National Front in the northern zone. Thomas also organized a meeting between Pierre Villon and a representative of General Giraud, who had parachuted from London and wanted to establish links with the Communist-led Resistance group Francs-Tireurs et Partisans (FTP). She tried to facilitate as many contacts as possible among diverse movements within the Resistance, whatever their political affiliation. Describing her role, Jean Guéhenno commented: "For me, the courage of the Resistance is symbolized by a woman like Édith."[17]

Parallel to *Les Lettres françaises,* an underground publishing house was created, an astonishing venture that had no equivalent anywhere in Europe.[18] The Éditions de Minuit were founded by the writer Pierre de Lescure and the draughtsman Jean Bruller. Although clandestine publishing would seem to be an oxymoron, the two men were determined to produce a series of volumes free of any concession to the enemy, books that would show real literary value and demonstrate to the world that the French spirit was still alive. Furthermore, the presentation of each book would be esthetically of high quality, from the paper and typography to the binding. All the difficulties of production and distribution confronted by the underground press were compounded in this ambitious venture. There was also the problem of finding authors willing to publish a book under conditions not only of danger but of anonymity as well. In his general preface, Pierre de Lescure affirmed the aim of the Éditions de Minuit: "Propaganda is not our domain. We intend to preserve our inner life and serve our art freely. Names are not important. Nor is personal fame. A difficult path is not important. It is a question of the spiritual purity of man." The purpose of these publications was twofold, to make it possible for French writers to be published in France without having to submit to censorship and, just as important, to project to the world an image of France that would counter the image projected by Vichy.

The underground Éditions de Minuit published its inaugural volume, *Le Silence de la Mer* by Vercors, in February 1942. The real identity of Vercors, a pseudonym taken from the mountainous Vercors region which later would become the scene of one of the bloodiest battles of the maquis, remained unknown throughout the war years "doubtless the only secret," Thomas writes, "of the literary Resistance."[19] At the CNE, the Éditions de Minuit were represented by "Madame Desvignes," occasionally accompanied by "Monsieur Desvignes," a mysterious character dressed in a large, gray cape, about whom Thomas and the others knew only that he was not the husband of Madame Desvignes. During the liberation they learned that Monsieur Desvignes was Vercors and that Vercors was the draughtsman Jean Bruller. His small book, smuggled abroad and republished in countries around the world, became the most influential and widely disseminated of Minuit's publications. The metaphor of the silence of the sea speaks to the hidden violence underlying the quiet surface of the story. In an article written many years after the war, Édith Thomas reflected on that metaphor in the context of what the book represented for the intellectual Resistance: "For us, in the torpor, the fear, the disgust, and the misery of those years—physical, moral, and intellectual—*The Silence of the Sea* was like a window that suddenly opened onto the sea. It proved that one could write committed literature that in no way recalled the chauvinistic vein of [Maurice] Barrès and others during the war of 1914."[20]

Silence was a pervasive theme in occupied France, constantly shifting between opposed and even contradictory meanings. Silence, first of all, was imposed by Vichy France and the German occupation—the silence of censorship, of oppression, and of death. There was the silence of conformity and accommodation to the realities of the time. But silence was also the silent choice of saying no, conveyed in titles such as Vercors's memoir *The Battle of Silence* as well as his story *The Silence of the Sea* and, most famously, Jean-Paul Sartre's 1945 essay, "The Republic of Silence."

Most of the narrative of *The Silence of the Sea*, which takes place over a period of six months in the winter and spring of 1941, consists of the monologue of a German officer as he speaks each evening to his unwilling hosts, an old man and his young niece who are obliged to lodge him in their home in the provinces.

Werner von Ebrennac is a musician, a man of culture and an ardent lover of France. His hosts listen to him in complete silence, the only resistance available to them. Day after day, he describes the marriage of complementary cultures that he has always dreamed of between France and Germany and that he hopes will come about, in spite of the war, in spite of Hitler, through the collaboration of their two countries. When he returns from a trip to Paris where his military superiors have summoned him, he appears in uniform before the old man and his niece to say farewell. He tells them that his superiors laughed at his notion of collaboration and made him understand that their idea of collaboration was to destroy France, not only its power but also its soul: "We will make [of France] a groveling bitch." In despair he has asked the officers for permission to be reposted to a fighting division headed for the Russian front, "to Hell."[21]

Vercors's message needs to be understood within the context not only of German occupation but also of Vichy propaganda in 1940 and 1941.[22] Vercors was writing in opposition to the official response of Pétain's government to the occupation, a response encouraged by Germany insofar as it served the Nazi regime, namely, that a politics of collaboration served the best interest of France. Although the seduction of that propaganda waned as the occupation became more brutal, it continued to have a certain appeal as long as the majority of the French were convinced of the inevitability of German victory. Vercors was also addressing those who had not given up their pacifism, who still allowed themselves to believe that collaboration could mean the rapprochement between France and Germany, a hope that had nurtured French leftist thinking until the Spanish Civil War. The ending of *The Silence of the Sea* transforms the meaning of what has preceded. Once von Ebrennac, this appealing and best of all possible German officers, learns the reality of German intentions for France, he does not rebel: all he can do is submit to orders that go against everything he believes.

The ambiguities of Werner von Ebrennac take on another dimension as they reflect the situation of an actual German officer in Paris during the occupation years who has often been evoked in connection with Vercors's main character. Gerhard Heller was the officer in charge of literary censorship, the Propagandastaffel, in Paris. Like von Ebrennac, he considered himself a Francophile, was deeply versed in French culture, and anti-Nazi. Heller, who died in 1990, relates his story in *Un Allemand à Paris, 1940–1944*, written in French and published in 1981. He emphasizes the Huguenot influence in the city of Potsdam where he was born in order to explain his early love for France, alongside his love for his native Germany. After studying Romance languages at the University of Heidelberg, he worked for the cultural services of German radio. Due to rheumatism and other health problems, he was not drafted for military service. Nev-

ertheless, in November 1940 he was given a uniform and the rank of Sonderführer (the equivalent of lieutenant) and sent to Paris. He claims that he succeeded in never swearing allegiance to Hitler.

By the nature of his position, most of the French writers Heller came to know
were collaborators, and he developed friendships with Marcel Jouhandeau and
Drieu la Rochelle, among others. But he also had close ties to Jean Paulhan, although of course the subject of the intellectual Resistance was never discussed
between them. Heller calls Paulhan his "master," in the sense of mentor, both
aesthetically and politically. Paulhan taught him about modern French art and
literature and, Heller affirms, freed him from the antisemitism he had absorbed
during his years in Nazi Germany. As Sonderführer, Heller was able to intercede
and prevent the arrest of a certain number of threatened personalities, including Jean Paulhan. For others, like the Jewish poet Max Jacob and the Resistance
poet Robert Desnos, he tried to intercede but was unable to save them. After the
war, he returned to Germany and became an editor of French books in translation, some of which he translated himself.

Heller's role was described with considerable sympathy by many writers in
the intellectual Resistance, including Paulhan, François Mauriac, Jacques Debû-
Bridel, and Édith Thomas. In an article about the diary of her CNE comrade
Jean Guéhenno, she comments: "It seems we were 'protected' by Lieutenant
Heller of the Propagandastaffel. I would very much like to meet Lieutenant
Heller."[23] Actually, it was only after the war that Heller learned where these
meetings of Resistance writers had been taking place. He writes in his book:
"What emotion, after the war, when [Édith Thomas] told me that the room in
which we were speaking was the same one in which the members of the CNE
got together!"[24] The encounter between them, perhaps inspired by the wish expressed in her article in 1966, must have taken place between that date and 1970,
the year of Édith Thomas's death.

Since then, there have been striking conflicts in the interpretation of Gerhard
Heller and his motivations. An extensive and favorable account, based on Heller's book as well as correspondence and interviews, can be found in the chapter "A German Friend" in Herbert Lottman's study of French intellectuals, *The
Left Bank* (1981). More recent analyses, however, have been far harsher. In *La Littérature de la défaite et de la collaboration*, published in 1995, Gérard Loiseaux
describes Heller's book as a piece of "stubborn revisionism" and analyzes what
he calls Heller's "calculated silences," pointing out that in order to keep his position, Heller had to enjoy the confidence of his superiors and of the terrifying
SD, the Sicherheitsdienst (in charge of the repression of subversive activities in
occupied territories).[25] Lottman and Loiseaux each emphasize a different side
of the paradox that Heller embodied by occupying the position he did, a para-

dox of which Heller himself was aware, although his account is, at the very least, highly selective.

Yvonne Paraf (Madame Desvignes), who bound all the books of the Éditions de Minuit at her home, had the idea of designating Minuit authors by regions of France with which they felt a special connection. At a meeting of the CNE in April 1943, Jean Paulhan gave Madame Desvignes a manuscript by Édith Thomas, which Pierre de Lescure had asked her to write. The *Contes d'Auxois* (Stories by Auxois), subtitled "transcribed from the real," were based mostly on stories of Sainte-Aulde and a few of Paris. Thomas takes her pseudonym from a slightly changed version of Orxois, a neighboring village. The book consists of seven vignettes of daily life in occupied France, brief chronicles which speak in a quiet voice of ordinary and extraordinary ways in which French men and women, young and old, workers, peasants and bourgeois—and even a German soldier—struggled to say no to the occupying Nazi forces.

In "The Professor and the Mussels" an elderly classics teacher waits with a long line of women in front of the fish store, which does not get him anything to eat but gives him a sense of solidarity and a hopefulness about human possibility that he had not found working in his study on the origins of the *Aeneid*. The affectionate portrait of the professor seems to have been inspired by Édith Thomas's father.[26]

In "La Relève" a French worker, encouraged by his wife, gradually comes to the decision that he will not leave to work in Germany. Thomas's title refers to the prisoner exchange accepted by Pierre Laval, Pétain's second in command, to provide three skilled workers who would go to Germany in exchange for each prisoner repatriated to France. When voluntary recruitment proved to be ineffective, the government's pressure on French workers became increasingly intense, leading to requisition notices and in 1943 to the STO, the Service de Travail Obligatoire. That measure, effectively drafting young men to work in Germany, created many thousands of *réfractaires* (dodgers) who decided to hide out and join the Resistance instead.

Thomas's initial telling of the story "The Arrest," which takes place in Paris, can be found in her diary. A young woman named Anne is visiting her mother's bedside in the hospital when the Gestapo comes to arrest her. Anne tries to reassure the old woman, although the reader knows she will not be returning. Sounds dominate the end of the story: Anne's heels resonate in the entryway, as hard as the boots of the German soldiers.[27] "The Arrest" was also published as a separate book in 1944 by La Bibliothèque Française, an underground press in the south of France founded by Aragon.

"Le Tilleul" (the French word for a herbal tea from the linden tree), which recalls *The Silence of the Sea* in its representation of an anti-Nazi German, is told from the point of view of la Renaude, the caretaker of a country chateau that has been requisitioned by the Germans. Three German soldiers have been stationed at the chateau to guard a railroad bridge nearby. One of them, Hans, speaks French and has been helping la Renaude with her daily chores. When he has a cold one evening, she offers him a *tilleul* and in the course of their conversation he says to her:

> "Hitler, this is what I think of him." He spit in the fireplace, and the flames sputtered.
>
> "Well then, I wonder why you took him as your leader," said la Renaude.
>
> "And you, why do you have your Marshal?" replied Hans abruptly. "You have him because you are defeated [*vaincus*]."
>
> "But you are conquerors [*vainqueurs*]," said la Renaude.
>
> "We are defeated," said Hans. "We have been defeated since January 30, 1933."[28]

For Édith Thomas, the "defeated" were all those internationalists, German as well as French, who had believed, before Hitler came to power, in the possibility of Franco-German reconciliation, a genuine collaboration between the two former enemies to construct a society that would be more just and more humane. In this respect, the Notice at the back of each volume of the Éditions de Minuit is revealing: "The printing of this volume, published at the expense of a patriot, was completed under Nazi occupation in Paris on . . ." followed by the date. In 1943, "a patriot" was changed to "a few patriotic people of letters" and "under Nazi occupation" became simply "under the oppression." Significantly, however, in these changes of wording, "Nazi" never became "German," a self-conscious decision on the part of the contributors to Éditions de Minuit. As Édith Thomas points out, the literature of the Resistance was fighting against an ideology of human degradation; it refused to take on a racial or national character—the French against the Germans.

Along with many others in France on the left who were to become part of the intellectual Resistance, Thomas had rebelled against the Manichean rhetoric of the Great War that she remembered from her childhood, and she was determined to free herself of all traces of what she called "bourgeois nationalism." When the Germans occupied France, however, she discovered that she loved not only a particular land but also a language, the heritage of a culture, a *patrie*. She interpreted that patriotism as paradoxically continuous with her earlier internationalism. France took on an emblematic meaning because in 1789 it was the country that had brought to the world the Declaration of the Rights of Man, an idea of France generally shared during the occupation years by all writers in the intellectual Resistance—Communists, liberals, Christians, secularists, Jews. It was only to the extent that France remained faithful to a universalist idea of rights and of humanism that it could claim a privileged place among nations. By taking a stand against national socialism, Thomas argued, French writers of the Resistance were also defending German culture in its universal aspect.

There is probably a personal factor as well in Thomas's diverse representations of occupying German soldiers and even officers, based on what she would have heard from her mother and neighbors in Sainte-Aulde. Roger Bacuet, employed as the Thomas's groundskeeper, grew up with Gérard and remained a close part of the family all his life. Bacuet's father was the *frère de lait* of Fernande Thomas, breast-fed by the same wet nurse. In 1994, when I went to see Bacuet in Sainte-Aulde, he told me the following story:

> In 1943 I got involved with the *réfractaires,* the men who did not want to work in Germany. A group of us hid them and found places for them. There was a German officer from Konigsberg occupying Sainte-Aulde who spoke fluent French and knew all about what we were doing. He had forty men under his orders. They didn't speak French and none of them knew what their captain was up to. A *réfractaire,* a young boy of seventeen or eighteen, was hiding in Sainte-Aulde in a lady's house. Someone denounced her to the Germans. The German captain came to the house and warned her: "Watch out. The Germans are coming to search the house." We got the boy out—he was able to stay for a few days with Madame Thomas [Fernande]—and three days later they came. I don't like Germans, that's just the way it is, but if that German came back—he would be about ninety years old now—I'd put my arms around his neck and I'd embrace him. Me and my brother, we owe him everything. When the Allies landed, he left Meaux with his men but first he came to see the people he had protected, to say good-bye. I said to him: "You protected us. Now it's my turn to protect you. We'll dress you in blue and no one will arrest you, and you'll be safe." But he wouldn't abandon his men. "I'm not going to surrender to the FFI [the Resistance forces]," he said; "we'd all get ourselves killed. But since I speak good English, I'll hide in the woods and I'll surrender to the Americans. I'll ask them to make my men prisoners of war. I deserve that for the good I've done the French. I hope they believe what I tell them."
>
> I never saw him again.[29]

For Thomas, the defeat of German civilization in 1933 was no less real than the military defeat of France in 1940. That universalist context gives added force to the last story of *Contes d'Auxois,* titled "F.T.P.," for the Communist led maquis group Francs-Tireurs et Partisans that supported active military engagement with the occupying forces. The story focuses on six men who meet at the edge of a forest to sabotage the railroad track where a train will be passing carrying German soldiers. As the locomotive crashes on its side, the soldiers, terrified, scramble out of the other train cars. Édith Thomas ends her story this way: "Then, calmly, the six began to shoot. With no more hatred than a surgeon. With no more hatred."[30] Much of the force of that ending comes from our having read the earlier story "Le Tilleul," and our awareness that some of the fleeing soldiers perhaps resemble Hans.

The participation of poets in the literary Resistance was at least as important as that of prose writers. On July 14, 1943, in remembrance of what had been Bastille Day, the Éditions de Minuit published *L'Honneur des poètes,* an anthology of twenty-two poets including, among the best known names, Paul Eluard, the editor of the volume, Louis Aragon, Robert Desnos, Pierre Emmanuel, and Francis Ponge. Édith Thomas, who contributed four poems under the pseudonym Anne, was the only woman included in the collection. Later that year, on October 30, General de Gaulle gave a speech in Algiers at the Alliance Française that paid homage to French writers and poets of the Resistance. If the sword is one pole of "national hope," he affirmed, the other is French thought, whose dignity is being saved "by those who did not accept the disaster." He cited these verses from the lament of "Anne," a young woman dreaming in the Tuileries Gardens:

Comme ces jardins
Sont abandonnés!
La Guerre est au bout de l'allée.
Nulle part je puis m'en aller.
Où donc est-il, mon amant?
Derrière les fils barbelés?
Ou bien dessus la mer allant
Rejoindre une armée triomphante?[31]

[These gardens,
How abandoned they are!
War waits at the end of the path.
Nowhere can I go.
Where then is my lover?
Behind barbed wire?
Or crossing the sea
To join a triumphant army?]

The poem was probably written early in the occupation and inspired by Édith's anguish and reveries about Stefan. It is not difficult, of course, to understand why this poem would have been especially appealing to de Gaulle.

In fact, Édith Thomas's original poem, as it was published in *L'Honneur des poètes*, was written in three stanzas (of six, four, and five lines), each line with eight syllables. The verses cited by de Gaulle have a somewhat modified rhyme, punctuation, and love theme. When de Gaulle's version of the poem was published as part of his Algiers speech in *Discours et Messages* (1970), Thomas wrote to him and included the poem as it originally appeared in the Éditions de Minuit collection. De Gaulle's letter of response, on July 23, 1970, suggests that the poem he received during the war was transcribed from someone's memory rather than from the underground book itself:

> Your beautiful verses—and so moving!—reached me during the war, their text truncated by obstacles and dramas. Such as they were when I read them, that is how I cited them in my Algiers speech in October 1943 and it is that speech, published and republished at the time, which is reproduced in the collection of my messages. However, the truth must be shown. I will therefore put a note of explanation in future editions of "Discours et Messages."
>
> At least I am happy to verify, once again, that what I cite of yours, although incomplete, was exact.[32]

A few months later, on November 9, 1970, de Gaulle was dead. Édith Thomas died the following month, on December 7. Subsequent editions of the *Discours* include a footnote that explains the circumstances in which the verses were cited and refers the reader to the "exact and complete" version of Édith Thomas's poem in *L'Honneur des poètes*.

In March 1944, Thomas was asked by her comrades at the CNE to write a piece about Frenchwomen for their *Almanach des Lettres françaises*, to be published by the Éditions de Minuit. The defensiveness that characterizes much of her public writing as a woman before 1945 appears in this article as well. After addressing her subject, she makes a point of adding that she personally does not think it necessary to insist on the role of women in the Resistance, since men and women worked anonymously side by side to accomplish the tasks that needed to be done. Putting aside what she calls "nuances of affect," which she dismisses as irrelevant, she argues that the reasons for men and women to become involved in illegal action were the same, while conceding that the place reserved for women in the Nazi system or in Pétain's New Order might provide an additional motive for some women.[33] The ambivalence in her article is palpable, in part because she clearly has not chosen her topic: as a token woman with *Les Lettres françaises,* she has been assigned to write it. Grudgingly acknowledging the persistence of what she identifies as the old Gaulois tradition of misogyny, she decides that it is perhaps "not useless" to remind people that women have had and will have their part to play in the liberation of their country.

The Éditions de Minuit published a second volume of poetry edited by Paul Eluard, *Europe,* to which Édith Thomas also contributed. The title of the collection was in itself both a provocation and a struggle to take back the meaning of an idea, a dream, and a word, at a time when "Europe" had come to mean collective submission to Nazi tyranny. *Europe,* which appeared in May 1944, includes translations of poems from Greece, Poland, Czechoslovakia, Holland, Norway, Yugoslavia, Bulgaria, and Italy as well as from Belgium and France. Of the thirty poets brought together, one third were in prison.

Between February 1942 and the liberation, the underground Éditions de Minuit published thirty-three books, each with the same elegant presentation, small enough to fit into a coat pocket. Thomas took pleasure in registering the copyright of each volume at the Bibliothèque nationale without the knowledge of either her comrades at the CNE or Bernard Faÿ, the fanatical collaborator appointed to replace Julien Cain, who was Jewish, as head administrator.[34]

𝒯

USES OF THE PAST

As a medieval historian, Édith Thomas felt a special irritation with Vichy's appropriation of the Middle Ages to bolster its propaganda for a New Order, the return to values of an idealized past that embodied eternal France. Periodically in her wartime diary she contrasts Vichy's representations of the medieval period with contemporary realities that evoke for her a very different image of that time. In the first months of Vichy she writes in her diary: "Certainly the Middle Ages, dear to our leaders, is not an empty word: famines, obscurantism, the hierarchy of individuals, castes, that's what the twentieth century is imitating."[1] A few months after the liberation, she points out how the medieval image of cathedral builders, "whose only function was to believe and obey," was politically useful to Vichy. Alluding to Pétain's regime, barely past, she describes it as "an astonishing period in which people believed everything they were told and no one asked any questions."[2]

In her diary, Thomas inveighs against the "medievalist bull" (*foutaises moyenâgeuses*) of fascist intellectuals, in particular Drieu la Rochelle.[3] She is specifically referring to his novel *Gilles,* in which the protagonist, taking on the Germanic pseudonym Walter, goes to Spain to fight alongside Franco's forces in the civil war. During a conversation with his comrades-in-arms, an Irishman and a Pole, he explains that like them he is there to defend "male Catholicism, that of the Middle Ages."[4] At the end of the novel Gilles returns once again to Spain, to Burgos. Finding himself in a town square that will be destroyed by mortars, he methodically begins shooting, exalted by the bloody death that awaits him. Drieu's admiration for what he considered the medieval ideal of virile and spiritual valor was inseparable from his visceral hatred of democracy, which he saw as synonymous with decadence.

Thomas also denounces the evasions, and what she sees as the implicit complicity with Vichy propaganda, inherent in the officially sanctioned literature and film about the past. On March 18, 1943, she records an extended and furious critique of Marcel Carné's film *Les Visiteurs du soir* (*The Devil's Envoy*), the most popular movie of the previous year and a critical success as well. After a scathing attack on the phoniness of this medieval phantasmagoria, its mediocrity, and its misunderstanding of the specific poetry of film, she comes to her real concern, the film's insidious influence. Its popularity provokes her to invent a new word, *troubadourism*, which she offers as if it were the diagnosis of a contagious but unrecognized illness. With the irony she favors when she attacks the stupidity—as distinct from the horrors—of the Vichy regime, she reports that *Les Visiteurs du soir* is symptomatic of a generalized and alarming malady. Continuing the medical metaphor, she defines troubadourism as "a malady of art and literature that appears in regressive periods and consists of an ingenuous sentimentalizing of an imaginary past. To make this past as imaginary as possible, it is pushed back as far as possible, to the point where public memory fades into legend. The Middle Ages does the job very well." Troubadourism, she writes, makes its appearance in the history of letters in the nineteenth century, between the end of the Napoleonic Empire and the beginning of the Restoration of Louis XVIII, a period of defeat, intellectual oppression, and "prudish silliness." Of course, she adds, "I would not dare make any comparison with our times. That would be slander or calumny. Everyone can see that the national renaissance is on the march."[5]

Les Visiteurs du soir takes place in an unnamed country in the month of May 1485. In the opening sequence, two troubadours on horseback make their way to a chateau where the baron is celebrating his daughter Anne's betrothal to the cruel and cynical knight Renaud. The troubadours, Gilles and Dominique, a beautiful woman (played by the actress Arletty) disguised as a man, are really envoys of the Devil. They join in the festivities and in the middle of a dance they cast a spell, immobilizing the guests. While Dominique seduces Renaud in order to enjoy the power of exercising her charms, Gilles has truly fallen in love with Anne. Following a series of episodes, some "realistic" and some prodigious, the Devil arrives to complete his envoys' work. Gilles is imprisoned and threatened with torture, having revealed his love for Anne. After she succeeds in deceiving the Devil and freeing her lover from prison, they escape to the garden where they had first declared their love. As they drink from the fountain, the Devil finds them and transforms them into statues. When the Devil approaches, he hears a rhythmic sound, which he is unable to silence. It is the heart of the two lovers that continues to beat beneath the stone.

The Devil is unable to silence the hearts of the lovers he has turned to stone
in *Les Visiteurs du soir* (1942). Museum of Modern Art Film Stills Archive, New York.

Like most French feature films of the Vichy period, *Les Visiteurs du soir,* written by Jacques Prévert and Pierre Laroche, had no intention of supporting Pétainist values. In Prévert's initial scenario, the Devil was supposed to represent
Hitler, who is defeated at the end of the film. Although there were episodes of
magic, the characters were to be in modern dress, suggesting the present. However, since any clear political allusions would not pass the censors, the director
and the screenwriters decided to set their story in the Middle Ages. In their attempt to disguise their intentions from the censors, they disguised their intentions from the audience as well, even those initiates, like Édith Thomas, who
would be most alert to a subtext of resistance.[6]

As a result, *Les Visiteurs du soir* had no problems with the censors. In spite of
the pervasive hunger and general scarcity, the film became, for the times, an extravagant production, with the principal actors costumed in velvet, satin, and
brocade. But ersatz materials were used whenever possible, and the director
filmed mostly in long shots to avoid close examination. For the hunt scenes, the
Republican Guard provided sleek, well-nourished horses in large numbers.
They could not, however, find the requisite packs of hounds, and the production had to make do with one pitiful pack, since breeders could no longer afford
to feed their dogs. The banquet scenes created another problem: extras were so

hungry that provisions tended to disappear as soon as they were placed on the table.[7]

The ending of *Les Visiteurs du soir* was generally interpreted as celebrating both eternal love and eternal France, which lived on in the beating heart of the two lovers. Of course, the comforting idea of an eternal France that all could embrace, whether they were for or against Vichy, was precisely the problem. Édith Thomas's critique of troubadourism precludes any easy notion of a cinema of escape to a sentimentalized past that would reassure audiences of France's continuing glory. She saw the reflection of France's defeat in the complicity between filmmakers and the public to promote that reassurance.

Several decades after Édith Thomas penned her private notations, critics of the cinema of Vichy France have tended to confirm this analysis. The American critic Evelyn Ehrlich points out a central paradox of French cinema under German occupation. Although most of the prestigious filmmakers of the time did not subscribe to Vichy ideology, "the refuge that filmmakers sought in history, myth, and allegory served Vichy's interest by promoting the glories of French culture and nationalism."[8] In order to glorify the new Europe, Nazi Germany wanted the French to continue making these films. The French critic Jean-Pierre Bertin-Maghit, using very different discursive methods, arrives at a similar conclusion. In his detailed structural analysis of a number of films of the period, including *Les Visiteurs du soir,* he highlights the gap between the films' intentions and their meaning as finished products. The propaganda he finds in French cinema under Vichy is not conscious political propaganda but a propaganda that exerts its action on the level of the unconscious. He sees these films as examples of conformist propaganda that promote, however unwittingly, the values of the group in power.[9]

The appropriation by Vichy of French history and particularly the Middle Ages raises the matter of Simone de Beauvoir's work in 1943 for a weekly program on the National Radio station, also known as Radio-Vichy. Her task was to select songs and poems written for festivals, from the Middle Ages to the nineteenth century. She obtained her position thanks to Sartre's connection with René Delange, editor of the literary journal *Comoedia.* Later she explained that since the documents she prepared concerned the Middle Ages, "they had nothing to do with the war or what was going on at the time." She therefore considered herself "not contaminated," and did not feel "any sense of guilt" in working for radio controlled by the Germans.[10] According to the unwritten code adopted by writers sympathetic to the Resistance, work for Radio-Paris, which had a German director, was unacceptable, but work for Radio-Vichy, whose entire staff was French, could be acceptable depending on the content of the work performed. A recent review of the actual scripts for Radio-Vichy confirms Beauvoir's assessment: she selected the texts to be presented, beginning the first week with the scene of a medieval fair and the following week with poems by François Villon. She made all her selections from a French tradition which focuses on "marginal individuals and rebels against the established order," hardly a tradition consonant with Vichy values.[11]

In the context of work, two points of comparison can be made between Simone de Beauvoir and Édith Thomas. On the one hand, although Jean Paulhan invited Thomas to write for *Comoedia,* she did not accept. On the other, it is only fair to point out that Beauvoir had just been dismissed from her university position, where she had earned a decent living. Thomas, thanks to her diploma as *archiviste-paléographe,* had access to a part-time post at the Archives nationales, a far less ambiguous place to work. It gave her relative independence from Vichy regulations and also enough money to support herself. Although she considered some of her tasks absurdly irrelevant, none of them could be perceived as compromising.

Simone de Beauvoir's record during the occupation is less troubling for what she did than for what she did not do. The most disturbing aspect of her history in those years is the enormous gap between her thinking and her life, the absence of any reflection of the ethics of commitment in her actions. Her Resistance novel *The Blood of Others,* like Édith Thomas's stories in the *Contes d'Auxois,* was completed in 1943, when the outcome of World War II remained uncertain. All indications, including the book's length, suggest that Beauvoir never considered publishing her novel anonymously with the Éditions de Minuit during the occupation. *The Blood of Others,* which appeared after the end of the war in 1945, supports the most violent and extreme kind of Resistance action. However, in Beauvoir's life during the war years, there is no indication of personal resistance on any level; she does not seem to have confronted the question, except as an intellectual problem. Nor did she offer moral support to intimate friends who were directly threatened.[12] It is undoubtedly true that Simone de Beauvoir's record is no worse than that of most French people and, for that matter, no worse than that of most writers during the occupation. It does not seem unfair, however, to expect more of Simone de Beauvoir. Existentialism is not a theory of language, like structuralism, or of texts, like deconstruction. It is a philosophy of existence in which terms like freedom, responsibility, and action imply an ethics. In 1944, just after the liberation, Simone de Beauvoir published *Pyrrhus et Cinéas,* a meditation on the problem of freedom, which she describes as the foundation of all human values. She calls the first part of her essay "Candide's Garden" and concludes that his advice cannot be of much help to us: "No dimensions can be assigned to the garden in which Candide wants to enclose me. It is not drawn in advance; I am the one who chooses its placement and its size."[13] It is disappointing that the garden she chose to cultivate during the occupation years—in contrast to the garden of Édith Thomas and many other shadow sisters—was so very small. In Beauvoir's case, it is as if she considered herself exempted from the imperative of commitment by the act of articulating its necessity—in writings that appeared, and were intended to appear, after the war was over.

In 1943 Jean Lescure, editor of the poetry journal *Messages,* published in Switzerland a wide-ranging collection of poems, fragments of novels, and essays which he called *Domaine français,* a manifesto "to affirm the obscure passion that binds us to the permanence of a civilization."[14] The epigraph for the volume is a French translation of the first half of "O Star of France" by Walt Whitman, a poem written during the Franco-Prussian War that is strikingly relevant to the trauma of France's defeat and occupation by the Germans seventy years later.[15] Among the fifty-six contributors to *Domaine français,* the best-known names include Louis Aragon, Gaston Bachelard, Albert Camus, Paul Claudel, Paul Eluard, André Gide, François Mauriac, Henri Michaux, Jean Paulhan, Jean-Paul Sartre, and Paul Valéry. Two women are represented: Elsa Triolet and Édith Thomas.

Édith Thomas's essay evokes a collective memory of the Middle Ages that counters the troubadourism of *Les Visiteurs du soir.* Her contribution, titled simply "Christine de Pizan," is also the most unambiguously feminist of Thomas's writings up to that time. In this meditation on both Christine and her contemporary Joan of Arc as feminine figures of resistance, she points out that we owe to Christine the only poem that celebrated Joan of Arc while she was still alive. Thomas, writing six hundred years later during a period of renewed offensive to send women back to the kitchen, honors Christine as the first French woman of letters. In her brief summary of Christine's life, Thomas is careful not to "troubadourize" her subject, an educated fifteenth-century woman who wrote for a public of prelates and lords. What she admires in Christine is "her will, her stubbornness, the patient violence" of this woman who took up her studies again after becoming a widow, when she had three children and was over thirty years old.

Édith Thomas celebrates feminine resistance in its two aspects, the spirit and the sword, as they were embodied by Christine and Joan of Arc during the Hundred Years War, with clearly recognizable allusions to Nazi-occupied France. She writes: "Paris belongs to the Bourguignons, and the invader has crowned a foreign king. Houses are in ruins, the countryside is devastated. . . . A secret police surveys everyone's words and acts."[16] Not surprisingly, Thomas makes no ref-

erence to the English identity of the enemy invaders. Quoting at length from
Christine's poem about Joan, she ends her essay with a repetition of the two
verses that evoke the year of Joan's victory in the siege of Orleans, a message of
hope for the French Resistance in 1943:

L'an mil quatre cens vingt et neuf
Reprint a luire li soleil.

[The year of fourteen twenty nine   -
The sun came out to shine again]

Both Édith Thomas's own diary during the war and Costedet's fictional diary contain a number of allusions to Joan of Arc. The ambiguity of Joan's mythic
status as a patriotic icon during the occupation years made possible her appropriation by forces of the Resistance and of collaboration. France's heroine gave
her life for her country and saved it from invading foreigners—who could be
read symbolically as the Germans or literally as the English. De Gaulle and Pétain both invoked Joan's name. The communist Claude Vermorel wrote a play
about her, *Jeanne avec nous,* and a fictional account of her trial by the fascist
Robert Brasillach, written in 1931, was reprinted during the occupation.

After the war, Édith Thomas's return to her vocation as a historian, which she
had abandoned after writing her thesis for the École des Chartes, can itself be
seen as a response to the experience of living under Vichy. Her *Jeanne d'Arc* is
the first biography she wrote and the only one that explores the life of a medieval figure. The fifteenth century was already familiar to her from her thesis
at the École des Chartes on Louis XI, who was the son of Charles VII, crowned
king at Reims after the battlefield victories of Joan of Arc. In revolt against the
troubadourism of the occupation years, Thomas considered her book an essay
in "demythification."[17] Noting in her introduction that a bibliography of Joan
of Arc in 1894 already included 2,127 entries, with certainly a few thousand more
in the half century that followed, she explains her own interest in writing the
book as a desire to return to the historical reality of Joan, against everyone's attempt to make her the symbol of their cause: "the monarchists, even though she
was abandoned by her king; the Catholics, even though she was burned to death
by the Church; the 'freethinkers,' even though she finally gave herself over to the
Pope and the Council; the patriots, even though the *patrie* did not yet exist. Others, on the contrary, treated her as a 'miserable idiot' (Voltaire) or as a 'hysteric'
(Anatole France)."[18]

What interests Édith Thomas is the project of demystifying Joan of Arc and
bringing her back to her fifteenth century, leaving her with her voices, her god,

and her king as she understood them. Thomas bases her narrative entirely on the documents of the time, which include extensive records of Joan's two trials, archival documents, and narrations of fifteenth-century chroniclers. In Thomas's account, the voices Joan hears do not require explanation; they are important because Joan believed in them enough to die at the stake for them. Her biography renders a world in which devils and angels mingled with men and women in their daily lives. She takes us among the people who fought against the English invaders, those peasants, artisans, monks, and gentlemen for whom France was "a kind of deep and rudimentary instinct, but one for which they were ready to sacrifice their lives." Thomas finds much of her evidence in the accounts of Joan's two trials. The first one, conducted by priests attached to the king of England, aimed to prove to posterity that Joan was a witch. The second was conducted after her death by priests attached to the kings of France and set out to prove to posterity that Joan was a saint. In the first trial, Joan herself speaks; in the second, it is the turn of the laborers, priests, bourgeois, and knights who witnessed her life. Remarkably, notwithstanding the opposed assumptions in each of the two trials, they converge in their description of Joan. "Few contradictory documents," Thomas writes, "are as perfectly complementary."[19]

Following her narration of Joan's life, Thomas moves to another kind of history, the posthumous life of Joan through different historical periods. Although Joan's transformation into a legendary figure began with her contemporaries, interpretations remained within a historical framework until the nineteenth century, when she became a mythical incarnation of the nation as well as a saint. Thomas considers Michelet the "heretical John the Baptist of this new religion," which needed sacred symbols. For Michelet, Joan of Arc founded French patriotism and France itself: "For the first time, one can feel it, France is loved as a person," Michelet writes. "And France, moved, began to love itself. Remember, Frenchmen, that the *patrie,* for us, was born in the heart of a woman, from her tenderness and her tears, from the blood she gave for us."[20] Thomas traces the contradictory representations of Joan through the nineteenth and twentieth century, culminating in Joan of Arc's extraordinary destiny during the occupation years.

In spite of the extensive archival work involved in her study, Thomas effaces her scholarship; there are no notes or bibliography to signal a work of erudition. She is primarily interested in what she calls "the person Joan, her courage, her intelligence, her frankness," in other words, her "style."[21] All quoted dialogues in the book—the words of Joan and her judges, witnesses for and against her— are transcribed from contemporary documents. At the same time, as many critics noted, the book reads like a novel. History and story come together in an engaging narrative that tries to be as faithful as possible to the documents of the time. Thomas chooses not to end with a conclusion, recognizing that in spite of her efforts to free Joan from accumulated myths, she cannot free herself from the contingencies of her own time and place, inevitable for any writer—and any reader.

Thomas's work at the Archives nationales during the occupation years consisted of organizing historical documents and making inventories. One such task, beginning in 1943, involved a little-known episode of the occupation and turned out to be of passionate interest. The Nazis had raided the Archives series of what was called *les religionnaires fugitifs,* fugitive Huguenots. After the revocation by Louis XIV in 1685 of the Edict of Nantes, which had assured religious tolerance to the Protestants, or Huguenots, many fled to Germany as well as to other European countries in order to escape Catholic persecution, which continued for well over a century. German descendants of these Huguenot refugees had French names. The Nazis requisitioned all the files and took them to Germany for intensive genealogical research, to determine whether families descended from these French Huguenots were really "Aryan." When the Nazis returned the files, Édith Thomas was asked to verify that every carton had been sent back and no documents had been removed. The existing inventories, called the TT series, did not allow her to make that determination, but she was asked to make a new inventory of the 464 cartons, some of which contained more than five hundred documents.[22]

The dossiers of fugitive Huguenots included information about where they came from, where they were going, which professions they pursued, what they owned, and what had been taken from them, along with certificates of baptism and marriage. The dossiers also listed the names of those who had been sent to prison for their beliefs. About one third of the Huguenot population left France; those who stayed either conformed to the behavior expected of "new converts" or took the risk of becoming voluntary outlaws, hiding in the Cévennes Mountains. Thomas was particularly fascinated by the accounts of those Huguenots who stayed in France and resisted Catholic oppression. She learned of a rebellion in 1702 which spread to five dioceses: Mende, Uzès, Alès, Nîmes, and Montpellier. Documents recounted the exploits of these "fanatic scoundrels" and the most effective means of opposing their crimes. It was decided that for every church burned down, thirty houses would be razed. There were descriptions of what was learned about resistance in the Cévennes from Protestants who spoke under torture. Another document "from the King" enumerated the villages to be destroyed, as inhabitants fled with their animals. Thirty years later, an official who had been stationed in the Cévennes declared that since the population was still indifferent to Catholicism, fines must be imposed to oblige the "new converts" to attend Mass. Reading through the narratives of persecution and resistance, Thomas found numerous analogies with the present: "Nothing seemed closer to us than the lives of these voluntary outlaws."[23]

Huguenot history helps to explain the extraordinary story of Le Chambon, narrated in the book by Phillip Hallie, *Lest Innocent Blood Be Shed,* and the French-American documentary film by Pierre Sauvage, *Weapons of the Spirit.* The Protestant village of Le Chambon in the Cévennes Mountains, a population of five thousand souls deeply imbued with the Huguenot ethic, succeeded in saving about five thousand refugees, mostly Jewish children, during the war.[24] For the most part, Huguenot Protestants did not respond well to Pétain's message that the French should follow him with blind confidence. French Protestants also tended to feel a certain affinity with Jews. Both were minorities imbued with a history of religious persecution, a predilection for knowledge of Scriptures without the intermediary of religious institutions, and a belief in the primacy of individual conscience. According to a frequently told story in the Cévennes Mountains during the war years, a Nazi officer asked a woman if she knew any Jews. "Yes," she replied. "In the Bible." Madeleine Thomas remembered that early in her high school years she was once falsely accused of being antisemitic. "How could I be antisemitic," she replied indignantly. "I'm Protestant."[25]

After the allied landing in North Africa in November 1942, Hitler announced that France would be completely occupied. German troops invaded the unoccupied zone, ending the fiction of anything resembling a "free" zone in France. By 1943, the ranks of the maquis were becoming far more significant, particularly after the promulgation in February of the obligatory service in Germany of French workers, the STO. Most camps were in the mountainous southern zone whose terrain was more propitious to guerrilla implantations. In the north there were no mountains, and few villages or farms were sufficiently isolated from roads.

For a long time Thomas had wanted to make contact with the Francs-Tireurs et Partisans (FTP), the Communist-led guerrilla group she had written about in her final story of *Contes d'Auxois.* Thomas's diary entry for April 30, 1944, consists only of a series of dashes, to mark it as the date of her departure for the maquis, which had been prepared a long time earlier with the help of Aragon in Lyon and the Communist film critic Georges Sadoul. She found herself in many of the same villages and mountain regions of the Cévennes that she had been reading about in her work on the Huguenots at the Archives nationales.

In *Les Lettres françaises* of June 1944, she wrote the first account of her trip, the only one published underground. The title of her article, "Un seul et même peuple" (One and the same people), about the FTP in the Cévennes, alludes to the tradition of resistance going back to the Camisards, those Protestants who in 1702 rebelled against the persecutions that followed the revocation of the Edict of Nantes. Now, in the region about which she is writing, every house takes turns sheltering young men going off to fight. "Everyone," she notes, the grocer, the butcher, the schoolteacher, the baker, even the police, supports the maquis. The schoolteacher often went at night to a cave twenty kilometers away that he had known about since childhood, taking with him a typewriter and the material necessary to make false identity papers for the *réfractaires*. He arranged for her to meet the head of the camp, who told her that they informed the local police sergeant before each operation so he could send his men, some of whom were "good" policemen but some "bad," elsewhere. The mountain path she followed to get back to the village was one of those marked out in the eighteenth century by province officials in their fight against the Camisards.[26]

Two other articles about her experience in the maquis were published in *Femmes françaises* just after the liberation. She was deeply moved by the young woman she knew only as "Claude," who accompanied her in the early part of her trip and helped arrange contacts with FTP leaders. Claude's husband had been sent to prison after refusing to serve with the STO. When he escaped, he once again took up his underground activities, along with his wife. It was often necessary for Claude, now pregnant, to accompany him, since women tended to arouse less suspicion than men. She would carry a large shopping bag that contained compromising materials and even weapons. Claude worried about the conditions in which the child she was carrying would be born and spoke to Édith of her hopes and fears, and about the escalation of reprisals. As liberation approached, the French militia, used as a reinforcement of the Gestapo, was receiving increased support from the Nazis, enabling more murderously effective reprisals against the Resistance.

Thomas spoke with the leader of an FTP camp in Saint Benoit-du-Désert, which she reached by climbing a winding mountain road in one of the few cars belonging to the Resistance. Everyone in the car except herself had a revolver, and she noted her "indescribable pleasure" at seeing Frenchmen armed. The thirty young men in the camp, between eighteen and twenty-five years old, were workers, peasants, and students. They joined for a variety of reasons: most were *réfractaires;* some were there out of patriotism; others had escaped from Vichy youth camps and were looking for adventure. Frantz, an Alsatian lieutenant, recounted the implacable discipline imposed by the FTP camp on these outlaw fighters. One of their wounded men who had been cared for by local peasants stole a blanket from them when he left. The blanket was returned and the young man was shot dead, a punishment meted out in order to demonstrate that larceny and pillage would not be tolerated.

Thomas concludes her second *Femmes françaises* article with a tribute to individual men she met and especially to her guide, Bertrand, an idealistic young worker from Lyon who joined the FTP as the best way to struggle effectively and immediately against the enemy of his country. When she learned that the train they were supposed to take through the mountains to the next village was out of commission, she proposed that they make the ten-kilometer hike on foot. He asked her about the positions taken by writers and artists in Paris, talked about the feeling among many of the men that the rest of the country had abandoned them, and reflected on the terrible anguish of killing a man.[27]

Thomas's extensive account of those weeks in her memoir is based in large part on a draft written immediately after her trip; it includes a wider geography, many other incidents, and a more complicated interpretation of what she saw, influenced by the conflicts of the post-liberation period. In all her reports, one is struck by the extraordinary endurance, force of will, and physical determination of this woman who had suffered from tuberculosis of the bone and then of the lungs and whose appearance was often described as frail. In one of many self-flagellating moments during the 1930s she wrote in her diary: "What is there for girls like me to do in life? They are not pretty; they limp. So they create a refuge or a subterfuge, God or the Revolution."[28] But a refuge or a subterfuge is also a choice. It is in no way inevitable that a girl who is not pretty, who limps, will choose to risk her life for the Resistance. From that same distress of feeling unlovely, she could have made other choices during those traumatic years: collaboration as a means of revenge or, like the great majority of French people, accommodation in one form or another with the Nazi occupiers.

Shortly after Thomas's return to Paris, she made a brief notation in her diary about the American offensive in Normandy on June 6, the beginning of the end of the long ordeal: "'They' have landed."[29]

8

THE LIBERATION OF PARIS
AND THE END OF THE WAR

In 1945, Édith Thomas published *La Libération de Paris*, an account of preparations for insurrection and a day-to-day report of maneuvers. As she points out in her introduction, if objective history is always an illusion, since it necessarily involves choice and interpretation, then a narration of events "as impassioned, gripping, and magnificent" as those that took place in Paris between August 19 and 25 will be particularly subjective, all the more since she writes as "an engaged witness."[1] She traces the phases of the insurrection as they unfold, with maps that locate the sites of combat and numerous photos of men and women putting up barricades, overturning German trucks, and taking German soldiers prisoner. Thomas was most directly involved with the Union of French Women, which was charged with implementing health measures, preparing kits of medication and bandages, and mobilizing nurses and doctors to organize first aid posts. She considers her narrative, written a few months after the events she describes and based to a large extent on diary entries, not as history but as useful testimony for those who will write history in the future. In *Le Témoin compromis* she returns to an account of those days, as they looked to her eight years later.

Thomas begins *La Libération de Paris* with news of the Normandy landings, as she tries to read the faces of people in the street to decipher what is different. The first visible change took place on Bastille Day, July 14. By then de Gaulle had arrived in Normandy; the Allied front was less than two hundred kilometers from Paris; people in Bayeux and Cherbourg were openly singing a Marseillaise "whose meaning is not shamefully distorted." In Paris, signs of hope burst out with the colors blue, white, and red appearing everywhere in defiance of the ban against all demonstrations, as if by a "secret watchword." As Thomas walked around the city she saw tricolored ribbons in lapel jackets, hair decorations, hat feathers; clothes in the three colors put together in myriad ingenious ways by Parisian women; bouquets in florist shops displaying all available combinations of blue, white, and red flowers. Shirts and blouses in the window of a dry cleaner repeated the same motif. On a balcony, blue work pants were hung out to dry, along with a red scarf and a white dishrag. In the working-class neighborhood of Belleville as well as on the place Maubert in the Latin Quarter, thousands of demonstrators gathered. People who were prudently watching from their door-steps looked on with stupefaction and Thomas imagined them thinking: "So it's *possible.*" The police arrived, but pulled back from the crowds, which dispersed only much later in the day when German police intervened. At the Porte de Vanves, a crowd burned an effigy of Hitler.[2]

Behind the scenes, underground groups were preparing the insurrection, which began on August 19. During the next few days, people put up barricades all over the city. Street fighting took place in working-class neighborhoods, in the Latin Quarter, and in the suburbs. Public services went on strike. For the first time, Resistance forces openly patrolled Paris and occupied public build-ings, factories, train stations. In the midst of repeated electrical failures, which made it difficult to get radio news, contradictory rumors abounded: the sur-render of Paris to the Americans was being negotiated; two German divisions specializing in street combat were being brought to Paris; the Wehrmacht wanted to abandon the city but the Gestapo and the SS were opposed; Paris was going to be declared an open city. While the Nazi flag with its swastika still hung over the place de la Concorde, the French flag was raised over Notre Dame and the Palace of Justice. Paris was oscillating between two worlds, two legalities, and two sets of symbols.[3]

Everyone could see clearly, however, that the German army was fleeing. Their cars and trucks were decked with foliage to conceal their retreat from bombs on the roads. "As in Shakespeare," Thomas notes in her memoir, "the forest was moving. But it was a forest in flight." In the pathways of the Luxembourg Gar-dens, children's games were no longer about bombs falling. "On their tricycles covered with leaves, they played at what we had all been waiting for during the past four years: the departure of the Germans."[4] With the triumphant entry of Leclerc's division and American tanks on August 25, Paris was a liberated city. French and American soldiers joined Parisians in the outpouring of joy. Thomas ends her account of insurrection and freedom with a quotation from Michelet about July 14, 1789, followed by her own exuberant commentary: "Yes, the peo-ple of Paris have proved once again that they are still the same people who took the Bastille."[5]

In that brief moment of exultation, the murderous divisions of the past four years were erased: "the people of Paris" were one people, united in their active resistance against the enemy, a feeling widely shared by Communists and anti-Communists, Gaullists and anti-Gaullists. For example, Jean-Paul Sartre, writing in *Combat,* describes General Leclerc's march into Paris in a decidedly uncharacteristic rhetoric of celebration: "They look, they shout, they smile, they salute us with their fingers shaping [a] V and we feel that their hearts beat in unison with ours. Some women and children have invaded the trucks and cars; cars full of FFI [the Forces Françaises de l'Intérieur of the Resistance] follow the tanks, civilians and military are one race: free French."[6] Most famously, de Gaulle's euphoric first speech in liberated Paris laid the groundwork for the myth of the Resistance that was to take over the national imagination in the immediate post-Vichy period: "Paris liberated! Liberated by itself, liberated by its people . . . with the support and help of all of France, of the France that is fighting, the only France, the true France, eternal France."[7] In de Gaulle's speech, the Resistance folds into "all of France." This exalted interpretation, which came to be called "resistantialism," would soon be contested. But for the moment, after four years of humiliation and atrocities, few wanted to question de Gaulle's narrative of "the true France."

La Libération de Paris describes a week that culminated in an extraordinary moment of collective jubilation. In contrast, Thomas's diary of the week preceding the liberation shows a chaos of emotions, sometimes on the same day—anxiety, disappointment, frustration at not knowing what is going on, anticipation, and finally, joy. At one point she exclaims: "How confusing it is to live historic events!"[8] Both *La Libération de Paris* and, seven years later, *Le Témoin compromis,* in spite of their efforts to take that confusion into account, impose the coherence of hindsight. In each of these accounts, omissions, additions, and changes reflect the moment at which the writing takes place.

A few of the differences among these versions are of particular interest. In one of Thomas's diary notations on August 23, she includes an astonishing poem that does not figure in either of the later accounts. It was written for her mother's birthday:

Paris n'est plus une fille fardée
Qui attend le client au coin d'une porte
Paris n'est plus une putain
Qui ouvre les jambes
Paris se bat. . . .

Dans les rues qui sont redevenues nos rues
Sous ce ciel d'été qui est enfin notre ciel
Au bord de la Seine qui emporte notre histoire
Sur son eau véritable
Paris se bat. . . .[9]

[Paris is no longer a tart with makeup
Who waits for her client in a doorway
Paris is no longer a whore
Who opens her legs
Paris is fighting. . . .

In the streets which have become once again our streets
Under this summer sky which is at last our sky
On the banks of the Seine which carries our history
On its real water
Paris is fighting. . . .]

The stanzas are brought together by the repetition of the line "Paris is fight-ing." After the long humiliation of being occupied and dispossessed of their beloved city, Parisians were engaged in active combat to win her back. The pros-titute image conflates the collective symbol of France as a woman with the ac-tions of individual men and women, specifically those who not only accepted French defeat but profited from it as well. A year later in *La Libération de Paris* the prostitute image reappears, again in contrast to the image of a Paris fighting for its liberation: "The moment has come to prove to the world that Paris is not a prostitute, spineless [*veule*] and indifferent, passed from hand to hand. The moment has come to prove that Paris is capable of liberating herself."[10] In her choice of the metaphor of the prostitute, Thomas translates one of many forms of sexual malaise, deeply embedded in the collective imagination of the time.

Vichy France offered its own sexualized interpretation of the national com-munity. Its repressive ideology of female virtue relegated French women to the role of mothers for the nation, defining those women who subverted their assigned feminine identity as unpatriotic.[11] At the same time, the Nazi occu-pation made visible both the humiliation of French masculinity and the con-tinuing absence of French men, over two million of whom were prisoners or forced laborers in Germany. The contradictions and hypocrisy of Vichy's sexual ideology permeate the atmosphere of Claude Chabrol's film *Une Affaire de femmes* (1988), released in English as *A Woman's Story*. It is based on the true story of Marie-Louise Giraud, who performed abortions during the occupation and was guillotined by the Vichy government. According to Pétain's analysis, France's defeat was a result of "too few children, too few arms, too few allies." Giraud's death sentence was based on a law passed in 1942 that made abortion a "crime against the state" and those who performed abortions "assassins of the *patrie*."[12]

The metaphor of a French-German couple, in which Germany was the man and France the woman, functioned as a kind of collective unconscious with diverse meanings for collaborators and *résistants*. Vercors's *The Silence of the Sea*, written at the beginning of the occupation as a call to resistance, can be read as a thwarted love story between Werner von Ebrennac, the Francophile and best of all possible German occupiers, and the French narrator's niece, who remains silent in response to his monologue of love for France and implicitly for her. The impossibility of love between them signifies the destruction of all hope of genuine collaboration, in which French and German internationalists had passionately believed between the wars.

Sartre's essay "What Is a Collaborator?", first published the summer after Brasillach's execution, describes the sexual imagery in collaborationist writing: "Everywhere in articles by Chateaubriant, Drieu, and Brazillach [*sic*], are curious metaphors that present the relationship of France and Germany under the aspect of a sexual union where France plays the role of the woman."[13] Writing from his position as a Nazi collaborator in February 1944 when the German defeat was imminent, Robert Brasillach evoked his own image of the sexualized French-German couple: "It seems to me that I've contracted a liaison with German genius, one that I will never forget. Whether we like it or not, we will have lived together. Frenchmen given to reflection, during these years, will have more or less slept with Germany—not without quarrels—and the memory of it will remain sweet for them."[14] His political journalism enacted the sado-masochistic implication of those words in the context of occupied France. As editor of the virulently pro-Nazi newspaper *Je suis partout,* Brasillach had denounced with shocking specificity Resistance fighters, Gaullists, Communists, and Jews, aiding the Gestapo in finding them and sending them to their deaths. Brasillach was brought to trial for treason and executed in 1945.

It can be argued that the choice to take action and join the Resistance, for women as well as men, reflected a determination to counter the role of submission, what Sartre calls the role of the woman, assigned to France by the invading German occupiers and accepted by the Vichy government. Since the French Revolution, France has been figured as Marianne, perhaps best known as she is embodied in Delacroix's dramatic painting *Liberty Leading the People.* Among the three national representations of the French Republic—Marianne, the tricolor, and the Marseillaise—only Marianne was officially banished by the Vichy regime. After France's defeat by Germany, Marianne was removed from town halls and postage stamps to be replaced by Pétain.[15] The change of icon from an embattled, desirable young woman to the defeated old man who represented France's collaboration with its conquerors carries its own eloquent commentary.

The occupation years gave new meaning to the traditional symbolic representation of France as a woman. On the first page of de Gaulle's wartime memoirs, following his famous beginning, "All my life I have had a certain idea of France," he writes that his "emotional side" tended to imagine France "like the princess of stories or the Madonna of frescoes, dedicated to a distinguished and exceptional destiny."[16] For many poets of the Resistance, the "distant princess" in Jaufre Rudel's medieval songs became emblematic of the national sense of loss and exile.[17] In Aragon's Resistance poem "The Reseda and the Rose," France defeated and invaded by the Germans is "the lovely captive," grieved by all those who worship her and who fight to liberate her, whatever their beliefs otherwise.[18] In an article written just after the war, Édith Thomas speaks of Paris during the occupation years in the feminine as "*une étrangère*," a stranger, a "beautiful, bound prisoner."[19]

In Thomas's diary, earlier on the same day that she writes the "Paris is fighting" poem for her mother, the image of Paris as a prostitute first appears as a metaphor attacking those who are passively waiting for liberation: "The impression pursues me that most of the population, without being hostile to the Resistance, would have preferred to see the liberation of Paris accomplished just by the Americans. No hassles, it's easier that way. Paris is a prostitute who is waiting, her legs open." She finds that only the working-class neighborhoods are there to "save the honor of that girl," an honor that was lost when France was defeated and Vichy decided to collaborate with the enemy.[20]

The experience of Nazi occupation as sexual humiliation of the *patrie* was a primal motivation in the ritual punishment of the head shaving of women, *les femmes tondues,* inflicted on as many as 20,000 women in cities, towns, and villages all over France, for the most part during the battles of the liberation.[21] Women suspected of "horizontal collaboration" were dragged to a public square where their heads were shaved and they were paraded as spectacles of derision. Head shaving was inflicted on women who had offered themselves to Germans, whether they were prostitutes, had had an affair, or even, in many cases, because they had collaborated as men did with the Nazis. No distinction was made between private and public acts. As the historian Henry Rousso comments, in the specific violence that targeted women as sexual beings, "they were symbolically accused of having been 'unfaithful' to the nation and having 'sullied' it through their own body, as if it belonged to the collectivity."[22]

Thomas writes in her diary on August 25: "On the boulevard St. Germain, they've shaved the head of a woman who collaborated, a *collaboratrice,* and the crowd follows her, screaming. The FTP, a force for order, protects her. Without them, the people would lynch her."[23] There is no hint of her own reaction to the episode. Her account in *La Libération de Paris* puts "*collaboratrice*" in quotation marks but makes no other changes. Eight years later in *Le Témoin compromis,* however, she adds a few sentences after her account, all of which was supposedly transcribed directly from her diary: "The crazed look of this *femme tondue* would be enough for me to be horrified by victory. I tell myself that a shaved head is better than a head at the end of a pike, the symbol of vengeance rather than vengeance itself. But that's because I've decided to console myself about everything today."[24] Her pained criticism reflects either a change of perspective after 1945 or an unwillingness to admit, in the joy of liberation, any criticism of Resistance actions.

During the liberation, Édith Thomas was asked by the leader of the Communist-led National Front resistance movement to serve as editor of a new women's journal, a vehicle of the Union of French Women, for which she had been writing underground tracts. As a good militant, she accepted the task assigned to her. But she was uncomfortable with her position as editor, in large part because she felt removed from the traditional assumptions about women's roles as housekeepers, wives, and mothers that had prompted the male leaders of the National Front to decide on *Femmes françaises.* At least sometimes, she notes in her memoir, the debate has to be raised "above the price of potatoes and carrots."[25] Although her editorial independence was severely constrained by Party directives, she was able to institute a book column and to hire Dominique Aury as well as her good friend Clara Malraux without requiring what she mockingly calls a *bulletin de confession* (literally, a certificate of belief), in this context a confirmation of Party allegiance. In theory at least, the Union of French Women, the journal's sponsor, welcomed all women who had participated in the Resistance, whatever their political affiliations.

In addition to her editing and publishing responsibilities, Édith Thomas wrote for each issue. When she needed to write more than one article, she would sign the additional piece with a pseudonym, Brigitte Chevance, to underplay her role. A number of her articles were of substantive interest, including an extensive interview with the psychologist Henri Wallon, focusing on his ideas for a coherent and progressive policy concerning children.[26] In other contexts, however, the double mission of *Femmes françaises,* the "defense of family interests" and the "liberation and reconstruction of France," were not always easy to reconcile. French women had only just won the right to vote, granted by de Gaulle's provisional government. The program of action for the Union proclaimed: "In their new role as citizens they do not forget their obligations as mother and wife,"[27] an ambiguous statement meant to allay fears that women would become excessively absorbed in political action. Translated into policy, the statement meant that positions of authority in the Union were given to wives or widows of Communist leaders whenever possible, and no decisions were made independent of the leaders' approval.[28]

By January 1945, the accumulation of conflicts about both the content of the journal and the role of the Party became intolerable for Thomas, and she made up her mind to resign. When she enumerated the reasons for her resignation in a letter to the Central Committee, she was asked to appear before their tribunal, where they informed her that these quarrels among members of the Party should not be known on the outside. They insisted that she rewrite her letter, giving reasons of health as an explanation for her departure. She complied, in spite of her feeling that these methods were, as she writes in her memoir, "detestable."[29]

Nevertheless, the following spring, on April 24, 1946, Édith Thomas accepted an invitation to join a delegation of the Union of French Women to visit Moscow and Leningrad for a few weeks. A comparison between her observations about that trip made at the time in numerous articles and her memory of those observations after she left the Party in 1949 reflects the changes in her perspective. In both time frames she records her admiration for the extraordinary confidence and hard work of the Russian people, who were struggling to overcome the war's devastation and to rebuild their country. Visits to stores and markets, factories and collective farms, convinced her that the life of Russian peasants and workers was an immense improvement over their life before the revolution.[30]

In her memoir, however, she also notes that she was disturbed by a number of things she was able to observe firsthand, even in a brief, supervised visit: the idolatrous cult of Lenin; the fact that secondary education, free in capitalist France, was neither free nor equal for boys and girls in the Soviet Union; the impression that in this proletarian state, workers had little to say; the awareness that even officially invited foreigners were considered potential spies. No hint of these reservations appears in the numerous articles she wrote, shortly after her return, for a wide range of Communist and leftist newspapers and magazines. In her memoir she comments: "For most of us, this trip took on the sacred character of a pilgrimage to the holy land. I went there in a rather different state of mind. Along with a favorable bias, my critical faculties were on the alert; I was determined not to be taken in."[31] Those alert critical faculties are decidedly hidden in the articles, where her enthusiastic account of life in the Soviet Union, uncomplicated by criticism of any kind, could win the approval of her most orthodox comrades in the Party.

With the end of the war, Thomas was elated to rediscover Paris. She walked everywhere, taking in the city as if she had just landed there after dreaming about it for the four years when it did not belong to Parisians. During that time, she writes, they were deprived of their city as they were deprived of bread. Parisians could walk in the street, but they were too attentive to the sound of the boots of the Wehrmacht and the muffled step of the agents of the Gestapo to listen to the personal message of the Seine and its poplars. As long as swastika flags were hanging from the windows of the place de la Concorde, Paris did not reveal its human face. Even after the liberation, while the enemy was not defeated and there was still war, in all that distress, the city she loved could not become itself again. Now, with peace in the world, Paris seemed like a gift. She almost couldn't believe that the quays and Notre Dame, the Louvre and the Sainte Chapelle, survived intact in the midst of Europe in ruins. She marveled at the beauty of the chestnut trees in the Luxembourg Gardens and across the Seine in the Tuileries, where dahlias and zinnias were once again in bloom.

After the long years of occupation when travel outside of France was forbidden, Thomas felt a physical need to cross the frontiers of her own country. She went first, in June 1945, to Switzerland. Although part of the purpose of her trip was to meet with the Swiss novelist Charles-Ferdinand Ramuz, a writer she admired, there was also the desire to return to a place that during her childhood had represented the pleasure of vacations. She describes her "childish joy" at arriving in this privileged country that had escaped two world wars, the enjoyment, for example, of a real breakfast, with real white rolls and real butter. In Geneva she was dazzled by stores full of clothing, shoes, and pastries "which belonged to a fairy tale world whose existence we could no longer imagine." The Swiss received her and her friends with solicitude, "like poor, ill, mad relatives."[32]

In July 1945 Thomas was given the assignment to do a report on the French occupation of Germany. When she crossed the Rhine and saw cities and towns in ruin everywhere, she finally had the certainty that Germany was defeated. She confides to her reader: "Should I say, can I say, that the ruins of Mainz are as painful to me as those of Brest? I am not made for scalp dancing." In the same article she enumerates the long list of German crimes and with each evocation she repeats: "Don't think I have forgotten." The question of French relations with Germany after the war, she insists, must be determined not in terms of vengeance or forgiveness, but in response to the historical and political demands of a coherent policy. As she traveled through Freiburg and Mainz, through Mannheim and Karlsruhe, through Pforzheim and Stuttgart and Konstanz, she found that French military governance was completely different from one city to another, even from one district to another. In most cities she hears, "We're going to make the Boches pay"; only in a few does she find French forces trying to bolster anti-Nazi elements in the population. She recounts a number of anecdotes of French soldiers intoxicated with the power of being on the side of the winners.[33]

The French zone of occupation was instituted just after the Yalta conference, at which the United States and Great Britain agreed to give up a part of their respective zones so that France could become an occupying force. Consisting of two triangles on either side of the Rhine, the French zone was the smallest and least populated of the zones of occupation. Thomas's analysis in 1945 of the French occupation is supported by recent studies, based on French and German archives opened in 1985. A German poll in 1947 attested that the French had the reputation for being next to the worst of the occupying powers, just after the Soviets. According to the French historian Cyril Buffet, they were seen by the Germans as "vengefully eager to pillage and dismember [Germany]."[34]

The end of the war meant that deportees and prisoners liberated from Nazi camps were returning in large numbers and that their accounts of the full horrors of the Shoah were beginning to be revealed. The universalist humanism invoked by Thomas and the literary Resistance became even more difficult to sustain. For the first time, she vacillated in the position she had held throughout the occupation, questioning how a fanatical gang of thugs could have committed so many atrocities without the complicity or at least the acceptance of an entire people. She writes: "I don't think there is any shame in admitting that it took me four years to discover hatred. For four years I was among those who tried to separate the German people from the Nazis, to remember that Oradour was the crime of a few S.S., and to think constantly about the day when we would have to proclaim out loud that distinction [between Germans and Nazis] which in my heart I had never wanted to stop making. Now, I don't know anymore."[35]

When she looks back at that time in her memoir, the anguished questions remain, although she tentatively returns to a universalist response, much darker than her humanism of the war years: "Doubtless there were brutes and sadists everywhere. But here there were doctors, so called men of science to conduct these experiments that were being described to us. I tried to hold on to something, anything. I even became racist. Until then I had always condemned both antisemitism and antigermanism as absurdities. I felt hatred for fascism or Hitlerism, never for the Germans. But neither Italian nor Spanish fascism had found intellectuals to carry out this work of refined and perverse executioners. I wanted to see in that the mark of specifically German excess. In so doing, it seemed to me that I was saving mankind in general. But at the same time I knew that I was deceiving myself. If I had been able to believe in the devil, I would have invented him in order to exonerate men."[36]

Thomas's memory of *les années noires,* the dark years, always remained concerned with the future as well as the past. She saw in the experience of her generation a warning for everyone. As she put it in a review of the Auschwitz memoir of Charlotte Delbo: "Tortures did not disappear with Hitlerism, nor did racism. We need to be vigilant to what happens around us and within us."[37] From that same perspective, and as a professional historian, she opposed any notion of a generalized German guilt that flattened all differences of individual behavior into a collective psychological essence. Her refusal to conflate Germans and Nazis was accompanied by her insistence that those who commit evil acts must take moral responsibility and that the notion of an original sin specific to Germans is a dangerous illusion.

9

STORY OF TWO WOMEN
Édith Thomas and Dominique Aury

Édith Thomas's brief position as editor of *Femmes françaises* proved to be a transformative moment in her life, since it was there that she met Dominique Aury. Dissatisfied with the first few issues of the journal, Thomas was determined to find a colleague who would provide an intellectual dimension. In November 1944 she wrote to Jean Paulhan, asking him to recommend someone. He suggested Dominique Aury: "She is courageous. She has demonstrated it. She is also unusual."[1] Paulhan had met Aury when she was working at Gallimard during the occupation; he would often give her articles and poems to read. One day she took out of her pocket a carefully sealed envelope containing the clandestine *Lettres françaises* that she helped distribute, gave it to him, and told him to be sure no one else saw it. She did not know, of course, that he was one of its founders. After the liberation, when Paulhan received Édith Thomas's request, he sent Dominique Aury a note to advise her that "a dear friend, someone quite remarkable, needs a literary collaborator for *Femmes françaises*."[2] Dominique went to see Édith and immediately took the job. She wrote a number of book reviews and a series of articles on women's struggle for the right to vote in France, England, and the United States.

The two women were able to share stories and complicities about the intolerable situation at the journal, although Dominique was always resolutely anticommunist and Édith was still a Party member. Dominique recalled their difficulties working with women in the Party: "When they had the slightest problem, they would phone the Party, and the Party would treat them like dirt. They needed the Party not only to tell them what to do, but what to think as well. It made Édith ill. It made me laugh." She remembered a reception for the

Soviet ambassador at the Hôtel de Ville that the women of *Femmes françaises* were asked to attend. Although he ignored the other women, in spite of their efforts to engage him in conversation, he talked eagerly with Dominique. Afterward, they wanted to know what she had said to capture his attention: "They called him Comrade. I addressed him as His Excellency. No officials anywhere love titles as much as the Soviets."

When Dominique, like Édith, decided she would leave *Femmes françaises,* she did so with a shrewdness that was completely foreign to her friend. Asked to write a review of what she called a "perfectly respectable" novel by a Russian historian, Dominique complied by producing a perfectly favorable article—to which she gave the title "Travail, Famille, Patrie," the slogan of Vichy France which had replaced the French Republic's "Liberté, Égalité, Fraternité." As she anticipated, she was fired, and thus able to collect the unemployment insurance she had coming to her.

Dominique was appalled by Édith's faith in the Communist Party and the communist ideal. During the 1930s, when Dominique began to support herself as a literary journalist, most of her friends were part of what she herself described as an extreme right-wing milieu. Her first books, published during the occupation, were far removed from the passions of the time: an anthology of seventeenth-century baroque poets appeared in 1941, and Gallimard published her anthology of French religious poetry in 1943. In contrast to Édith's abiding political commitment, Dominique was vehemently averse to all politics: "What idiocy," she said to me, "to bring a moral judgment to bear on political ideas. One can die for people or for things, but not for an idea. An idea is always malevolent once it is put into practice." Nevertheless, she took risks for the Resistance, transporting and distributing underground newspapers and books. In reply to my question about the apparent contradiction between her statement and her actions, she insisted that the Resistance had nothing to do with politics: "One's homeland, the country one loves, is not an abstract idea, it's concrete." Her response points to the differing motives of patriotism and antifascism among those who joined the Resistance, although these motives were by no means mutually exclusive.

After the liberation, Dominique returned to her work as a literary critic, which she continued until a few years before her death. In February 1946 she wrote a review of the two novels by Édith Thomas that had recently been published, *Étude de femmes* (Study of women) and *Le Champ libre* (Free and clear). *Étude de femmes* opens with the words of the three witches from *Macbeth*, spoken by three adolescent girls—two sisters, Claire and Dominique, and their friend Yvonne—practicing their lines with the best English accent they can manage as they move gracefully in the August moonlight, talking about their roles in the play and wondering about their future. Their interwoven lives, defined by men who disappoint them, show different aspects of the problems confronting educated women in French society during the 1930s. Thomas took the epigraph for *Étude de femmes* from Balzac: "When Buffon depicted the lion, he completed his lioness in a few sentences, whereas in society, woman is not always the female of the male." In Aury's review, she sees the three characters as three contradictory aspects of the same woman and points out that Thomas's characters "yield to *amour-passion,* while the truth of their heart is *amour-estime.*" In all the couples evoked, she notes, "each woman remains locked in her solitude."[3]

Le Champ libre, published by Gallimard, is more directly autobiographical, although the parents of the heroine, like those of *Le Refus,* have little in common with Thomas's own parents beyond their social standing. Refusing the prospect of the pedigreed husband she can expect in exchange for her impressive dowry, Anne chooses instead to pursue her studies toward an advanced degree in philosophy so that she can earn a living as a lycée teacher in Paris, scandalous ambitions in the 1930s for a woman of her class. She soon finds that she has exchanged one form of alienation for another. Her dual quest for what she calls salvation, through a great love and through commitment to irrevocable action, clashes with the cynicism of a modish intellectual world in which she finds no place. After she becomes pregnant by Renaud, a man she does not love who belongs to the same caste and has the same values as the man she was initially expected to marry, she decides she wants to keep the child. Traumatized by a miscarriage, Anne feels the need to be elsewhere, and in July 1936 she finds herself in Barcelona amidst the distress, confusion, and hope of the civil war that has just broken out, although she remains an outsider. The novel closes with the discovery that her childhood soul mate and hero, who had disappeared from her life after his adolescent rebellion against family and class, is now in Spain and seriously wounded. She searches for him frantically only to learn, in the final sentence of the novel, that he is dead.

In spite of the shift to a political context in the last part of the novel, Thomas's heroine, like the characters of *Étude de femmes,* remains locked in her solitude and obsessed with an impossible love. Dominique Aury's reflections in her review seem to be less about Anne than about Édith, words of comfort and tribute addressed by Dominique to her friend: "For Anne has perhaps lost the world, and all hope, but she has not lost herself. . . . Anne carries within, without knowing it, her own light. . . . For those who observe her, her radiance makes warm and alive the night in which she despairs. In this struggle between bitterness and courage, the victory, in spite of appearances, belongs to courage, at least to that form of courage that is expressed by silence, by the refusal to complain, by modesty and *courtoisie.* The Stoics know of no higher virtue. Anne resembles them."[4]

When Dominique Aury and Édith Thomas began their love affair in 1946, Dominique was thirty-nine years old and Édith thirty-seven. Briefly married and a mother when she was in her early twenties, Dominique had considerable sexual experience with men and episodically with women—in contrast to Édith, who had little sexual experience with men and none with women. Her first affair with "Renaud" was followed by one or two brief encounters during the period of the liberation. On October 27, 1946, Édith Thomas writes in her diary: "This morning D. said to me: 'Édith, I've drawn you into a trap.' She was pale, ill, agitated. 'I love you the way a man loves a woman.' What to do? My God (who doesn't exist), what to do? I feel friendship, respect, deep affection for her. We agree on what is essential; we experience things, people, books in the same way. I love her delicacy, her intelligence, her exceptional quality of being. If she were a man, I would be infinitely happy about her love for me. If I were a man, I would love her. But she is a woman and I am a woman. What should I do?" She continues the next day: "I never thought that homosexuals and lesbians could be in love outside their closed network. And here I discover the love of one of them for a physically normal being."[5] Once she and Dominique became lovers, what counted for Édith was that she had found someone to love who loved her. Dominique's gender was no longer an issue.

The tone of Dominique's recollection of the beginning of their love affair is quite different. She says of herself: "I was the bad boy in our story, it's true. I enjoyed that role." However, the casual playfulness of her remark in conversation almost fifty years after the affair belies the language of passion in which she first declared her love, in a letter written the same day as Édith's first diary entry about her. This is her letter in full:

> Édith, my darling, forgive me. I have been struggling for such a long time. Forgive me, I couldn't take any more. I still want to be near you, to tell you that I love you, to embrace you. I know that I seem absurd to you. And also that I am selfish. But I am trembling before you, because I am afraid to frighten you, and to hurt you. And I can't control myself any more. Your gentleness overwhelms me. You don't know what it is to burn with love, to have your soft hands on my lips, or your soft black hair, or the down on your cheeks, just below the ear. For months I haven't let myself think about that. I've never loved a woman as I love you, Édith.
>
> I've never loved a girl for whom I feel at the same time respect and admiration and this friendship which in spite of love has nothing to do with love, but rather with tenderness, and which resembles what is strongest in a camaraderie of combat. Ordinarily, I don't have many scruples. Up to

now, it has never happened to me to think about a girl: leave her alone; you don't have the right. If I've thought that about you, it's not out of obligation, but out of tenderness. But you're so much stronger within me than I am. When I held you for one second in my arms, I had to throw myself against the wall, my legs buckling and my cheeks pale. And you looked so anxious and so sad that I want to ask your forgiveness for loving you. Yet I love you. I kiss your hands, Édith.

   Dominique[6]

In spite of the rhetoric of uncontrollable emotion, her expression of desire is both timid and literary, reminiscent of a medieval knight courting his lady. In retrospect, one can discern in the letter a prescient self-awareness of what will be durable and what will be transient in her feelings. For all its intensity, her romantic passion does not run deep. She seems to know, with some guilt, that if Édith responds to her desire for a sexual relationship, it is Édith who will inevitably be hurt. The uniqueness of this love in Dominique's history is on a different level. Over the years, in spite of all obstacles, her actions will demonstrate the other emotions she names: respect, admiration, friendship, and tenderness. Why, she asks elsewhere, is nothing ever said about tenderness? "The tenderness that remains when desire, when pleasure have passed, isn't it the most extraordinary gift of life?"[7] Her letter bends masculine and feminine assumptions, particularly in the link she creates between tenderness and "what is strongest in a camaraderie of combat," an image that corresponds to her fantasy of what she calls, in the single interview she gave as Pauline Réage, a "suppressed military vocation."[8]

   At the time Dominique wrote her letter, she was having an affair with a man, whom she left for Édith. Among the mass of Édith's papers was a five-page handwritten poem, "On the love of Urania and Philis," by the seventeenth-century court poet Benserade, an imitator of Ovid.[9] Dominique did not remember the circumstances of sending the poem, transcribed in handwriting clearly recognizable as hers, to Édith. Benserade's verses are addressed to his mistress, who has left him for someone else. In his lament he complains that not only has someone else replaced him but also, to compound his disgrace, the new lover of his mistress is a woman. The poem seems to have been part of Dominique's courtship of Édith, to give her pleasure at the thought of being preferred by Dominique to a man.

   In our conversations, Dominique often spoke with admiration of Édith's courage: "The courage to live when one is very ill, the moral courage to surmount her depression. She was always in fragile health and lived with the constant threat of a recurrence of tuberculosis. Her illness left her with the feeling

Dominique Aury, circa 1946. Gift of Philippe d'Argila to the author.

of being cut off from the world. But this constant danger gave her a kind of flame that I found very beautiful, a charming ferocity, and an exceptional energy for work." Dominique's letters over the years give substance and context to that admiration. All her life she suffered from periods of severe migraine headaches and exhaustion, which sometimes left her incapable of getting out of bed. Unable to overcome the extreme fatigue that overwhelmed her, she would feel depressed and remorseful. Although Édith also suffered from constant health problems and depression, many friends commented on the paradox of her remarkable energy, in spite of her melancholy.

In that respect, Dominique found in Édith a model of courage she wished she could emulate:

> I admire and I envy you. . . . Give me a little of your energy, my darling, a little of that regularity of work that I have not yet learned and which is so lacking in me. You can't imagine how much you shame me, and all my fa-

tigue doesn't change that, as deep as it is, as slow to disappear, as invincible. Precisely because it seems invincible to me, it is obvious that I must act as if it weren't there, since nothing can be done about it. Tell me that I have to work, my darling, immediately. If it's you who tells me, I do believe I will obey."[10]

That kind of formulation about obedience notwithstanding, they often argued, especially about politics. "When Édith said no," Dominique said to me, "she was stubborn as a mule. When it was no, it was no. You could stay and argue for three hours, she would not change her mind. Of course the same was true for me."

Dominique seems to have confided much about herself to her new friend, in spite of the radical differences in their experience of the world. Just after Dominique's initial declaration, Édith writes in her diary, without specifying further: "She spoke to me piecemeal about her life, as unedifying as could be. And yet I consider her one of the healthiest, most honest, most loyal beings I ever met." The first time they made love together, sex for Édith became passion: "I'm burning. I'm like a bundle of firewood, like a handful of straw. I'm thirsty. I'm like someone walking in the desert. I'm hungry. Can you be my orchard, my source of water? Or only this devouring fire which, when it withdraws, leaves me mortally unsatisfied?"[11]

At other moments, passion was transformed into a form of spiritual, even mystical connection. Going to see Dominique one day in February when she was ill in bed, Édith writes: "Suddenly I felt invaded by such a deep tenderness that it seemed to me—just for a moment—that through her, through me, I touched another reality. . . . One or two sensations like that and I will begin to understand what is real for the mystics." And a few months later: "Whether you are a man or a woman doesn't matter to me. I love your caresses and the beauty of your body, and the beauty of your forehead and your eyes. And my abandon to you and yours to me. This loyalty and this equality between us, my love."[12]

On Dominique's part, looking back, she was drawn physically and emotionally to a primal contradiction in Édith. "She was not a woman," Dominique said, "she was a child. She had the body of a ten-year-old girl. And a young girl's naiveté. She was also resolute and fierce. Like a great, exiled lord." Dominique's description speaks to the division of feminine and masculine that intrigued her, in images of feminine and masculine that are also images of a child and a man, of powerlessness and power. "Exiled" suggests, in a single word, the feeling shared by Édith and Dominique of the world as a place of exile.

Édith's passion made her increasingly fearful of losing Dominique. Writing in her diary in the middle of the night, she was plagued by worry about her wrinkles, her limp, and all the women and men more beautiful and younger whom

Dominique could love. She worried, too, that their adventure in love would compromise their friendship: "I believe in the duration of friendship more than that of love." Just over nine months later, Édith thought about a compliment paid by Paulhan to Dominique the day before, when the three of them were together: "I'm convinced that Paulhan is beginning to love D., and since she admires and loves him, my love will not weigh very much in the balance. Thinking about that, I cried for two hours. I wrote an imaginary letter breaking up with her: I would rather lose D. than share her. I feel as jealous as a tiger."[13]

As Édith guessed, Dominique Aury did fall in love with Paulhan, who was not someone younger, as in Édith's phantom fears, but twenty-three years older than Dominique and married. He was devoted to his wife, who had Parkinson's disease, and he did not consider leaving her. Jean Paulhan and Dominique Aury began a love affair in August 1947 that was to last until his death in 1968. She was determined, however, to keep her attachment to Édith alive and took the initiative of calling her every day, against Édith's impulse to break their relationship completely.

"Édith was more exclusive, more possessive than I was," she said. "Sexual freedom was not at all natural to her. I was the one who continued to call because she did not want to weigh on me. She was hurt and jealous." For Dominique Aury, one could love several people at the same time. The important thing was that the loved one "still loves you and does not leave you."[14] Her idea of fidelity required a faithfulness of hearts rather than bodies. The worst thing in life, she felt, was to be separated from those one loves, and she did not want to let that separation take place between herself and Édith. In spite of Édith's feelings of pain and rejection, the strength of their reciprocal attachment is evident in both their private letters and their published writings over the years.

Dominique Aury's presence in Édith Thomas's fictional imagination can first be traced in *Ève et les autres,* a little book that re-creates tales of women in the Bible. It was published in 1952, although many of the tales appeared separately before that date. In "The End of Gomorrah," directly inspired by her relationship with Dominique, Thomas makes Lot's wife, unnamed in the Bible, her own namesake.[15] The fictional Édith is irritated by her husband's patronizing airs, his pulling her along behind him as he leaves the city, his "family vice" of carrying on about the Almighty. She wants to stay in Gomorrah with her friend Deborah, the only person with whom she can be herself, and refuses to accept the judgment of God and Lot that their love is a sin. When Lot in his anger turns around to look at her, she becomes a pillar of salt, a statue of sparkling crystals with its face turned toward the city. The idea for this story can be found in Thomas's diary on November 5, 1946, when she imagines Gomorrah, a metaphor for the love affair with Dominique that has just begun, as her "lost homeland" and wonders about the regrets of Lot's wife, "who must have been my grandmother," as she looks back at the burning cities.[16]

A few months after the beginning of Dominique's relationship with Paulhan, she suffered an attack of appendicitis. Just after her operation, while she was still recuperating, Édith also became stricken—with appendicitis. Édith writes from her hospital to Dominique at hers: "Is it imitative magic or the most vulgar of intellectual plagiarisms that 'inspired' my attack of appendicitis Monday morning? I think rather it's a kind of dialectical materialism, a way to pray for you, to commune with you. One does what one can, even if the result is not very intelligent. Since I'm as unable to go see you as if I were in the Black Forest."[17] And Dominique replies: "You are playing terrible tricks on me, on yourself. What an idea for you, too, to have appendicitis. As long as you're at it, what a pity you didn't have it sooner. They could have given you a room here next to mine—and communicating with mine. . . . It's my bad magic, my darling, or your baneful dialectical materialism."[18]

Not surprisingly, many of Édith's letters after Paulhan's entry into Dominique's life are passionate, demanding, and unhappy. Then she is regretful, and turns on herself: "Forgive me for having sent you that ridiculous letter. I should be silent at those moments instead of letting myself go in emotional disasters. I'm angry with myself afterward. And very ashamed, as if I had committed an indecency." And in another letter: "Why must I always attach myself so exclusively to one person? You are much wiser than I am." Sometimes their exchanges are playful historical musings. When Dominique wonders what Édith would have been like if she had lived at the end of the eighteenth century, she replies: "I can reasonably suppose I would have been for Marat and Robespierre, and at the same time ogled the Girondins [the moderate revolutionaries]. Unless I was hopelessly in love with Saint-Just [the Jacobin purist]. And my head would have been cut off in any case."[19]

In a conversation with Dominique Aury during the summer of 1991, we discussed my ongoing transcription of Édith Thomas's handwritten diaries that she had given me on loan. When I asked whether revealing their relationship in the biography of Thomas that I was planning to write could present problems for her, she smiled: "You know, as far as scandal is concerned, I'm an armored truck," and proceeded to tell me of her bout with the French censors concerning *Story of O*, taking it for granted that I knew she had written it. Dominique asked me if I had read the sequel to *O*, or the single, book-length interview she gave, still anonymously, almost twenty years after her novel was published. As a response to my reply in the negative to both her questions, she offered to give me copies of the books. When we emerged from her favorite Chinese restaurant near Gallimard, she whisked me away in her old Ford with the speed, style, and aggressiveness characteristic of Parisian drivers; soon we reached her home in a working-class Paris suburb. Its plain facade, no different from others on the street, opened up to a house with a gorgeous private courtyard, filled with plants and light. We stayed just a few minutes, long enough for her to agree to sign her book. What she especially wanted me to have was not the book itself, *Return to the Château*, which she considered "very poor," but the preface, titled "A Girl in Love." It is an astonishingly beautiful essay about love, writing, and identity, "the only true story I ever wrote," she told me. She signed it "Très ·amicalement, Pauline Réage," enjoying the game. "One should be consistent in life," she said.

The preface contains a hidden tribute to Édith Thomas, first of all in Dominique Aury's choice of pseudonym, as well as in allusions to the text of *Story of O*. She borrowed the first name Pauline, she writes, from "two famous profligates," Pauline Borghèse and Pauline Roland.[20] Pauline Borghèse was a sister of Napoleon and married one of his generals. Pauline Roland, a socialist and feminist during the first half of the nineteenth century, was the subject of Thomas's first major biography and a woman with whom she intimately identified. Dominique's letters show that Édith was beginning to work on *Pauline Roland* while Dominique was writing *Story of O*.

From the outset she confided in Édith about her project. She writes from Lausanne on October 5, 1950: "I continue my strange enterprise as best I can, isolated from any counsel or encouragement, and I am sending the pages, about fifteen or twenty, as I write them." Although she did not name the person to whom she was sending these pages, it is clear that the recipient was Paulhan, a name and a subject she avoided as much as possible with Édith. "It seems to me," she continues," that it's like jumping into the fire, and I'm dreadfully afraid. But isn't there an axiom that says you shouldn't put your hand to the plow if you're going to let go of the handles? We'll see. In any case, it's an astonishing stylistic exercise. . . . I don't like not being able to phone you, or to see you. Tell me about Pauline Roland, and don't be too much in love with the handsome Dalmatian," a Yugoslav diplomat with whom Édith was infatuated at the time.[21]

It is not clear whether Dominique sent Édith the manuscript of *O* before it was published. In response to Dominique's letter she writes: "How much I'd like to read your manuscript, my darling! With what curiosity, and also with what anxiety! Because you've often told me that these are subjects one could not approach with me."[22] After the publication of *O* in 1954, Dominique Aury once again linked her "Pauline" to Édith's Pauline Roland: "In a very small circle this Pauline you're talking about has caused quite a stir, generally attributed to me, an honor I share to a small extent with Leonor Fini and Louise de Vilmorin. I'm very pleased that your Pauline has received the anticipated subsidies."[23]

In Dominique's preface to *Return to the Château*, she explores the autobiographical traces of the characters in *O*. For Anne-Marie, she writes, "I don't know at all." But then she continues: "One of my woman friends (whom I respect, and I am slow to respect) could well be Anne-Marie, were it not for the fact that she is the epitome of purity and honor: I mean that Anne-Marie might have got her rigor and her resolve from her, and the straightforward, unequivocal way in which she exercised her profession."[24] The link between Édith Thomas, writer and curator at the Archives nationales, and Anne-Marie, a strong-willed prostitute, would be less than obvious without Dominique's allusions in her preface. Going back to *Story of O*, however, one can readily find connections between Anne-Marie and Édith Thomas, beginning with specific details. Like Édith, Anne-Marie lives near the Observatoire; she is a slender woman, her hair black and gray, with the air of a "great, exiled lord," the same image that Dominique used to describe Édith in one of our conversations.[25] Anne-Marie's chaise longue recalls the one in Édith Thomas's apartment, where she would sit very straight with her bad leg stretched out, an intimidating position in the eyes of many who came to visit her. Anne-Marie is in complicity with O's adored male lover Sir Stephen, which could be read as a complicity Dominique would have wished between Édith and Jean Paulhan. Two of the young women who whip O, following Anne-Marie's orders, are Claire and Yvonne, the names given by Édith Thomas to two of the three women in *Étude de femmes* (the third woman is Dominique), the novel reviewed by Dominique Aury in 1946. O thinks that Anne-Marie "was less interested in making a spectacle of her power than in establishing between O and herself a sense of complicity." O pleasures Anne-Marie, as she demands, but she does not possess her: "No one possessed Anne-Marie."[26]

When Édith Thomas read *Story of O*, she was "horrified, scandalized." "But I know you like Fénelon," was Dominique's surprised and surprising response. The abbé Fénelon (1651–1715) was a writer and priest denounced by the church for his subversive doctrine of quietism. He is perhaps best known, insofar as he is still read at all, for his progressive treatise *The Education of Girls* and his equally forward-looking didactic novel of a young man's education, *Telemachus*. What particularly fascinated Dominique Aury, however, was Fénelon's mysticism, elaborated in his spiritual writings. In the only collection of her literary essays published in her lifetime, she calls the first piece, about Fénelon, "Le Pur Amour." The book appeared in 1958, just four years after the publication of *O*. Reading her interpretation of Fénelon's quietism, one can immediately see how his doctrine of pure love inspired *Story of O*: "What do those who are tortured for their truth find in their sufferings, in the very midst of their groans and their tears, if not the same atrocious happiness that Fénelon wishes for his followers (*aux siens*) when they suffer? . . . Profane love and sacred love are the same love,

or should be. Only the object changes, if one can accept that it is decent to use
the word object for God. The pure love in which Fénelon in the exact sense of
the word annihilated himself is the single discourse of his *Spiritual Writings*."[27]
O's terrifying desire to be sexually degraded and destroyed by the lover to whom
she ascribes absolute power is inseparable from her yearning to be freed from
herself and given over completely to the transcendent being she adores. On that
level, *Story of O* is a work of pornographic mysticism.

The identity of the author of *O*, a secret self that Dominique Aury called
Pauline Réage, remained elusive even to herself. In a letter to Édith she writes:
"A small echo in *Carrefour* proposes three possible authors for this story (which
has just been forbidden by the police): J[ean] P[aulhan] or Mandiargues or me.
The most probable, they say, is Mandiargues, because he has the most energy.
But the book is being reprinted, with an additional ending. It's strange to make
a stir without anyone being sure that it's you. Also strange is this clandestine vocation, which has been pursuing me now for twenty years, in one form or another."[28]

For Dominique Aury, the secrecy of clandestine relations, whether in a fantasy, a love affair, or the Resistance, corresponded to her pleasure in having a self
or selves separate from the world—not solitary, but shared with her special ac-
complice(s). She remembered her adolescent fantasies always beginning, as in
Story of O, with a lover taking her to a secret place. By not signing *O* with her
name, she felt she could write freely, as someone else, knowing she was not compromising anyone. In fact, Dominique Aury was already a pseudonym. She was
born Anne Desclos and decided to adopt another name after her divorce in the
1930s when she began to work in journalism as an art and literary critic. The an-
drogyny of the name Dominique appealed to her and she liked the Breton sound
of Aury, which was also the first half of her mother's name, Auricoste. The initials D. A. reversed her own initials as well as those of her adored father, Auguste
Desclos. Beyond the social discretion implied by her use of a pseudonym, she
was attracted to an identity of multiple selves, in contrast to Édith Thomas's desire for coherence.

Dominique and Édith shared a need to take risks, although it took strikingly
different forms. She told me of the stories she recounted to Édith about a good
friend who "would sleep with everyone, the wildest girl I ever knew. And I know
what wildness means," she added, without elaborating. In Dominique's telling,
Édith did not understand the girl's courage in living that way: "She could return home one evening beaten, strangled. It's about adventure in the most
extraordinary sense of the word. She had a lot of courage, that girl." What seems
to have mattered for Dominique was the risk of danger, freely chosen, whatever its nature.

The opposed sensibilities of the two women in relation to the question of a coherent identity become blurred when we consider the role of fantasy in their writings and their lives. Part of the fascination of Édith Thomas's diaries lies in the tension between her willed coherence of identity and the underground selves that it could not contain. On June 10, 1944, possessed by the fever of those days and weeks preceding the liberation, she records a political fantasy as self-annihilating as Dominique Aury's erotic fantasies. In each of four passages she builds on a rhetorical structure that begins, "If they said to you," and ends, "I would answer: 'All right, that's fine.'" Whatever is demanded of her, she accepts, in the exaltation of believing that the utopia she desires will be achieved. Each passage takes her a step further in her imagined submission to the impersonal will of this ideal world. The last two stages take her fantasy to its extreme limit of death and degradation:

> If they said to you: "Don't think we will use you; we will keep you out of the way and we will create without you the world you desire"; I would answer: "All right, that's fine."
> If they said to you: "You will be put in prison and slandered, and you will die ignominiously in a way that will make everyone believe you were against us, but we will create the world you desire"; I would answer: "All right, that's fine."[29]

When Édith Thomas was confronted with the reality of such self-sacrifices in the postwar political world, her reaction was one of dismay. In her public statement of resignation from the Party in 1949, she specifically alludes to the rigged confessions of Rajk in Hungary, executed for treason, as well as the false accusations against Yugoslavia's Tito. In all her political writings, from the 1930s through the 1960s, she categorically rejected Stalinist reasoning that the end justifies the means. During the war years, however, once the Soviet Union had joined in the struggle against Nazi Germany, her diaries and memoir show that she was periodically tempted by the fantasy of ecstatic submission to the revolution, an impulse that found no place in her critical thinking about revolutionary politics.

In *The Second Sex* Simone de Beauvoir explores the profane translation of woman's desire to lose herself in a transcendent being. If the lover's demands, she writes, however odious, are perceived as reflecting his "divinity," then "it is intoxicating joy to feel herself the prey of another's free action": "One wearies of living always in the same skin, and blind obedience is the only chance for radical transformation known to a human being."[30] Her analysis of *l'amoureuse* can be read as a feminized version of the terrifying passion to sacrifice the self to a being—or an idea—that is perceived as superhuman, however tyrannical and arbitrary it might be. For Dominique Aury and Édith Thomas the fantasy of self-immolation, in the name of love or revolution, was a safeguard that enabled the independent lives they actually lived.

Reflecting on the origins of the self-annihilating fantasies of *O*, Pauline Réage writes: "Whence came to me those oft-repeated reveries, those slow musings just before falling asleep, always the same ones, in which the purest and wildest love always sanctioned, or rather always demanded, the most frightful surrender, in which childish images of chains and whips added to constraint the symbols of constraint, I'm not sure which. All I know is that they were beneficent and pro-tected me mysteriously."[31] A letter to Édith in 1954 gives voice to that conviction in immediate, physical terms. She notes that she has not had a migraine head-ache for several days: "I've thought a lot about the reasons for this change. René [Dr. René Wolfromm, the personal physician at the time of both Dominique and Édith] thinks there is one. You, logical girl, must be of the same opinion, as am I, although I am not logical. Well, I've discovered that the only element that has intervened is the publication of *Story of O*. . . . Unfortunately for science, I can hardly offer that explanation to René. But you will let me know what you think of it."[32] Her theory is intriguing, although it seems that the reprieve from her migraines did not last long.

The female signature of the text matters. Before Pauline Réage's identity was clearly established, the critic Nancy K. Miller wrote: "I prefer to think that this positioning of woman [in *Story of O*] is the writing of a masculine desire at-tached to the male body." Miller acknowledges that if the heroine of *O* were proven to be a female creation, "I would then have to start over again." "But," she adds, tellingly, "it would be a different story, since the story of the woman who writes is *always* another story."[33] With its highly stylized characters and rit-ualized settings, costumes and accoutrements, *O*'s story is a work of the imagi-nation brought into being by a woman who circulates, as creator, through all her characters: not only O, but also René, Sir Stephen, and Anne-Marie. Do-minique Aury's mastery of her narrative, which she elaborates with extraordi-nary formal skill, acts as a counterpoint to O's submission.

For Dominique Aury, an underground self can exalt the desire for self-anni-hilation in the name of love, a desire at least partly in contradiction to the life she led. Capturing in words the world of an underground self gave her control, she seems to suggest, and freed her from the need to live her fantasy. Édith Thomas's fantasy of self-annihilation in the name of the revolution served a similar function, although it found its expression in a diary rather than a fin-ished work of art. In radically divergent forms, with different dosages of reality, Dominique Aury and Édith Thomas shared the fantasy of being dispossessed of the self and given over to a master will in the name of their god, love or revolution. Distinguishing between a fantasy and its enactment can be crucial. Fantasy tends to simplify the ambivalence, the conflicting valences, of human yearning. The fantasy of a desire is not the same as the desire for that fantasy to be realized. In Dominique Aury's words, alluding to O in conversation, "Fantasies are unlivable but they help in living."

Paradoxically, the author of *Story of O* represented for Édith Thomas her only love affair grounded in the reality of another person. Her relationship with Dominique Aury also seems to have been Édith Thomas's only affair with a woman. Édith's intimate relationships with men, lived or fantasized, tended to be solitary inventions reminiscent of lovers in Proust, a favorite novelist of both women. In *Le Jeu d'échecs* the narrator's tribute to Claude gives another unexpected turn to the complexities of Édith Thomas's relationship with Dominique Aury: "You've taught me what it means to love someone in spite of everything, I mean to love someone not just as one has invented them but as they are, as they might become. To prefer the person who is to the person one has imagined."[34]

10

FEMININE HUMANISM
VERSUS EXISTENTIALISM

Thomas's first written reflections connecting humanism and women go back to 1934, when she writes in her diary: "If it is difficult for a man to attain humanism, that perfect equilibrium, what a problem for a woman. There isn't even a word for it (mockery of 'feminism'; and the 'femininity' of a [D. H.] Lawrence is a masculine creation)."[1] After the war years, she created the term *humanisme féminin,* to which she repeatedly returned in her writings and interviews. Although its emphasis shifted and became more political over the years, sometimes highlighting feminist consciousness and sometimes social ethics, the inclusive, universalist ideal it represented remained intact.

Many of Thomas's writings seem to prophesy the women's movement in France, which came into focus the year she died, 1970. Her play "Sappho," written in 1941 and produced on Radio Paris in 1946, emphasizes Sappho as a writer and an independent woman rather than as a lesbian. In the central dialogue, Sappho's protégée Atthis reproaches her for awakening in women a longing they cannot fulfill, leaving them dissatisfied in a world that is not theirs. Lamenting that she was born too early, Sappho wants women to exist in the public world even as they continue to be wives and mothers. And Atthis tells her that this must come later, perhaps many centuries later, when the world will be different.[2]

From 1947 to 1949, Édith Thomas wrote the stories of *Ève et les autres,* the most feminist and also the most playful of her fictional works. Her heroines subvert the lessons of obedience to the authority of God and man, displacing the biblical heroes and acting out new meanings of choice, rebellion, and desire. The tales highlight anachronism and word play, displaying a writerly pleasure of the text unique in her fiction. Thomas's opening story, "Eve and the Serpent," is a precursor of feminist interpretations since the 1970s. Eve has become bored with the perfection of earthly paradise, to the perplexity of Adam. Although Adam warns her that the Almighty does not like questions, she wants to know why they have been forbidden to touch the tree of the knowledge of good and evil. She learns only that if she touches it, she will die: "And what does that mean, to die?" she asks. "To live in time," the Almighty tells her. She becomes intrigued with the serpent and learns the pleasures of rebellion and secrecy. After she and Adam eat the apple, she resists the Almighty's judgment that she will now be subservient to Adam: "'I will create my own freedom,' said Eve," which becomes a motif for all these biblical women who refuse to adhere to the moral imperatives dictated by men.[3]

From 1947 to 1949, while she was writing *Ève et les autres*, Thomas also put together a historical anthology she called "L'Humanisme féminin." It is quite possible that her idea for the project was born with her essay on Christine de Pizan during the occupation years. She evokes Christine as the first French woman of letters, defined as not only a vocation but also an economic necessity: the woman of letters is obliged to earn a living with her pen. In her remarks about Christine, Thomas emphasizes a theme that was central in French feminist writing over the centuries: the importance of an education for women that will enable them to exercise their intelligence outside the home.

The title of Thomas's anthology highlights the historical exclusion of women from humanist thinking about "man." Her manuscript consists of writings by forty-three women and two collective petitions, the 1789 "Petition of Women of the Third Estate to the King" and the 1848 "Petition to the Provisional Government." She sees the forty-five texts as constituting in themselves a history of women; her own commentary, except for the introduction and the conclusion, is limited to a paragraph or two on each text, in which she situates the author in relation to her times. Thomas's writers include many women, especially those who lived before the nineteenth century, whom contemporary feminists have only recently begun to study. The last chapter of Thomas's anthology was supposed to be a report by Jeannette Vermeersch, companion of the leader of the French Communist Party, on "Women in the Nation." Vermeersch's name is crossed out in the Table of Contents, although her speech is still included in Thomas's manuscript. It is highly unlikely that the chapter would have remained had the book been prepared for publication after her resignation from the Party.

"L'Humanisme féminin" plants the seed for Édith Thomas's major historical works, which bore fruit in the next two decades, when she focused her intellectual energies on writing biographies of women. Texts by all the individual subjects of her biographies are represented in chapters of the anthology: Pauline

Roland, George Sand, and Louise Michel, along with writings by a number of
the women who will figure later in Thomas's two collective biographies, *Les
Femmes de 1848*, published for the centennial commemoration of the Revolution of 1848, and *The Women Incendiaries*, about the women of the Commune
uprising in 1871.

Like Beauvoir, Thomas rejects the term "feminism," which she sees as representing the movement for women's liberation in the nineteenth century, in
the context of economic and political conditions particular to that time. Her
own term affirms the universalist and individualist implications of humanism
while giving it a different inflection: "To give to each human being, man or
woman, the possibility of developing fully and harmoniously."[4] The definition
she offers, however vague otherwise, implicitly criticizes the masculine assumptions underlying humanism and delineates a project that is genuinely inclusive of both sexes. She allies herself with what will later be called a feminism
of equality rather than of difference. In her introduction Thomas does not attempt a philosophical analysis of women's situation but focuses instead on a
brief history, from prehistoric times to the present, starting from the observation that in every society, within a given social class, woman is always considered secondary.

Thomas's manuscript is of particular interest as a document exactly contemporary with *The Second Sex*. An interview with Thomas in November 1947
indicates that she conceived her conclusion, along with the introduction, when
she began her project. Two years before the publication of *The Second Sex*,
Thomas poses the question: "Why should only the eternal feminine be eternal
and escape history?"[5] In the conclusion, she declares the need for women to demand political equality as well as equality of education and the professions, allowing them a more complete destiny, a fuller involvement in society. Her last
words, however, sound a very different note: "While economic autonomy must
be the basis of their dignity, it seems that women can only realize themselves
fully as part of a couple and through a child. Humanism is finally accomplished,
therefore, through love. But love has a thousand and one faces. Those of the future are still veiled to us."[6] The last page of *The Second Sex* shows a similar emphasis: "When we abolish the slavery of half of humanity, together with the
whole system of hypocrisy that it implies, then the division of humanity will reveal its genuine significance and the human couple will find its true form." Beauvoir supports her affirmation with a quotation from Marx: "The direct, natural,
necessary relation of human creatures is the relation of man to woman."[7] It is
striking that both these feminist works, written by two French intellectual
women at exactly the same historical moment, conclude with a celebration of
the couple. Their divergences, however, are equally significant. Beauvoir speaks

of the couple finding its true form. Thomas, fresh from her passionate affair with Dominique Aury, prefers to evoke the thousand and one faces of love.

In contrast to Beauvoir's hostility to the biological as well as the cultural conditions of maternity, Thomas would always consider the maternal role as positive. Although in 1947 she was still a member of the Communist Party, there is no indication that she followed the Party's pro-natalist position. Thomas's only allusion to the issue of abortion can be found in her novel *Le Champ libre* (1945), in which the narrator accidentally becomes pregnant. When Anne confides in her housekeeper, who gives her an address, she admits to herself that abortion had always seemed to her "as monstrous as infanticide," something that until then she had never imagined for herself.[8] Nevertheless, she accepts the possibility of making that choice, but is repelled by the dangerous circumstances of an illegal abortion. Her decision to keep the child (shortly thereafter, she suffers a miscarriage) is ultimately the expression of personal desire rather than principle.

The table of contents in the typescript of "Humanisme féminin" shows Simone de Beauvoir as a name added after the final listing, clearly inserted at a later time. Thomas's comments succinctly describe Beauvoir's project as an attempt to take up in its totality the question of woman from the biological, historical, social, and philosophical points of view, posing woman's freedom in existentialist terms. Without specifying her criticism, she declares that she will not follow the author in her conclusions, nor in "certain errors (particularly concerning history)." But she praises Beauvoir's study as a "courageous effort of elucidation."[9]

Thomas's earlier articles about Beauvoir show a tangle of admiration and hostility aroused by her more famous contemporary. In a review of Beauvoir's novel *All Men Are Mortal,* Thomas uses her as an example to protest the condescension implied in the term "women's writing" and asserts: "There are not many men who can write in as virile a style as Mme de Beauvoir."[10] The positive implication of "virile" in that context is clear, suggesting one of its dictionary definitions, even now: vigorous, energetic, and courageous. In the same article she describes Beauvoir as one of the best writers of her generation. Nevertheless, in spite of Thomas's numerous book reviews, she never reviewed *The Second Sex,* a telling statement in itself.[11]

Her ambivalence toward Beauvoir is inseparable from her hostility toward existentialism, particularly its Sartrean incarnation. She reluctantly admires *All Men Are Mortal,* finding in the book a continuation of the eighteenth-century tradition of philosophical tales. But she criticizes what she sees as Sartre's contaminating influence, as evidenced in the novel's conception of its protagonist, the immortal man Fosca, who resembles "like a brother" Sartre's Roquentin in

Nausea and Mathieu in his *Roads to Freedom*. Although she begins a review of Beauvoir's essay *Pyrrhus et Cinéas* by declaring what she will not do, namely, discuss existentialism, she cannot resist an occasion to attack the philosophy she considers an adversary. For Thomas, existentialism is both antihumanist and anti-Marxist. Noting her own agreement with the position of the Marxist philosopher Henri Lefebvre, she assails existentialism as a doctrine of nothingness and complacency in despair, which has become, as she puts it, "fashionable with the defeat and the occupation."[12]

Claims to humanism were a subject of intense debate after the war and a major stake in the competing ideologies of existentialism and Marxism, both of which presented themselves as humanist, although Sartre and a number of Marxists had derided humanism in the 1930s. The cultural historian Michael Kelly has pointed to the extraordinary revival of humanist discourse in France at the end of the war across a broad spectrum of political, philosophical, and religious thought. He argues convincingly that the divergent ideas contained in the term "humanism" were held together by the political task of building unity rather than any conceptual coherence. Humanism provided a broadly inclusive framework that could offer "a commonality of aspirations" after the bruising divisions of the war years, while drawing on France's long-standing tradition of universalism.[13] In that context, it is hardly accidental that the celebrity status of existentialism was consecrated in Sartre's wildly successful lecture in October 1945 titled "Existentialism Is a Humanism."

Several months before his lecture, Sartre had written a summary of its themes for the communist journal *Action,* in response to Marxist attacks on his writings that began to appear as soon as the brief euphoria of the liberation had dissipated. In rebuttal, Henri Lefebvre wrote an article in the same journal outlining the Marxist position, a polemic he elaborated the following year in *L'Existentialisme,* cited by Thomas in her article about Beauvoir. Lefebvre wrote his book as a self-described former existentialist, an allusion to the philosophy of consciousness he developed as a young man in 1925, before the reading of Hegel and Marx led him to reject his earlier subjectivist thinking. After a brief exploration of the history of existentialism in Kierkegaard, Nietzsche, and Husserl, Lefebvre focuses on his contemporary targets, Heidegger and Sartre. Heidegger had joined the Nazi Party in 1933. While his reputation in Germany declined after the war, in France it was revived, in part because of his influence on Sartre. Lefebvre's polemic conflates both the metaphysics and what he views as the social implications of the two philosophers, since he considers Sartre to be Heidegger's direct disciple. "On the horizon of Heideggerism," he writes, "we can see the outline of mass graves. And it is truly unbelievable that this philosopher and his disciples claim to be humanists and defenders of freedom."[14]

On November 24, 1945, an extended article in *Les Lettres françaises* titled "What Is Existentialism?" includes interviews with Sartre and two of his adversaries, the poet Pierre Emmanuel and Henri Lefebvre. The article, which shows an openness to both sides of the heated debate and displays a friendly curiosity about existentialism, was written by one of the postwar staff writers for *Les Lettres françaises:* Dominique Aury. Lefebvre, in Aury's interview with him, uses the occasion to repeat his well-known protest against the preponderant role that existialism assigns to ennui and anguish: "I contest it in the name of Marxist humanism, which accepts the totality of life." Citing *Being and Nothingness* in particular, he asserts that existentialism reveals "something morbid, which is linked to the decomposition of bourgeois culture."[15]

From the Marxist point of view, at least during the immediate postwar years, existentialism could not be reconciled with humanism. In January 1946, Édith Thomas wrote an article for *Les Lettres françaises* that she called "De l'avilissement" (On degradation). Her title refers to the hellish testimonies of concentration camp survivors, which had begun to appear in large numbers. After describing these narratives of unspeakable horror, she examines the crisis they reveal as not just a German catastrophe unleashed by Hitler but a catastrophe for humanity, which has found nothing to put in the place of Christianity other than nihilism: "We see this thinking in areas that are no longer those of politics: in all the fashionable literature that revels in nothingness, the absurd, anguish, despair, and degradation." Later in her article she focuses on the "furious rage" against innocuous objects as well as against the human body that is found in this nihilistic thinking, all of which, she declares, would be "absolutely comical and ridiculous if one did not see in it another symptom of the intellectual phenomena that led men to conceive and execute the plans for Auschwitz or Buchenwald." She contrasts the focus on despair and nothingness with the effort of those who live a harsh life and are trying to change it, and make of their condition "a human condition."[16]

Although she names no writer in particular, her attack is aimed first of all at Sartre, as the allusions to disgust with existence and the human body make clear. A few days later, she received a personal letter of reproach: from Albert Camus. The letter reads as follows:

> Madame, I was going to thank you for sending me your *Champ libre* when I came upon your article in *Lettres françaises*. And I confess, although I have become resigned to a certain kind of attack, this article left me only with a profound sadness. I will not respond to it publicly, having renounced defending myself on that level. But I cannot help writing you to express my feelings of reproach. For this article is signed with the name

of a former comrade in combat. For there had never been anything between us, to my knowledge, but simple sympathy. Have I seemed so monstrous to you since then that you can calmly write that a certain kind of thinking puts me on the same spiritual level as the executioners of Auschwitz? Have you at least weighed those terrible words and can I be sure that you condemn me so definitively, and with full knowledge of the facts?

Oh! I understand very well the feelings you express in this article. I consider that you are making a plea for happiness. I too have something to say about the question. But your intelligence judges badly in this case. It is not pessimism that leads to cruelty and degradation. If that were so, an immense tribe of great minds should have wallowed in the mud. But what matters is the consequences one draws from it. You did not see that from pessimism, German neo-romanticism drew the glorification of instinct and consequently of the beast. Whereas all of contemporary pessimism draws from it the idea of lucidity, which is its opposite, and which should have explained why you found me at your side during a certain period. But you have forgotten that and if I still care about giving you these explanations, it is perhaps in memory of the sympathy I spoke about and doubtless because I still keep an absurd confidence in the human heart.

In any case, I cannot be truly angry with you and I want to tell you here only my sadness and my indignation. No, one doesn't write what you wrote knowing what you know. That is my feeling about it. I would not have expected you to cause me such bitterness. I wanted you to know that also.

Yours,

Albert Camus[17]

Thomas's article, not one of her more carefully reasoned pieces, leaves her exposed to precisely the argument made by Camus. Condemning on moral grounds any philosophy whose starting point is despair, or in Camus's case the absurd, she does not consider the divergent ethical consequences that can be drawn from those assumptions. As the case of both Sartre and Camus makes clear, their starting point can lead to commitment as well as to nihilism. Like Thomas, Camus makes no direct allusion in his letter either to existentialism or to Sartre. Their names were constantly linked, particularly in the postwar period, although both men repeatedly explained the differences between existentialism and Camus's philosophy of the absurd. In his letter to Édith Thomas, Camus chooses to ally himself with Sartre through his reference to "contemporary pessimism," his inclusive term for the literature of "nothingness, the absurd, anguish, despair, and degradation" in her wide-ranging condemnation.

For many years, Thomas was attracted to the optimistic reading of human possibility she found in Marxism. From a Marxist perspective, unmodified by psychoanalysis or a philosophy of subjectivity, she could attribute the frequent bouts of despair she suffered to her singular temperament, a condition that was irrelevant in the general scheme of things. She found an odd comfort in thinking of her own situation as merely personal, as if that made it less threatening to confront than the universal anguish and absurd in the philosophy of Sartre and Camus.

If it is true that Édith Thomas, like Camus, pleads for happiness, as he affirms, his notion of happiness is contained in the present moment, whereas hers depends on hope for the future. His letter makes only a passing, nonphilosophical, but surely deliberate reference to the absurd, a key concept in his thinking, when he speaks of his "absurd confidence in the human heart." However, Thomas's mention of the absurd in her attack may in itself have sufficed to provoke Camus's pained response.

Prior to Thomas's article, her only specific reference to Camus was a brief, neutral notation in her diary, followed by a quotation. She writes in November 1943: "Read successively *The Stranger* and *The Myth of Sisyphus* of A. Camus. Two panels of a diptych." The passage she transcribes from *Sisyphus*, without additional commentary, would seem to speak to aspects of her own thinking: "Thus I draw from the absurd three consequences, which are my revolt, my freedom, and my passion. By the mere activity of consciousness I transform into a rule of life what was an invitation to death—and I refuse suicide."[18] One might expect, given the ordeal of tuberculosis each writer suffered, as well as their shared temptation of suicide, that Thomas would have felt an affinity with Camus. They were both active *résistants,* as his allusion "you found me at your side during a certain period" attests. Camus frequently attended meetings of the Comité national des écrivains in Thomas's apartment during the periods he was in Paris. It is not clear whether she opposed Camus, for ideological or personal reasons, or whether he was drawn into her attack by association with Sartre.

There is no evidence that she responded to Camus's letter. It is quite possible that she shared the dismissive attitude of most French Marxists at the time, particularly those in the Communist Party, who tended to focus their hostility on Sartre and ignore Camus. A few years later, however, when Thomas decided to resign publicly from the Party, she chose to do so in the pages of *Combat,* whose history is closely linked to that of Camus. As she well knew, *Combat* was founded as an underground newspaper during the struggles of the Resistance, and Camus was part of its first team as writer and editor. After the liberation, *Combat* became a major daily newspaper of the noncommunist left and Camus served as its editor in chief until 1947.

During Thomas's visit to the Soviet Union a few months after her article appeared, she gave a lecture on the literature of the Resistance in which she attacked Sartre's philosophy in the same language used by his Marxist adversaries: "Existentialism is one of the myths and the mystifications of bourgeois consciousness which has lost the sense of the real and struggles with metaphysical contradictions because it is incapable of posing problems on this earth." She acknowledges Sartre's anti-Nazi attitude and his claim that existentialism is meant to complement Marxism. But then she continues: "Heidegger, the father of existentialism, joined the Nazi party. Sartre excuses him by saying that one can be a great philosopher and lack character. But nothing is fortuitous." This part of her speech, which voices some of the same themes as her article, significantly omits the idea of the absurd in its condemnation of existentialist philosophy: "The doctrine of nothingness, of anguish and despair can easily be adapted to National Socialism. It is its philosophy. It is prepared to accept all forms of adventure to escape the stranglehold of its destiny."[19]

Paradoxically, Thomas's attack on Sartre took place during the period when his thinking focused on ethical questions close to her own preoccupations, as opposed to both his earlier and his later philosophy. She was always repelled by the disgust with the natural in all its manifestations, which dominates Sartre's early works. And after the war she gradually distanced herself from the Communist Party, which she left at the time Sartre was moving closer to it. However, many of Sartre's works in the 1940s, specifically *The Flies, Anti-Semite and Jew,* and *Existentialism is a Humanism* show affinities with Thomas's voluntarism, her Cartesian rationalism, and the themes of lucidity and commitment.

As Sartre has observed, people of the same period and the same community, who have lived through the same events, ask or avoid the same questions.[20] Thomas's "Prométhée," an unpublished radio play written in 1940, is curiously evocative of *Les Mouches* (1943). The strongest scene in her play, an encounter between Prometheus and the Sorcerer, mirrors the confrontation in *The Flies* between Orestes and Zeus in its use of Greek myth to dramatize resistance against oppressive authority in general and Pétain's cult of repentance in particular. After Sartre's Orestes has killed Aegistheus and Clytemnestra, Zeus appears as God the father figure, offering Orestes and Electra rest and protection in exchange for a little remorse. When his coaxing fails, he inflates himself into the terrible God of Creation. Similarly, the Sorcerer offers magic chants to appease the pain of confronting truth and suggests to Prometheus the division of humanity between them: Prometheus can take with him those who can bear to see things as they are, as long as he leaves behind all the others, the great herd of women and slaves. With a feminist twist decidedly absent from *The Flies,* Prometheus proclaims that "slaves and even women must be liberated" and refuses the Sorcerer's bargain. Rejecting the Sorcerer's warning that he will forget at his peril the masses who follow the Sorcerer's word, whether they need to be consoled or need magic to affirm their domination over others, Prometheus chooses war with the Sorcerer over peace.

In the final act of Thomas's play, Prometheus encounters Death, who tells him: "But this world is deaf, naked, ugly. This world is horrible to bear if suffering is not the expiation of sins according to a divine and incomprehensible plan." Death then asks: "What is left for you, Prometheus?" to which the rebel replies: "Nothing. And I must build my joy on the lucid acceptance of that nothing."[21] The spirit of Prometheus's words is not very different from that of Orestes telling Zeus: "Human life begins on the far side of despair."[22]

More than two decades later, in a review of a personal memoir of the Resistance, Thomas explains why those years were both an ordeal and, for some, a privileged moment as well. For those in the Resistance, it was a period that favored an accord between thought and action, what she calls in other contexts "coherence." "Many," she writes, "have remained nostalgic for that accord." She describes how the struggle of men and women stripped of everything, even their identity, "enabled them to discover the truth that is forgotten in the routine of everyday life: that man is never more than the sum of his acts and that his life has no meaning other than that which he has chosen to give it, here and now."[23] The unmistakably Sartrean echoes of Thomas's article recall the language of "Existentialism Is a Humanism."

Thomas's deeply intimate hostility is directed at a specific aspect of Sartre's writing: his horror of biological life and the flesh. Notwithstanding the verbal sorcery which succeeds in portraying nausea toward existence as phenomenology, Sartre's anti-vital obsessions are rooted in his sensibility rather than in existentialist philosophy. In the private reflections of Thomas's "Lettre à mon frère," written in 1967, she returns to issues she raised in "De l'avilissement" more than twenty years earlier: "What I hate in the work of Sartre, in that of Simone de Beauvoir, is the extent to which they degrade man, always taking him by his lowest, most repulsive side. As if Sartre's ugliness had made him detest bodies and attach a ridiculous significance to natural secretions, which in themselves have no importance." She is haunted by a scene in *The Reprieve*, the second volume in Sartre's trilogy of novels *Roads to Freedom*, in which "Sartre describes the 'horizontals' of Berck only in their secretions. As if the fact that one needs a basin diminishes a man."[24] The scene to which she refers takes place in September 1938 at the Berck sanatorium, which specialized in care for patients with tuberculosis of the bone. It was decided that the patients of Berck should be evacuated, because the sanatorium was in an area in the north of France considered especially vulnerable to German attack. Many patients at Berck who could not move had to be placed on the floor of freight trains that were taking them southward. Paradoxically, the scene in *The Reprieve* between Charles and Catherine, which shows both of them physically helpless and desperately struggling to control their excretions, is one of the rare scenes of romantic tenderness between a man and a woman in Sartre's fiction.

For Thomas, since her first illness, the sanatorium of Berck symbolized her worst fears that she would become one of the horizontals, a terror she tried to exorcize with *La Mort de Marie*. It is not surprising that she would find this scene in *The Reprieve* unbearable, an intimate violation by a writer she distrusted. In her diary entries of the postwar period, written during bouts of depression that often coincided with periods of poor health, depression and existentialism became synonymous. After one of those bouts in 1948 she was diagnosed with appendicitis and welcomed the prospect of an operation with relief and even a kind of pleasure (*volupté*). "Will the surgeon's knife," she mused, "cure me of this crisis of existentialism I've been fighting against, in vain, for months?"[25] After the operation, feeling much better, she decided that such a cure might indeed have happened, since the removal of her appendix, along with a rereading of *War and Peace*, seemed to have worked wonders. At one point, many years later, she even asked her doctor about her "existentialist" anxieties—the degree of irony in her question is not clear—and he reassured her that he did not think she had an "incurable existential ennui; everyone has periods of ennui."[26]

Édith Thomas struggled to counter her "existentialism" with an affirmation of biological life. The diaries show that she considered suggesting to a few men that she would like to have a child with them, although it is not clear whether she made that desire explicit. In any case, Dominique Aury made inquiries for her early in 1949 about artificial insemination, consulting some doctor friends who were interested in the highly unusual case of a single woman wanting to give birth. They were ready to find her a suitable donor. At first she was intrigued by the possibility, confident that the doctors would find her a donor "endowed with all the desirable physical and intellectual qualities: spermatozoids do not have political opinions." She soon dropped the idea, however, as "satisfactory for the mind" but "rather inhuman."[27] At one point, briefly, she thought about adopting a child, but didn't consider that option seriously, in large part, it would seem, because her desire for a child was inseparable from her need to affirm herself biologically as a woman.

A few months later, as she was walking through Montmartre for an article she was writing about the poet Gérard de Nerval and his *Promenades* in that neighborhood of old Paris, she encountered "Renaud," who was now married and the father of two children. They renewed their relationship and she told him of her wish to have a child for which she would take full responsibility. She was now forty years old. Her doctor reassured her that she was healthy enough to "get married" and have a child. She confided in her brother, who promised that if anything should happen to her, he and Madeleine would take care of the child—as he assumed she would take care of their children if something happened to them. Édith and Renaud were together sexually at occasional intervals, and she had brief affairs subsequently with a few other men, but she never became pregnant.

11

THE COMPROMISED WITNESS
Leaving the Communist Party

Le Témoin compromis: choosing that title for her political memoir is hardly characteristic of a woman who conceived her life as the quest for a coherent accord between her actions and her conscience. Her memoir represents a crisis of doubt and self-division which required that she justify herself in the eyes of the imaginary male other to whom she addresses her narrative. From time to time in her earlier autobiographical writings she confided in an intimate alter ego who served as the companion to her solitude. In "Lettres à Ariane" (1940), for example, written in the form of a literary diary she kept every day for two weeks, she whispers her reflections to a sister and soul mate who like herself is suffering from tuberculosis. In her personal diary, in 1942, her "Letter to myself" begins: "My dearest friend . . ."[1] Her interlocutor in *Le Témoin compromis,* however, takes on the role of stern judge rather than confidant. His disdain for the bias of subjectivity inherent in the project of writing a memoir suggests that the *tu* she invokes, especially at the beginning of her narrative, functions both as the ghost of Communist intellectuals she has loved and the projection of her own suspicion of autobiographical writing.

Thomas began to write her memoir during the summer of 1952, at a time when the wounds inflicted by leaving the Communist Party in December 1949 were far from healed. The general themes of her disillusionment are familiar: the Party's theological orthodoxy, which left no place for criticism; its unquestioning allegiance to the Soviet Union; the systematic practice of lies in the name of the defense of the proletariat. After the liberation, Thomas's grievances against the Party, especially in relation to its intellectuals, accumulated to the point of becoming intolerable. In contrast to the 1930s, when the preferred tactic was to persuade and encourage hesitant fellow travelers, the Party in the post-war period, finding itself much stronger on the national scene, took a harder line toward its intellectuals, demanding the same discipline it expected of all its militants.[2] Thomas rebelled against the claim of a self-appointed few, Aragon in particular, to speak in the name of all the intellectuals in the Party. In January 1948 she wrote a satiric article against that practice, specifically targeting the Party's use of the personal pronoun "we." She compares the various uses of "we," favored, she notes, by kings and police chiefs and writers, and points out the particular problems posed by this "we" when it is employed by the Communist writer, especially if he enjoys a certain notoriety. Since the abuse of "we" by Communist writers seems to be becoming "contagious," she wants it known that as far as she is concerned, she is responsible only for what she signs, and she has not entrusted anyone, "pope, beadle or church warden," to speak in her name. "Please," she concludes, "leave the 'we' to the chief of police."[3] Her article was turned down by the two Communist publications to which she submitted it, *Action* and *Les Lettres françaises.*

In another postwar statement of protest, she objected to the condemnation by French Communists of Richard Wright, a writer she considered an "autodidact of genius and character." Wright, who had joined the American Communist Party in 1932 and resigned in 1944, moved to Paris in 1947. She describes his first experience of reading a novel, evoked in his autobiography *Black Boy,* as "comparable to Pascal's illumination, or to Descartes's dream: a new man is born."[4] The French Communist Party disapproved of his implied critique of the Party in *Native Son* and found it easiest to condemn him altogether, "adding for good measure a few insults to those who might be naive enough not to be of the same opinion."[5]

In lectures and articles, Thomas protested against the idea of political laws that could govern artistic creation. Although none of the major Communist writers, Aragon least of all, actually practiced Zhdanov's "socialist realism" in his own writing, his doctrine was accepted as dogma, the inspired application of Stalin's definition of the writer as "the engineer of human souls."[6] The Party's demand that intellectuals follow the Soviet notion of cultural orthodoxy extended even to the sciences. Thomas was appalled by the absurdity of expecting scientists to reject hypotheses verified in the laboratory so that they could embrace the theories of the Soviet biologist Lyssenko, who advocated a "proletarian" science. By 1948 Thomas had decided that "staying in the Party would be an *imposture*" and recorded in her diary the letter of resignation she planned to send, a polemic against the "dictatorship" of Aragon and Elsa Triolet. After showing the letter to her brother Gérard, he helped her write a "petition for divorce" in more polite terms, which she accepted but did not act on.[7]

That same year, on the occasion of a centennial commemoration of the revolution of 1848, she was invited to Poznan, Poland, along with two French Communist legislators who found themselves abroad for the first time. Fiercely anticlerical, her two companions were as shocked as she was pleased by the manifestations of Catholicism that were still pervasive in the cities and the countryside. In her comments later, she saw this coexistence of religion with communism as an expression of Poland's capacity to transform itself according to its own national genius. The symptoms of a hardening of the Party line, however, were already becoming apparent, particularly in the "fusion" of socialism and communism, which in fact meant the absorption of the first into the second. As in Thomas's articles about the Soviet Union in 1946, only her praise of Poland found expression in what she wrote at the time. Later, in 1950, she recorded a joke she heard in Poland:

> A Polish dog meets an English dog in London.
> "Well, old chap," says the English dog, "have you come here for bread?"
> "No," says the Polish dog.
> "For meat? Sausage?"
> "No, no," says the Polish dog.
> "So what are you here for?"
> "To bark," says the Polish dog.[8]

Thomas's trip to Poland reinforced her conviction that each country needed to accomplish its revolution in accordance with its own specific culture and traditions.

When she returned to Paris she learned that Marshal Tito, who had been worshipped by the Communists since the liberation as the great Yugoslav war hero and disciple of Stalin, was now considered a traitor. In 1948, having dared to declare his independence from Moscow and distance himself from the Soviet line, Tito was suddenly transmogrified from savior to heretic. Accused by Stalin of being a fascist and an agent of American imperialism, he was excommunicated from the Party. Shortly thereafter, the Hungarian party official Rajk, whose arrest and trial Édith Thomas followed closely, was condemned to death after a rigged trial in which he confessed—falsely—to "Titoism."

When Thomas left the Party in 1949, she chose to make her decision public, explaining the reasons for her resignation in two eloquent and relatively moderate articles she called "Critique et auto-critique" (Criticism and self-criticism) which appeared in *Combat*. She pointed out that she would have preferred to voice her objections in the Communist newspaper *L'Humanité*—but if that had been possible, she would not have needed to resign from the Party. For many years, she wrote, she had accepted the constraint of silence with the hope that

French Communist Party officials would eventually realize that a change was needed in their way of operating, since the people they were trying to convince happened to belong to a national culture that valued critical thinking and debate. She had learned from experience that the practice of "self-criticism," whatever the phrase might imply, actually meant that the intellectual was expected to submit to Party diktats. With the Tito affair, along with the rigged trials of Rajk and many others, it had become clear to her that "traitor" simply meant someone who disagreed.[9]

In the report by *L'Humanité* of Thomas's resignation, the writer cites a speech of Maurice Thorez, head of the Party, in which he declared that it is inevitable for "the weakest elements" to "lose their way": "They become frightened, they cannot accept struggle." This is particularly true, he adds, for those from the petite bourgeoisie "who came to the Party in periods of relative ease."[10] The reporter neglects to specify that for Thomas this time of "relative ease" was 1942, when being a member of the Party was sufficient reason to be deported or shot by the Nazis or the Vichy police.

In an attempt to preempt Thomas's initiative, the neighborhood Communist cell to which she belonged unanimously voted to exclude her. Their letter took cognizance of her resignation and the articles she published in *Combat.* "In spite of her absolute denials," it proclaims, "Édith Thomas has passed into the camp of the enemies of the working class." Drawing the "appropriate" lessons from her "treason," they proposed the "definitive exclusion of Édith Thomas in order to manifest by this decision the contempt she has aroused in the ranks of the working class."[11]

A few months before her resignation, in the course of a meeting with Jacques Duclos, Thorez's second in the Party hierarchy, Édith Thomas told him of her decision. "Leaving the Party is death," he replied.[12] In fact, the break became for her a social death. From one day to the next her former comrades either vilified her or would have nothing more to do with her. The writer Dominique Desanti describes Édith Thomas as a "rigorous *chartiste* whom I had loved as a friend since the war." However, after the article in *L'Humanité* appeared, she notes: "From then on, when I met Édith, I had to pretend not to see her."[13] The phrase is revealing. Relegated outside the Party, she is invisible, since she does not exist.

For Édith Thomas as for so many thousands of other Western intellectuals, leaving the Party meant leaving the faith that for years had given meaning to life. She reopened the emotional wound of that break a decade later in her review of *Autocritique,* Edgar Morin's powerful and moving narrative of his own devastating experience with the god that failed. For Thomas, Morin's book is addressed not to those who remained outsiders but to those who engaged what they felt was the best of themselves, drawn into "the madness of commitment as one used to speak of the madness of the Cross." Morin's frequent use of religious language recalls her own fervor and the disillusionment that was its counterpart. What Orwell called "doublethink," Morin calls "the vulgate," and he examines the way it functions for intellectuals in the Party until the crisis, different for each individual, when faith is no longer possible. At that point, before a new beginning, there is despair: "Outside the Party, there is no hope, no salvation." Thomas admits to finding it difficult, still, to embrace as he does "this world without a dream and this history without an absolute."[14] Morin wrote a letter thanking her for her article—"that of a human being who has recognized another human being," bringing "the oxygen one needs in order to live."[15]

Even in the private intimacy of family, Thomas's resignation caused painful tensions, especially with Gérard. He had joined the Party at the time of the liberation, when his tuberculosis of the spine had begun to ease, and he would remain a member until his death in 1967. His wife, Madeleine, who joined at the same time as her husband, also stayed loyal to the Party for the rest of her life. After Édith's exclusion, the Party demanded that Gérard denounce his sister, following the common practice of demanding a denunciation from the person most intimately related to the person excluded. In spite of his disapproval of her decision, he refused to do so, offering instead a "self-criticism" of his own actions.

In the course of writing her memoir, on November 18, 1952, Thomas learned of the death of the Communist poet Paul Eluard. In contrast to her ambivalence about Louis Aragon, she felt an abiding affection as well as admiration for Eluard, and suffered from not being able to participate in the tribute to him by *Les Lettres françaises*, since she was no longer in the Party. During the occupation years she had seen him frequently and remembered him as carrying within himself "an extraordinary poetry, so evident that one day, near the Odeon metro, a dragonfly, a large blue and green dragonfly, came to rest on his hand." After she and Eluard exchanged various underground documents, the discovery of which would have been sufficient to arrest them, Eluard took her to some bouquinistes selling bric-a-brac on the quays of the Seine. A few days earlier he had noticed a turn-of-the-century statuette of a bronze car raising a bronze cloud: "The absurdity of it delighted him. But we never found it again and perhaps he had only imagined it."[16]

Thomas's break with the Party was all the more devastating because she experienced the act of joining as a moment of harmony with her most deeply cherished ideals. By September 1942 she had overcome her previous reservations. She reasoned that the dissolution of the Komintern had loosened the ties that linked Moscow to other Communist parties, since the war made it necessary to take into account the specific situation of each country. In France, the constitution of a National Front had broken the Party's isolation, allying it with all those who were resolved to fight against the occupying forces, a struggle in which the Communist Party was the most active element.

The most lyrical pages of her memoir describe the privileged moment when Thomas joined the Party. Her comrade Claude Morgan had arranged a rendezvous at the Dauphine metro stop near the Bois de Boulogne: "A young man, his hat pulled down over his forehead, emerged from nowhere." There was no introduction; the young man knew who she was; she in turn understood that the Party had put him in charge of "verifying personnel." The two of them "plunged" into the Bois de Boulogne: "It was about five o'clock in the afternoon, in September. The trees were turning yellow, there were places in the underbrush touched by the sun, and I felt a joy in this clandestine walk that no romantic encounter could have given me. It seemed to me that all the inner debates, all the hesitations, all the doubts that for almost ten years had loomed at every turn were finally overcome, left behind like a dead skin. . . . I experienced the feeling that inner simplicity can give."

Writing this account in 1952, she needed to add: "Or rather I imagined I experienced it. Later I would realize that nothing had changed and that I would always stay in the uncomfortable position of critical doubt."[17] But even with disillusioned hindsight, the romantic perfection of that political epiphany remained intact, distilled in a language that transformed the young man's interrogation of her identity—the actual subject of their exchange—into an experience that was both erotic and mystical. She gave herself to communism in an ecstatic act of faith, at a moment of history when she could feel in perfect accord with what the Party represented. Ironically, the judgment of Maurice Thorez in 1949 was correct, if one gives his words a meaning exactly opposed to what he intended. He referred then to those in the bourgeoisie who came to the Party "in periods of relative ease." For Édith Thomas, choosing to join the Party in 1942, the time of greatest danger, was easy precisely because it was difficult. Many of her comrades had been shot. Becoming a Communist no longer meant accepting the contorted dialectical justifications that had distanced her from the Party in the 1930s; it meant risking her life for a cause in which she could completely believe.

After the war, in addition to the many other reasons for doubt and opposition, her Party loyalty was severely undermined by a specific incident that she does not allude to in "Critique et auto-critique," but which conflicted directly with her sense of professional integrity. As a *chartiste* historian as well as a *résistante,* she was asked in 1945 to serve as one of three vice-presidents of the Committee for the Study of the History of the Second World War, with particular focus on bringing together testimony and documentation about the Resistance—a difficult task, since the conditions of the Resistance demanded that its members not leave any written trace of their activities. The secretary for the Committee asked her to put him into contact with the director of the Communist National Front, which had not responded to their inquiries. After a meeting with Jacques Duclos, who did not want to take the responsibility for a decision, she learned that the Central Committee had decided the Communists would not reply. They gave her two reasons: first of all, the inquiry could be used by the police; and secondly, "bourgeois" historians would never give the Party the place it deserved in the Resistance. For Édith Thomas, this reasoning meant simply that the Party wanted to be able to fabricate any truth it liked, according to the political line of the moment, without being hindered by documents.[18]

In her memoir Édith Thomas returns to the trip she made in the spring of 1944 to report on military groupings of the Communist-led Francs-Tireurs et Partisans. Articles about her trip had appeared in the underground *Lettres françaises* and, after the liberation, in *Femmes françaises,* excerpted from a thirty-eight-page manuscript she titled "Voyage au maquis," dated May 1944. When she revisited that narrative in 1952, the memory of her confrontation with the Party's Central Committee was a likely trigger for including in *Le Témoin compromis* a disturbing story that she had left untold in previous versions: the torture of a member of the fascist militia by FTP militants, following orders they were given by their superiors. She had been asked to communicate her account of the trip to a military leader of the Party, whose name she crossed out in the memoir manuscript. Her report had made the political argument that if methods of this kind became known, as was likely, they would provoke legitimate indignation against the FTP and alienate badly needed sympathies. She knew that leaders of the maquis took severe measures against theft and pillage; she demanded that they also punish those militants who had recourse to torture. In her memoir she notes that she refrained in the report from addressing the anguished ethical questions that preoccupied her most of all: "What world will we create if we degrade the adversary—who is still a human being—and thereby degrade ourselves? Since we claim to defend the dignity of man, do we have the right to use dishonorable methods? How do means act on and determine ends?" The moral passion underlying her political argument must have been clear, in spite of her efforts to focus on pragmatic questions of effectiveness. After reading what she had written, the FTP leader looked at her "with a kind of hatred" and threw the report into the wastebasket. "There is no absolute morality," he said.[19]

In her memoir she recounts another such incident that took place during the liberation. "While we," she writes, "the virtuous ladies of the steering committee of the Union of French Women, on the second floor of the building of the National Front, were discussing all kinds of generous resolutions, a member of the militia was being tortured in the basement." This time she spoke with a member of the Front who was not a Communist. His reaction was different but finally the same: "He looked uncomfortable and changed the subject."[20]

The "Voyage au maquis" of May 1944, written immediately after her return, contains a narrative about the subject of torture that is more in line with what she wants to believe. "Pierre" tells her that the FTP, following information from people in the region, arrested a policeman and his wife who had often been seen with a member of the militia. "We interrogated them and . . ." At that point, thinking about the torture chambers of Lyon and what was inflicted on *résistants* who were arrested, she has misgivings and interrupts him: "What methods do you employ to get confessions?" The tall, blond young man (he seems to be the Alsatian "Frantz" of *Le Témoin compromis*) looked her in the eye and said: "Do you take us for the militia?"[21] It is entirely possible that this story about the refusal to torture is also true.

Thomas's resignation and subsequent exclusion from the Communist Party can explain the perplexing notation in her handwriting on the folder containing the manuscript of "L'Humanisme féminin": "published by the Éditions Hier et Aujourd'hui." The manuscript was not published. Hier et Aujourd'hui, the same collection of the Éditeurs français réunis that had published Thomas's *Jeanne d'Arc* in 1947, was linked to the Party. It seems clear that when she resigned in 1949, they simply decided to withdraw their offer. In the discouragement of a recurring loss of confidence in the worth of her writing, exacerbated by her sense of political isolation, she did not attempt to take the anthology elsewhere.

The Éditeurs français réunis appear to have decided that the withdrawal of their offer to publish "L'Humanisme féminin" was insufficient retribution. In the spring of 1950, Édith Thomas learned from a number of friends who had requested her *Jeanne d'Arc* at various bookstores that the book was "missing" or that it was "being reprinted." She asked one of her Communist friends, Albert Soboul, a distinguished historian of the French Revolution who was also director of the Hier et Aujourd'hui collection, to contact the Éditions directly for further information. He was told that the book had been withdrawn from circulation, but they could give him some personal copies. At that point, in July, she wrote to the Société des gens de lettres, of which she was a member, asking them to arbitrate the conflict. After written documentation by the bookstores involved affirming that they were unable to obtain *Jeanne d'Arc,* the Society asked the Éditeurs Français Réunis to give Édith Thomas 2,500 copies of her book free, as compensation for the harm they had inflicted on her. The judgment was remarkably mild; in a letter to Jean Paulhan, she remarks that the Society seemed to be "trembling before Aragon."[22] Nevertheless, the Éditeurs made clear that they would destroy all the remaining copies of *Jeanne d'Arc* and use the opportunity of having settled this affair "amicably" to let the Society know that it had allowed itself to be "exploited" by Édith Thomas. As evidence, they cited the fact that one of the bookstores in question was being run by the wife of an official of the Yugoslav Embassy in Paris: "When one knows the attitude of Mlle Thomas, putting these facts together allows us to affirm that all this has been staged." These remarks needed to be made, the author of the letter continues, so that "the Société des gens de lettres of France can judge with full knowledge the attitude of both parties and know on which side there was bad faith."[23]

In the spring of 1950, just before this incident, Thomas accepted an invitation by Marko Ristic, the Yugoslav ambassador in Paris, for what she called a "study trip" to Yugoslavia. In fact, she had first been invited to Yugoslavia a year earlier, just after the Tito affair had exploded, but declined at that time so she could resign from the Party when she was ready, rather than being immediately excluded. During this initial trip to Belgrade she met at length with Milovan Djilas, who at the time was still secretary of the Political Bureau of the Central Committee of the Yugoslav Communist Party and a close ally of Tito. He had been instrumental in working out with Tito the strategy for breaking with Stalin in 1948. Her conversations with Djilas focused on the situation of intellectuals in Yugoslavia. In response to her question about the reaction of intellectuals to Lyssenko's doctrines before the break of 1948, he told her that there were no biologists on the Central Committee. Scientists were asked to experiment in their laboratories, discuss their questions among themselves, and report their conclusions. As far as literature was concerned, Djilas pointed out that a major state prize was given to the writer Davidcho, although the Communists did not agree with his surrealist esthetic. "But," Djilas added, "we consider him to be a great writer and we think he should be able to continue his explorations."[24] She saw in Djilas's attitude the possibility of a different kind of Marxism, one that would allow social transformation without alienating people's freedoms. Her concluding article, which spoke for many disillusioned idealists among the European intelligentsia, makes for painful reading today, over a half century later: "Yugoslavia in 1950 is for the international proletariat what the USSR was in 1920: a promise and a hope. The future will tell if we are still right to hope."[25]

When Thomas returned to Paris, she was asked by the France-Yugoslavia group to give a talk on the subject of "Women in Yugoslavia." The vituperative account of her lecture in *L'Humanité*, written by a woman, is worthy of the invective spit out by male leaders of the Party when they excluded Thomas from their ranks: "We had the feeling of finding ourselves face to face with the Nazis of the Gestapo. . . . And it is hardly surprising that Mme Édith Thomas was parading next to such individuals. This is the fate that awaits all those who abandon the struggle for peace. . . . This renegade is fleeing the side of peace simply to flee the risks and sacrifices that are inevitable in any struggle. It is her frantic egotism, her fear, and her sordid attachment to her personal interest that dictate her conduct."[26] The woman who wrote the article had worked with Thomas at the Union of French Women and had been part of the delegation of French women to the Soviet Union in 1946.

Thomas's trip to Belgrade was the first of several trips she made to Yugoslavia in the early 1950s, among them an international writers' conference in Dubrovnik and a peace conference in Zagreb. The delegation to Dubrovnik included a number of leftist writers, among them her good friend Clara Malraux, who described her as "the human being whose integrity could least be doubted."[27] Thomas was named vice-president of the France-Yugoslavia group and was awarded the Commander of the Yugoslav Flag medal, an official recognition by the Yugoslav government of her contributions. She participated in numerous activities on behalf of the Yugoslav experiment, enthusiastically supporting Tito's reforms in the direction of decentralization and self-management, which countered the Soviet dogmas of a centralized and planned economy. On one of her trips she met a handsome young Slav with whom she had her most romantic encounter, a first night by the Adriatic Sea under the stars, although their relationship did not last long.

By the mid-1950s Thomas's hope for Yugoslavia had already dimmed. The independent thinking of Djilas, whom she saw as a symbol of possibility in Yugoslavia, went too far for Tito. In 1954, after demanding more freedom of expression for Yugoslav Communists, Djilas lost his party post and in 1956 was arrested and imprisoned for approving the Hungarian insurrection against Soviet tanks. A year later, while in prison, his book *The New Class,* a scathing attack on the privileges and tyranny of the Communist bureaucracy, was smuggled out of Yugoslavia and published in French. Thomas confided to her friend Anne-Marie Bauer: "Communism doesn't work anywhere, not even in Yugoslavia."[28]

Many other French intellectuals transferred their faith from the Soviet Union to Yugoslavia and then to successive third-world revolutions in China, Africa, and Latin America. Édith Thomas, while continuing to be committed to leftist social democratic values, was not tempted again by a utopian vision of revolution. In the years following her resignation from the Communist Party, she gave a number of lectures with a new emphasis on the importance of rights "that are called the rights of man." The inclusion of rights for women, she notes, adds "a distinctive nuance."[29] She continued to agree with the critique formulated by Marxists attacking the French Revolution's abstract idea of freedom: the freedom of a banker is not the same as the freedom of someone who is unemployed. "But," she declares, "this critique of bourgeois freedom should not make us forget that it has also included positive aspects: the right not to be imprisoned and judged arbitrarily; the right not to be tortured so one will confess; the right to be able to express one's disagreement without being sentenced to prison, deported, or executed; the right not to be forced to admit to crimes one has not committed. In other words, the right to dignity."[30] The "positive aspects" she lists are those negative freedoms at the heart of any conception of human rights. In spite of her knowledge of Stalinist crimes and her experience of Nazi occupation, it was only after she left the Party that she was able to formulate these fundamental rights for men and women.

12

THE COMPROMISED WITNESS
The Quarrel with Jean Paulhan

Édith Thomas's break with the Communist Party is one explanation for the title of her memoir and the need she felt to defend herself. Another break, a few months before she began to write, came from a different direction. In January 1952, Jean Paulhan published his *Lettre aux directeurs de la Résistance,* a pamphlet against the purge of collaborators that took place after the war, and the purge of French letters in particular. In his pamphlet, Paulhan does a kind of deconstruction of the Resistance, making it into a virtual collaboration: the Resistance refused to collaborate with Germany because it had decided on a different form of collaboration—with the Soviet Union. During the purge these potential collaborators, who constituted the majority of judges, magistrates, and jury members in the courts, were charged with bringing to justice the actual collaborators. Paulhan's argument, a deliberate provocation, was aimed at the role of the "directors" of the Resistance—meaning the Communists. But he addressed his attack to the entire Resistance. On the first page he declares: "I am a *résistant.* . . . However that fact no longer gives me pride. Shame, rather." And a little later: "It is to the *résistants* that I am speaking."[1] Paulhan's *Lettre* enraged most of his former comrades in the intellectual Resistance, including the noncommunists.

Thomas's professional, literary, and political relationship with Paulhan went back to 1933, when Gallimard accepted her first novel for publication. At the time, he was already an influential editor. In January 1940, from the sanatorium in Assy, she sent him her "Lettres à Ariane," which he turned down, with the response that he preferred her earlier, "more substantial" work.[2] Their relationship began to grow more complex during the occupation, well before either

Édith Thomas or Paulhan became intimate with Dominique Aury. Although Thomas always admired the literary acumen of Paulhan and his early commitment to the Resistance, they were made not to understand each other. She distrusted the elusive and paradoxical style that characterized his life as well as his writing, a style that was contrary to her own need for directness and consistency.

In 1941 when Thomas returned to Paris after her convalescence in Arcachon, she went to see Jean Paulhan in the hope he could give her some suggestions as to how she might earn a living. Looking back on that encounter in her memoir, she remarks that although she has known him since the publication of her first books, "everything about him intimidated me"; she felt they would never find a shared language allowing real communication. On the other hand, his actions since the beginning of the German occupation inspired her confidence. First of all, he resigned from the directorship of the *Nouvelle Revue française,* which was taken over by Drieu la Rochelle, although critics now believe that he kept control of the journal through his office at Gallimard, located in the same building and on the same floor as the *NRF.* Second, Paulhan was involved in the network of the Musée de l'Homme, one of the earliest Resistance groups in the occupied zone. The Gestapo executed ten of its members on February 28, 1942. Paulhan, accused of hiding the duplicating machine for the group, was taken into custody and unexpectedly released thanks to the intervention of Drieu on his behalf.

Thomas describes herself as "a little surprised" when Paulhan proposed that she collaborate either with the *NRF* or with the theatrical journal *Comoedia,* both officially sanctioned by the occupying forces.[3] Her perplexity was based partly on the assumption that he himself would not write for either journal. In fact, Paulhan wrote two essays for *Comoedia* in 1942, one about the novelist Duranty and the other about Georges Braque. His position on the question of silence in the official press was characteristically ambiguous. In his notebooks the novelist Louis Guilloux quotes what Paulhan said to him on the subject: "People say: 'By collaborating (for instance with *Comoedia*), you're playing into the hands of the Protective Authorities who allow publication only of what serves them. So keep quiet!' But: If the P.A. have the power (and the intelligence) you say, how can I know that it isn't my silence they want?"[4]

In the same paragraph of her memoir in which Thomas wonders what could incite Paulhan to suggest that she write for official journals, she records that for herself "the situation was simple: the journals were German, the radio was German. It was out of the question to work with them."[5] However, the situation was not as simple as she indicates. Among the Resistance writers, only a small minority abstained totally from working with official journals. Even fewer refused to work with official publishing houses, which were generally considered less involved with the enemy. Thomas's own abstention was not as total as she claims. She reports that she had finished a novel, *Étude de femmes,* that she "resolved" not to publish. But an attentive reading of her diary shows clearly that in fact she tried a number of times to publish the novel, under another title and in different versions, with Gallimard. Although she expresses doubt about the possibilities of publication given the political circumstances, she never raises the question of refusing to publish. The novel was not accepted by Gallimard and appeared in 1945 with the Éditions Colbert.

In 1942 Claude Morgan visited her at the Archives to urge her to see Jean Paulhan, since she knew him and he knew the membership of the original Comité national des écrivains (CNE). She notes that even though Paulhan had made the "strange suggestion" to her that she collaborate with the *NRF* or *Comoedia,* she believes he "is not someone who would betray others' trust,"[6] adding in a later account, after their reconciliation, that he received her with "extreme kindness and total confidence."[7] Paulhan gave her the names of the six people, besides Jacques Decour and himself, who were part of the original CNE. On September 1, 1942, Paulhan writes to her: "Dear Mademoiselle, I need to see you, on the subject of that novel. Can you come Friday evening at 6:30 to the *nrf*? Please. Very cordially, Jean Paulhan." "That novel" is in fact an allusion to the CNE.[8] Paulhan participated regularly in the clandestine meetings at her apartment about *Les Lettres françaises* and the Éditions de Minuit.

During those years and until their break in 1952, Thomas seems to have sent Paulhan most of her writings, although she knew all too well the renowned severity of his literary pronouncements. He begins a letter to her in February 1943 without naming or making any direct allusion to the text he is criticizing: "Too bad, I am going to reproach you severely: there is something *common* in your style, a little vulgar, the reason for which is paradoxical (but in literature there is scarcely anything that is not paradoxical): it's because you have always counted only on yourself, your own genius, and never paid much attention to the way you were writing." Like a strict schoolmaster, except that his parentheses deliberately subvert his message, he tells her "there are two books you should know by heart (even if you detest them; it's not a bad thing either to detest them): *Esthetics of the French Language* by [Rémy de] Gourmont and, by [Marcel] Schwob, *Moeurs des Diurnales.*"[9] Paulhan's allusion to Gourmont and Schwob, relatively unknown even at the time, can be explained by his interest in both these critics as subjects of his provocative book on the art of writing, *Les Fleurs de Tarbes* (The flowers of Tarbes), published in 1941.

At the end of the letter, Paulhan's tone softens. He quotes a passage he likes from Édith Thomas's 1933 novel, *Sept-Sorts,* and counsels that she can regain control of her writing by "stronger convictions"—by which he seems to mean stronger esthetic convictions—and by "a more conscious technique." In her response, she begins by countering his criticism but ends by taking on the role of a pupil seeking to learn whatever the master can teach her: "I need to determine exactly how my style is vulgar and common. Is it because I write short sentences? But it is not necessary to plagiarize Proust. Is it because my sentences are simple? But I hate the 'artistic' style. . . . How do I overcome this vulgarity? . . . I have no resources until I am aware of the reasons for [it], until I discover a canon external to myself. Will Gourmont be of help? And you? You see, I question you as if you were the Delphic oracle."[10]

His response was certainly worthy of the ancient Delphic oracle in its ambiguity, but the suggestions he offered, governed by his endless delight in paradox and rhetorical effect, were unlikely to have been of much help. "Your style," he explains in his next letter, "will be commonplace as long as you think it is extraordinary. It won't begin to become truly extraordinary until the day you think it is commonplace. . . . You are lucky: in sum, to become a great writer, all you need to do is rid yourself of an illusion. . . . Of course I am not giving you advice. Rather, I am asking you questions, to which you will respond only if it amuses you."[11] Whether or not she was amused, they both chose to keep the exchange alive. In the debate about originality and banality, they support their respective positions with quotations from André Gide, and Paulhan comments: "We argue like the Arabs, using verses from the Koran."[12] Then he turns to Rémy de Gourmont, whose theories Thomas criticized as full of the "naivetés of the time." "It is useful and even necessary," Paulhan insists (inserting parentheses to modulate his emphasis), "for a writer to have believed for a moment (even if he subsequently rejects the suspicion with horror) that style is the essential element of literature, just as it is useful for him to have gone through the opposite conviction (in which all of us are now immersed)."[13] Paulhan's statement reveals, perhaps inadvertently, his distaste for the moral constraints imposed by the situation of writing what will later be called *littérature engagée*.

In another letter, among a list of various stylistic objections, Paulhan pens a critique of Thomas's "L'Étoile jaune" (The yellow star) and admits that the whole story "annoyed me a little." Since Jean Paulhan effectively acted as literary director of the Éditions de Minuit, it is probable that his letter of disapproval prevented or at least discouraged Thomas from submitting "L'Étoile jaune" with her other stories in *Contes d'Auxois*. It was not published until after the war. The dates involved would also support Paulhan's role: he wrote his letter to Thomas on April 20, 1943; we know that her *Contes* were received by the Éditions de Minuit that same month, April 1943.

What was it that annoyed Paulhan in this story? He comments: "You make things too easy for yourself" (*Vous vous faites la part trop belle*), without ex-

Jean Paulhan, 1945 or 1946. Photo by Henri Cartier-Bresson. Magnum Photos.

plaining what he means. He could be referring to the physical appearance of Thérèse Lévy, which counters prevailing Jewish stereotypes. She has green eyes, blond hair, thin lips, and a short, slightly turned-up nose that recalls "the faces of certain medieval virgins." Thomas's description reads like a demonstration for the entry in her journal on June 24, 1942, after the imposition of the yellow star, when she declares that there is no Jewish race. As we have seen earlier, "L'Étoile jaune" is narrated from the point of view of a young Jewish woman as she sews the yellow star on the garment of her eight-year-old daughter. Thinking about her family history, Thérèse articulates without naming them the republican values that date from the French Revolution. The emancipation of the Jews was based on the doctrine that they were to be granted full rights as individuals and as citizens; in exchange, they would renounce any claim to communal autonomy within the French nation.[14] Édith Thomas clearly has that history in mind when Thérèse Lévy says to herself: "There was no longer any Jewish question." Jean Paulhan, countering Thérèse's assertion, writes to Édith Thomas, "But yes, on the contrary, it all seems to be the proof that from now on [*désormais*] there is a Jewish question since ... and since ... and even for Thérèse."[15] The ellipses in Paulhan's letter signal the prudent self-censorship that he felt the subject required. His argument, hidden behind the ellipses, is reduced to a perplexing declaration. However, one word in Paulhan's statement seems to modify his protest and imply agreement with Thomas: *désormais* (from now on). He does not indicate when "from now on" might have begun. With the imposition of the yellow star? With the General Commission for Jewish Questions in March 1941? Or earlier, with the first measures against the Jews? It is puzzling that Jean Paulhan, the master of paradox, does not see the double meaning of Édith Thomas's sentence "There was no longer any Jewish question"—a sentence as paradoxical as his own. The reality of the situation "from now on"—that is, the persecution of the Jews by the Germans and by Vichy France—demonstrates Paulhan's point that there is a Jewish question. The reality of the situation also demonstrates Édith Thomas's point, the necessity of fighting against the idea of a Jewish question. Perhaps a key to Paulhan's surprising declaration can be found in his other criticism, "You make things too easy for yourself." He could be suggesting that the Jewish question would be more difficult to deny if Thomas had chosen as her protagonist not a Jewish woman who was assimilated and French, but rather a foreign-born Jew. That distinction was pervasive in French opinion and Vichy policy, with tragic consequences for Jewish immigrants in France. But the distinction between French and foreign Jews does not change Édith Thomas's argument—or the argument of Jean-Paul Sartre in 1946—that the Jewish question is an invention of the antisemite.

Although Thomas usually deferred to Paulhan in literary matters, she stood up more confidently to his political criticism, especially when it concerned disagreements with the CNE, which placed her in solidarity with others in the literary Resistance. A major argument broke out in relation to an article written by Édith Thomas and Claude Morgan in the July 1943 issue of the underground *Les Lettres françaises*, "L'Agonie de la NRF" (The death throes of the *NRF*). When Drieu la Rochelle, whose temperament was ill suited to the role of editing a journal, resigned from his position, Paulhan made a strenuous attempt to keep the *NRF* alive, trying to rally a team of respected non-collaborationist writers who would ensure a purely literary endeavor. However, the effort was doomed to failure, since those he tried to recruit remained unconvinced that such an enterprise was possible under the circumstances. As Thomas and Morgan argue, there was no way the *NRF* could bypass the German Propaganda Office, which would exert its power just as it did for directly collaborationist journals like *La Gerbe* and *Je suis partout*. In 1943, with Germany on the defensive, they write that the aim of the Propaganda Office is to neutralize intellectuals, allowing them to believe there can be a place for art that is neutral and relatively free: "An *NRF* that considers itself purely literary, especially if it actually succeeds, responds to that aim. By its existence alone it is insidious and dangerous. Its raison d'être is to demonstrate that French thought and French culture can readily accommodate the Nazi regime, and that the claim of oppression is just an invention of malevolent minds."[16]

In response, Paulhan writes privately to Thomas: "A propos of (silly) questions of pride: was it nice, was it loyal to show so much distrust in the journal I founded with J[acques] D[ecour]? It seems to me that one could have said to oneself (as you surely did) that as soon I was involved with the journal, either it would blow up, or it would be sufficiently different, beginning with the first issue, for the difference to be obvious to anyone."[17] In fact, the only explicit allusion to Paulhan himself, which occurs in the first part of the article, the part written by Thomas, is flattering, a comparison of the *NRF* before and after 1940. She affirms, "Drieu's journal had nothing in common with that of Rivière, Gide, Paulhan, Claudel, and Benda, which won the respect of the entire world."[18] In any case, Paulhan's letter to her remains friendly and includes a thank you for defending him (in an unspecified context) to Aragon and Elsa Triolet.

In its first meeting after the liberation of Paris, on September 5, 1944, the Comité national des écrivains declared its commitment to "refuse any collaboration with journals, revues, collections, etc. which would publish a text signed by a writer whose attitude or writings during the occupation brought moral or material aid to the oppressor."[19] That declaration, published in *Les Lettres françaises,* was followed a week later by what became known as *la liste noire,* the blacklist, which named the targeted writers. It should be emphasized that this French Resistance blacklist against collaborators, in sharp contrast to the American cold war McCarthy version some years later, had no legal power. As Édith Thomas points out, the CNE list did not prevent designated collaborationist writers from publishing their work, an interdiction left to decisions in the courts. She notes simply: "We were saying that we did not want to encounter a certain number of people, even on the professional level."[20]

From the beginning, however, the list was caught in a maze of contradictions. No attempt was made to include publishers on the list, although all the prestigious publishers of the time, including Gallimard, had made serious compromises with the occupying forces. In addition, many Resistance writers made special pleas to leave out their collaborationist friends. Moreover, the post-liberation Comité national des écrivains bore little resemblance to its clandestine counterpart. At its first open meeting in September, over a hundred people suddenly appeared, at least eighty of whom, Jean Guéhenno wryly observes, had never been seen at the secret meetings in Édith's apartment.[21]

The most vehement objections to the blacklist came from Paulhan, who considered that for writers, the basic right that needed defense was what he called "the right to error."[22] The CNE blacklist, he asserted, was a demonstration that the former democrats of the Resistance had become "fascists."[23] Even while the war was going on, Paulhan considered the reconciliation of opposing forces, especially among writers, to be a paramount task of the postwar period. In one of

his letters to Vercors, he gives the example of Marcel Jouhandeau, a collaborator whom he considered a writer of genius and with whom he shared a passionate friendship, as their correspondence makes clear. Reproaching Jouhandeau
for his trip to Germany during the war as part of an official delegation of writers and artists, Paulhan nevertheless insists that Jouhandeau remained a patriot. His letter to Jouhandeau in September 1944 is instructive of Paulhan's own
position in that regard: "You acted and wrote as you did, at a time when you
believed (and there were great, serious reasons to believe) that France was definitively conquered, to assure a better treatment for France on the part of the
conqueror."[24]

Paulhan's comment to Jouhandeau takes on its full meaning in light of his
own interpretation of the respective roles of de Gaulle and Pétain. In August
1940 he writes in a letter, "I like de Gaulle and his speeches. But the work of Pétain can be useful."[25] Paulhan took the same position in a radio interview in
1952: "After all, Pétain doubtless did what he could. I suppose without him we
would have had a hundred times more martyrs and deaths. And it is France's
good fortune that she had both de Gaulle and Pétain, those who resisted and
those who obeyed, the first to save principles, the others to save—to the extent
possible—the men and the land of this country."[26] Paulhan, an admirer of de
Gaulle, made a distinction between Pétain and Vichy. While he had some sympathy for Pétain, he had none for the Vichy regime. The idea that Pétain and de
Gaulle served complementary patriotic functions was widely believed in the
first twenty-five years after the war. This theory, which came to be known as the
shield and the sword,[27] has been opposed by countless historians since 1970, in
terms that elaborate Stanley Hoffmann's powerful indictment:

> Vichy's interest in collaboration far exceeded the "necessities" of shielding
> France. . . . Vichy France made moral choices that no government should
> be willing to make—about which hostages should be shot (Communists),
> which Jews should be delivered (foreign ones, including children the Ger-
> mans had not planned to grab). It lent France's police, judicial apparatus,
> penitentiary administration, not to mention its controlled media to the
> Nazis, or used them (as in anti-Resistance repression) for purposes that
> served the Nazi cause. Next to this, homilies about Pétain's good inten-
> tions, harangues about Laval's good deeds, hagglings about comparative
> results all wilt.[28]

Paulhan resigned from the CNE in 1946. Although Thomas's positions were
quite different from his, she found herself allied with him in his opposition to
Aragon and Elsa Triolet, whom she saw as consolidating their personal domi-
nance over the group in conformity with Communist Party directives. A year

after Paulhan's resignation from the CNE, Thomas resigned as well, along with many others who had become disgusted with the degradation of the CNE mission from the *mystique* of the occupation years to the squabbling *politique* of the postwar period.

After the war, many of the letters between Thomas and Paulhan focused on her belief in communism and his personal campaign to disabuse her, even when the ostensible subject of a given exchange was literary. Paulhan's praise for one of her stories, "La Vieille du chef-lieu" (The old woman of the township), inspired this reflection on his part, entirely convincing in view of Thomas's history: "How I wish that a good, solidly established communist society would finally let you discover that your anxiety is less social than mystical (or more precisely metaphysical)."[29] In her response, she thanked him for his remarks about "La Vieille," adding: "You know how much your judgment is precious to me." Her reservations about the man and his politics did not lessen her desire for his approval of her writing. Thomas's own interpretation of the "anxiety" in question reflects long-standing conversations with herself going back to the early 1930s, when she first began to move toward a political commitment:

> Perhaps you are right, perhaps this anxiety is *also* metaphysical (it was, I don't deny it). But oriented in that direction, anxiety has remained sterile for as long a time as there have been thinking human beings, who have not found any solution. Anxiety directed toward the social side is rather more effective. It would already be a considerable achievement to create a world in which everyone had the material possibility of being happy— which perhaps does not bring happiness. But for those who don't have that material possibility, one doesn't have the right to neglect its importance. In any case, it's a life hypothesis—a little like Pascal's wager on an earthly level—and enough to occupy the average sixty years of a precarious and absurd existence.[30]

On numerous occasions, in various ways, Paulhan speaks of his desire to convince her "a little."[31] To which Thomas responds at one point, stubbornly digging in because it is Paulhan, "No, dear friend, you cannot convince me."[32] In 1947, Paulhan wrote her a letter that seems to be his reply to her protest against the positions he took in *De la paille et du grain* (Of chaff and wheat), published that year, which already contained many of the themes he would elaborate later in his *Lettre aux directeurs de la Résistance*. He insists that he is a "democrat" and concludes with this prediction about her future as a Communist: "I leave you to your little intellectual aristocracy of yesterday. You'll suffocate in it (if you are the person I suspect you to be) one of these days. With friendship, Jean P."[33] His accurate suspicion in 1947 that she would not stay in the Communist Party much longer was surely reinforced by Dominique's knowledge of her friend's increasing doubts.

Until the break between Paulhan and Édith Thomas in 1952, nothing in their correspondence reveals any change in the relationship between them after Paulhan and Dominique Aury began their love affair. Paulhan's single reference to Dominique occurs in the context of Édith's health. In his 1948 New Year's note, graced with an ink drawing of a friendly butterfly, he tells her he is pleased with "the good news from Dominique Aury. . . . People assure me that convalescence from appendicitis is the freshest and most joyous of all convalescences."[34] There is no mention of Dominique in Édith's letters to him.

In 1947 Jean Paulhan and Dominique Aury edited *La Patrie se fait tous les jours* (The homeland is created day by day), their collection of Resistance essays, stories, and poems which brought together writers of all political points of view, showing a unity of struggle against the oppressor that had long since been shattered. Thomas was represented by three poems that had appeared in underground publications. Paulhan's reflections on patriotism in his preface to the volume perhaps illuminate the paradoxical postwar positions of this *résistant:* "To be truly a patriot, one would therefore have to combine successfully in oneself the rational and the emotional; loving one's homeland as it is, but wanting at any cost to make it different; demanding that it be normal and just and yet cherishing it in its injustice and its strangeness. In short, adoring one's homeland, but finding it intolerable. There is the enigma."[35]

When Paulhan liked something Thomas had written, he could be genuinely helpful, in words and in action as well. He thanked her for sending him *Jeanne d'Arc*—even remarking, "What a beautiful cover, where Joan resembles you so nicely." The icon of Joan chosen by Thomas shows the maid of Orleans as a warrior rather than a saint or a martyr, her sword raised, riding a white horse. She has dark hair and the Kalmuk eyes of Thomas's self-description. Paulhan continues: "I read it with great pleasure. I like its liveliness, its seriousness, its conviction. I like the naturalness of your characters—I like especially that great silent character: the people, whose presence you make us feel so well at every moment, the first among historians of Joan of Arc to do so."[36]

After Thomas's break with the Party, when the Éditeurs français réunis withheld *Jeanne d'Arc* from circulation, Paulhan encouraged her efforts to redress the situation and eventually succeeded in persuading Gaston Gallimard to take the remaining copies of the book, which was subsequently republished with a Gallimard imprint. In the warmest of all her letters to Paulhan, the only one she signs "affectionately," she thanks him for his "constant kindness" to her, which she "feels deeply" even though, she writes, she has difficulty expressing it.[37]

Just over a year later, Paulhan suggested a meeting that would take place on

"What a beautiful cover, where Joan resembles you so nicely."
Detail, photo of Joan of Arc by permission of Bibliothèque nationale de France, Paris.

December 29, 1951, at 5 P.M. in her apartment, "as in the good old days," to discuss the pamphlet he had just finished writing, *Lettre aux directeurs de la Résistance*.[38] He and the publisher of *Arts,* where it was supposed to appear, wanted to know the reaction of his old Resistance comrades before its public distribution. Thomas accepted his suggestion and invitations were addressed to François Mauriac, Albert Camus, Jacques Debû-Bridel, André Malraux, Jean Blanzat, Vercors, Jean Cassou, André Chamson, Jean Guéhenno, Maurice Merleau-Ponty, Jean-Paul Sartre, Georges Duhamel, and Claude Roy.[39] It is difficult to imagine the reaction Paulhan expected to his pamphlet, in which his outrage at the excesses of the

purges after the liberation, along with his visceral anticommunism and his lin-
guistic issues around the notion of *patrie* converge, calling into question the Resistance itself. He takes no account of the passions unleashed in 1944 and 1945 by
the atrocities of a war that had not even ended, and that had been not only an occupation by Nazi Germany but also a French civil war. A number of his notations
are factually inaccurate. He claims that between 60,000 and 200,000 people were
summarily executed by their countrymen and 400,000 Frenchmen "executed,
sent to jail, ruined, consigned to national indignity and reduced to the rank of
pariah."[40] These numbers, inflated even in relation to the figures provided by his
own maximalist camp, ignored reliable statistics that were available at the time
and have since been confirmed in recent studies by historians: there were 10,000
"extra-judicial" executions and 125,000 legal condemnations.[41]

The timing of Paulhan's letter is even more surprising. By 1952 the intense
emotions of the liberation period had diminished considerably. A year before
the *Lettre* was published, the first major amnesty of collaborators had taken
place, a fact that is not mentioned anywhere in Paulhan's pamphlet. Why then
write such a diatribe in 1952? A convincing argument is made by the historian
Anne Simonin that the *Lettre* was meant to cover the literary return of the "great
outlaws" of collaboration, Louis-Ferdinand Céline and Lucien Rebatet, who
were being published in 1952 by Gallimard.[42] For Jean Paulhan, as Dominique
Aury often said, no cause was more sacred than that of literature.

In any case, Paulhan's comrades were furious and *Arts* decided not to publish his *Lettre*. The pamphlet appeared instead with Éditions de Minuit, the
publishing house whose underground beginnings symbolized the literary Resistance at its finest, thus creating even more of a furor. Venomous exchanges of
letters ensued, in *Les Lettres françaises*, in *Le Figaro littéraire*, and elsewhere. Although Thomas did not participate in the polemic, she allowed her friend Louis
Martin-Chauffier to use her name in public letters he wrote against Paulhan.
Among the accusations in Martin-Chauffier's first letter, titled "Letter to a renegade [*transfuge*] of the Resistance," there is this: "You solicited [the verb in
French is *racoler*, as in soliciting a prostitute] for the very official *Nouvelle Revue
française* of Drieu."[43] Paulhan denies the accusation and asks him: "What writers,
what articles?"[44] In his reply, Martin-Chauffier specifically cites Édith Thomas.
Privately, Paulhan writes to her: "I'm a little unhappy with the use M[artin]-
Ch[auffier] makes of your name in an article whose bad faith, I think, does not
escape you. But is the fact true? Did I really 'solicit' Édith Thomas for the *nrf* of
Drieu? Answer me on that, please."[45] In response Thomas cites his suggestion
to her in 1941 about writing for the *NRF* or *Comoedia,* an anecdote she acknowledges having told a number of times since then. When Martin-Chauffier
asked for authorization to cite her, "I had no reason to refuse."[46]

Over the years, intense disagreements between Paulhan and Édith Thomas found a place within the boundaries of their friendship—or what both of them at various times called friendship. Paulhan's initial letter to her about the Martin-Chauffier matter displays the kind of contentiousness that often characterized their exchanges. The private letter that follows, however, quoted here in full, is of a different order:

> Yes. You did have a reason to refuse. You knew that the article by Martin-Chauffier was an article in bad faith. For you do not believe, finally—nor does he—that I wrote my *Lettre* out of "opportunism," or that I was a *résistant* out of hypocrisy. Just as recalling that anecdote in an article by you would have been acceptable, by the same measure it became unacceptable once Martin-Chauffier used it to bear witness against me. This was no longer the friendship that sometimes existed between us. It became treachery. Unless you really think I am an opportunist, and a hypocrite. But in that case as well we no longer have anything to say to each other.
>
> I must add that it seems to me base, in any case, to turn a favor I was ready to do for you to my disadvantage. Eluard and Guillevic were writing for the *nrf;* my proposal therefore had nothing injurious to you. It would not have been easy for me to follow through, and Drieu, if I had written him, would have doubtless objected that I could very well collaborate with the *nrf* myself.
>
> Farewell then. What I liked about you on the contrary was that great and gracious uprightness of spirit that you sometimes show. I don't know where your hatred of me might come from. I don't want to know either.[47]

From a political point of view, Paulhan's pronouncement of a definitive break with Édith Thomas is decidedly uncharacteristic of a writer who believed in the importance of reconciliation among writers and defended their "right to error." His moral support of collaborationist writers was not affected by the position they took during the war years. Yet in 1952, many years after the war, he was willing to end a friendship because of what he perceived as "treachery" in a quarrel between *résistants* that involved Thomas only indirectly. As Paulhan presents the specific argument, he is right: if she knew how Martin-Chauffier was going to use her anecdote, she should not have given him permission to do so. There is something incommensurate, however, in Paulhan's response. For someone as dedicated as he was to reconciliation, in the context of issues far more terrible, his definitive rejection of Thomas cannot be adequately explained by the incident that provoked it. As the last two sentences of his letter make clear, the issue between them is personal rather than political. Paulhan projects onto her what emerges in the letter as his own anger, with the disingenuous claim of not knowing where her "hatred" of him might come from. The anger on his part is apparently not tempered by the fact that in their romantic rivalry for Dominique Aury, it is Paulhan, after all, who won.

In distress and panic that she would lose Dominique, Édith seems to have sent her Paulhan's letter. Dominique tried to reassure her friend, mistakenly as it turned out, that Paulhan's reaction was temporary: "With a little time and patience, everything will be eased without your making any gesture."[48] She also lets Édith know that he had been ill for several weeks. Before or after the note from Dominique (all these letters are undated), Édith wrote the draft of a letter to Paulhan, which she kept with his letters. She began by bringing up for the first time the subject of Dominique, as if they could find some way to heal their rift for her sake. Édith's own anger, however, was too great to sustain even a semblance of conciliatory language. She claimed the break as if it were her own initiative, dating it from her reading of his *Lettre*. Her affirmation that had she been aware of its contents, she would not have agreed to host the meeting of *résistants* in her apartment is convincing. In relation to Martin-Chauffier, she explains that she accepted his request as a means of marking her disagreement with Paulhan's position. Tellingly she adds: "Moreover, if I had refused, I would have considered myself a coward."[49]

In response to Paulhan's rhetorical questions, she knows him too well to believe he acted out of opportunism or an intention to betray the Resistance, although her denial of such motivations on his part takes the form of a different kind of attack: "You are much too subtle and complex for commonsense explanations to account for your actions." She spells out their fundamental disagreement on the issue of the specific responsibility of the writer, which she sees as "that of everyone, with something more," the additional responsibility that comes with being a writer. Although she tries to conclude on a note of caring, "I know you are ill and I want to tell you that I hope you are feeling better," the stiffness of her expression of concern does little to soften the letter's hostility.[50]

It is highly unlikely that Thomas actually sent this letter to Paulhan, which in any case would not have altered the situation. According to Aury, in our conversations, Paulhan insisted that she break off all contact with Thomas, which she steadfastly refused to do. Nevertheless, for at least a year or two and perhaps considerably longer, Dominique made every effort to hide her continuing relationship with Édith from him. In October of 1953 or 1954 she writes to Édith from Lausanne: "J. P. is arriving the day after tomorrow. I will continue to write to you; don't answer me. I don't want to have anything here to show, or to hide, nor do I want to be caught in the act of hiding your letters. There is so much that is and has always been clandestine and necessarily silenced in my life and that must surely be my fault since it's constant. It's painful, and from time to time discourages me." But she seems to want to draw Édith into a feeling of complicity between them: "You are for me a human face, someone with whom I don't have to dissimulate, who allows me, even in spite of myself, not to dissimulate. I'm probably taking advantage of that."[51] In spite of Dominique's efforts, Jean Paulhan and Édith Thomas were not reconciled until fifteen years later, a year before his death in 1968.

In *Le Témoin compromis* Thomas reflects on the various reasons that prompted individuals to join the Resistance, viewing their motivation through the prism of postwar conflicts. She evokes what she calls different "dosages" of antifascism, attachment to the Soviet Union, and patriotism. Her reflections about her own decision take the form of a curious dialogue with herself which shows how disturbed she was by Paulhan's accusations in his *Lettre,* although her memoir makes no direct allusion to their quarrel: "If . . . the invader had imposed communism, wouldn't I have counted myself among the collaborators? I hesitated to answer. Yes, I thought honestly. But I added immediately: only if France were allowed to live on, if the invader did not impose either his language or his conceptions of culture, if France could accomplish its social transformation according to its own particular genius."[52] In spite of the ambiguity of those qualifications, Édith Thomas's writings and actions during the occupation years demonstrate that the most significant "dosage" in her motivation for joining the Resistance was antifascism. It is equally clear that for Jean Paulhan it was patriotism.

Thomas's defense plea in *Le Témoin compromis,* insofar as it concerns the Resistance, takes on its full meaning in relation to historical memory, what the historian Henry Rousso calls the "unfinished mourning" of the decade following the war's end, marked by ambivalence.[53] Édith Thomas's ambivalence cannot be separated from the memory of what the Resistance has become, "a kind of myth, a subject of exaltation for some, horror for others." In defending herself, she also defends the Resistance in general, "which certain people are embarrassed to have joined."[54] She argues that the errors and even the crimes of the Resistance—and she insists on a reminder of the conditions under which they were committed—do not sully the moral fact of resistance.

Her target, of course, was Jean Paulhan, but she was also rebelling against the prevailing state of mind at the time, which preferred simply to erase *les années noires,* the dark years of the occupation. In a tribute in 1956 to Father Maydieu, one of her comrades in the CNE who had just died, she wrote: "It is in bad taste today to evoke the Resistance period. Those who have not forgotten . . . , those who do not want to disown the commitments they made to themselves back then, look like spoilsports, nut cases, and even worse, like the inactive soldiers, bitter and out of fashion, under the Restoration."[55] Although she declares, "As for myself, I have not changed,"[56] she has lost the inner harmony and the fragile connection of trust among a diverse group of writers briefly united as a community by their shared struggle. Édith Thomas's own "unfinished mourning" grieved the loss of fervor that accompanied those years.

13

FROM NOVELS TO WOMEN'S HISTORIES

One of the questions of interpretation provoked by Édith Thomas's writings is the chronological puzzle of her choice of genres. Whereas all but one of the seven novels were published between 1934 and 1945, all her historical studies are dated after the liberation. With the single exception of *Le Jeu d'échecs*, which appeared the year of her death (1970), there seems to be no chronological overlap in the writing of the novels and the historical essays. In the novels the theme of solitude dominates, expressed as loneliness and the absence of love. In the historical essays, solitude is energized and transformed by the protagonists into a positive force of action, overcoming, at least in privileged moments, the solitude of the individual. Thomas's participation in the Resistance gave her a means of breaking through the feeling of difference, what she calls singularity, which separated her from others. The submerged discourse of loneliness resurfaces as a dominant theme in her last novel—the only novel, however, for which she writes a hopeful ending.

After the war years, Édith Thomas turned to the writing of history as a means of reaching beyond her own experience, which she had not been able to do in her autobiographical novels. The history she decided to write took the form of biography, her way of breaking through what had become a novelistic impasse. Biography satisfied her narrative impulse and at the same time allowed her to bring to life a particular historical period, the nineteenth century in France, which she found of compelling interest. Although most of her biographies depend on exhaustive archival documentation, she considered history "very close to art." In *Pauline Roland* (1956), her first full-length biography, she describes Michelet, that most literary of historians, as the greatest French historian, "with all his passion, his uncertainties, even his errors." Using Michelet as an example and a justification, she emphasizes the resemblance between the historian's art and that of the writer of fiction. For Michelet, she argues, history was a vision, "a vision imposed on the reader, just as the novelist imposes for a moment the vision of the world he has conceived."[1]

The subjects of Thomas's biographical histories are always individuals with whom she feels a special affinity, women—and one man—who were passionately involved in social issues and had in common a need to follow their conscience, wherever it might lead. Her choice of method thus followed completely different imperatives from those of the dominant *Annales* school of history as it evolved in the 1950s and to which she refers obliquely in the introduction to *Pauline Roland*. While she considers the focus on institutions and economic questions a salutary shift from the overemphasis on "great men," her own project is to bring to life individuals who were not "great men" but were engaged with special intensity in the historical struggles of their time.

Thomas's studies of women are inscribed within a conception of women's history as having taken place at the margins of history, raising questions specific to that situation. She writes her essays from an explicitly feminist perspective, although the contemporary women's movement in France did not begin until 1970 and "feminism" during the preceding decades was a pejorative term even for women. In 1949 Simone de Beauvoir published *Le Deuxième Sexe,* her pioneering and uniquely ambitious attempt to explore within a philosophical framework all aspects of woman's situation. Yet Beauvoir begins her monumental contribution by apologizing for what she calls her "irritating" subject and hastens to disassociate herself from the "quarreling over feminism, now practically over."[2] It was only in 1972 that Beauvoir first declared herself a feminist. In 1963 Édith Thomas also says that feminism is "thought today to be outmoded," but she continues by asserting that this is "a means of conjuring away the problems it posed, problems that are still very far from being resolved."[3]

In Thomas's initial biographies, *Les Femmes de 1848, Pauline Roland,* and *George Sand,* which focus on the first part of the nineteenth century, she weaves into her stories a body of thought, that of the utopian socialists, which intrigued her as it did her subjects. After her disillusionment with revolutionary Marxism, she read widely in the ideas and failed experiments of Saint-Simon, Pierre Leroux, and especially Charles Fourier. One of her objections to Marxism had always been its almost exclusive concern with economics and insufficient attention to questions of human emotion and ethics. In Fourier's ideal city, which he named Harmony, girls and boys receive the same education; the activities of each man or woman or child are chosen in complete freedom and according to the dispositions and tastes of the individual. Fourier believed that the extension of women's rights, including an education equal to that of men, was the measure of social progress. He also argued against the convention of marriage and placed sexual freedom at the heart of his values. In spite of the ponderous theoretical titles of Fourier's works, he wrote with an optimistic verve and imagination that delighted her.

She began to be interested in Fourier after the war years through an odd circumstance. His unpublished papers had been housed in the École Normale on the rue d'Ulm. The minister of national education under Pétain, concerned that these writings would corrupt French youth, had them removed from the school and transferred to a dusty attic of the Bibliothèque de documentation internationale contemporaine. According to legend, they disappeared in a library fire in 1944. In fact, they were not destroyed, and Thomas found them and moved them to the Archives nationales, where she made an inventory of all the manuscripts.[4]

In *Pauline Roland: socialisme et féminisme au XIXe siècle* Thomas explores Roland's life in the context of the utopian socialist ideas she espoused, against the backdrop of the miseries of industrialization for an emerging proletariat that had no social or economic protection of any kind. As a sheltered young girl in the provinces at the beginning of the nineteenth century, Pauline read with fervor Father Enfantin, an apostle of the new faith, and decided she would go to Paris to join a group of Saint-Simonians so she could give herself fully to what she believed. Pauline Roland's life story, like that of George Sand and Louise Michel, follows the trajectory of many male fictional protagonists of the time, including Balzac's Rastignac and Stendhal's Julien Sorel, who move from the provinces to Paris in search of a greater destiny. The mythical allure of Paris takes on feminine and feminist form in Pauline, who dreamed of an exalted love, body and soul, in freedom and equality. She met her first lover, a fellow Saint-Simonian, at the age of twenty-eight and they agreed not to marry, preferring love as a free choice without promises of any kind. Aware that she might become pregnant, she decided she would take charge of the child herself: "I want to be a mother," she writes, "but with a mysterious paternity."[5]

Pauline Roland gave birth to a son with her first lover, and to a son and daughter with her second. Although she was open about her situation, she insisted on keeping the names of her lovers secret. Her beliefs emphasized responsibilities as well as rights. In spite of the difficulties of motherhood outside marriage in nineteenth-century society, Roland supported the children on her own, working sometimes as a journalist, sometimes as a teacher. Her second lover, like her first, was a Saint-Simonian, which proved to be of little help in resolving the complications of their relationship. At one point, describing

Roland's role in a romantic triangle, her biographer makes a comment that could be addressed to herself: "Pauline found one of those subterfuges that are always available to moral souls, who justify themselves much more than they accept themselves."[6] With her three children, Roland sought refuge in the utopian community of the philosopher Pierre Leroux, who strongly influenced her thinking as he did that of George Sand. In the community of Boussac, she directed the school for young children and was able to apply Leroux's progressive methods of education. At the age of forty, she remained single but no longer rejected the principle of marriage, as long as it was based on love and complete equality between man and woman.

By early 1848, the economic situation of the Boussac community had become increasingly precarious and Pauline Roland moved back to Paris. At a time when there were neither unions nor any legislation regulating work conditions, she became involved in a teachers' association, part of the network of workers' associations that had begun to be organized, although they were considered illegal and subversive by the authorities. She was imprisoned in 1850, released a year later, and then arrested once again. The second time, accused of participating in the insurrection against Louis Napoleon's coup d'état of December 1851, she was deported to Algeria, where prisoners furnished cheap physical labor for the new French colony. After several months she was pardoned and released thanks to the efforts of her oldest son, who had become a lawyer. Exhausted and ill from her ordeal, she died a few days after her return to France. Victor Hugo wrote a lengthy poem of tribute to Pauline Roland (not one of his best), hailing her love for justice and freedom.

Thomas's relation to Pauline Roland is always sympathetic, even when she criticizes the effusiveness of her writing style and the limitations of her utopian ideas. While acknowledging "our" smiles at Roland's grandiloquence, she renders her excesses with affection as well as irony. At one point Thomas speaks of "the secret complicity that is always established between a biographer and her subject" and draws her reader into that complicity.[7] While most nineteenth-century feminists demanded political and social equality, Roland was also concerned with the biological aspects of women's rights. Thomas is especially intrigued by her affirmation of the right to choose to have children outside masculine rules of marriage. The only limit Roland put on her own freedom was the responsibility to assure the support of her children. What appeals to Thomas most of all is what she calls Roland's "logical passion" or her "coherence," the desire to live her life in accord with her convictions, a determination close to Thomas's heart.

Her study *George Sand* (1959), a little book written as part of a series about nineteenth-century "classics," reads as a lively and perceptive introduction to

Sand. Thomas emphasizes the richness of her contradictions, including her ambiguous feminism. Her maternal passion, at the center of her emotional life,
drew her to male lovers like Musset and Chopin who were younger than she, in
poor health, emotionally fragile, and in need of protection. Although she herself took on a man's name and often a male role, she saw women as fundamentally different from men and herself as an exception. She fought for changes in
women's personal lives, especially the conventions of marriage, but was deeply
distrustful of their struggle for rights in the public world. Thomas considers
Story of My Life Sand's masterpiece, although, she writes, "it is no more authentic than other memoirs, which are always self-justifications or self-accusa-
tions, to be read with a critical mind," a telling assessment of her own memoir
as well. She judges Sand's life story, along with her correspondence, "the most
fascinating novel she wrote."[8]

In 1960, ten years before the beginnings of the contemporary women's movement in France, the Lucien Mazenod Art Editions published a two-volume
encyclopedia called *Les Femmes célèbres,* a lavishly illustrated cross-cultural exploration. The books are organized historically, by categories of fame and
achievement. Among the nine collaborators, both Édith Thomas and Dominique Aury made significant contributions.

Aury was responsible for the section "Women of Letters," whom she separates from two other kinds of writers: on the one hand, those women she calls,
borrowing Thomas's term, the fighters for *l'humanisme féminin* and, on the
other, *les inconscientes,* "who write not because they want to write, but because
they are possessed and prisoners: I am referring to women in love and mystics.
Saint Theresa and Mariana [Alcoforado], [Saint] Marie Alacoque and Héloïse
are sisters. Let us leave them to their gods." Her earlier entry on Mariana Alco-
forado, the Portugese nun who was believed to be the author of the *Portugese
Letters,* written to the French lover who abandoned her, includes a wonderful
irony. The author of *Story of O,* a novel that many believed had to be written by
a man, notes that the identity of Mariana is not certain. "But one thing is impossible," she affirms, "that these letters were not written by a woman."[9] In fact,
recent scholarship has demonstrated that the letters were indeed written by a
man, Guilleragues, the seventeenth-century Frenchman who until recently was
thought to have been the person who found the letters of Mariana and translated them.

The conclusion to Dominique Aury's contribution on "Women of Letters"
celebrates her own generation as the beginning of a groundswell of writers
whose importance, in a future that turns out to be far less distant than she imagined, will be inevitable: "When, in a hundred years, the encyclopedia of *Femmes
célèbres* will have to be redone (like all encyclopedias), whatever our errors, how-

ever debatable our contribution, we will remain, we of the 1950s, witnesses to something new and irreversible. We are the anonymous soil. We are barely beginning and we are beginning today. Just wait."[10]

Édith Thomas, in her section on "Women and Power," wrote biographical entries for Queen Elizabeth, Christine of Sweden, and Catherine II of Russia as well as the general essay on queens and empresses. She notes that since monarchical power does not depend on the personal value of individuals but on their predestination for that role, Roman empresses were deified just as their husbands were. It was therefore not shocking that a woman, although considered inferior to a man, would exercise such power if she was destined to do so by her birth. In the subsection on political women, Thomas makes this pointed and disenchanted observation: "Women who have had a political role to play did not act differently than if they had been men. . . . Their actions are the result of a completely masculine civilization and merge completely with it. In the midst of the successive disasters called history, women, when they have been involved, have shown themselves to be neither better nor worse than the worst and best of men. They have shown as much cunning and intelligence, subtlety and toughness, courage and cynicism as men. In short, when they had the chance, they proved themselves in every way men's equals. Which is not always praise."[11]

Thomas reserves her genuine admiration for the different kind of political women she puts under the rubric of *humanisme féminin*. Her articles include biographical entries for, among others, Olympe de Gouges, Mary Wollstonecraft, Flora Tristan, Pauline Roland, Susan B. Anthony, and the woman she clearly considered a special soul mate, Rosa Luxembourg, quoting words which had become particularly resonant since her traumatic break with the Communist Party: "Freedom is always the freedom of those who think differently."[12]

Just before *Les Femmes célèbres* appeared in 1960, Thomas sent its publisher, the Éditions d'Art Lucien Mazenod, a proposal for a very different kind of history: "Les Fleurs du temps," a history of flowers and their artistic representation over the centuries in different cultures, including the Arab world and the Far East as well as the West. A carton at the Archives nationales has preserved Thomas's preparations: her preface, a draft of the text, documentation and correspondence, a list of illustrations she planned to use.[13] Lucien Mazenod regretfully turned down Thomas's "charming book project" for financial reasons.[14] In her thesis on Édith Thomas, Sonia Madrona has pointed out the "premature originality" of "Les Fleurs du temps," noting that such a book would be much more marketable in France today, when gardens are a frequent subject in magazines and on television, reflecting what has become a widespread leisure pastime.[15]

The unmitigated pleasure at the source of "Les Fleurs du temps" makes it unique in Thomas's work, an expression of the sensuous and indispensable role flowers played in her surroundings and her imagination. Her apartment, otherwise austere in its minimal furnishings, was always graced with an array of flowers, artfully arranged. In Édith's letters to Dominique, botanical references could become a tongue-in-cheek allusion to their relationship, as in this birthday letter of September 1948: "I'd like to bring you carnations or zinnias for your birthday. I'm just sending a sprig of ivy which, as everyone knows, is a symbol of fidelity. What I should send you is a bunch of ivy, whose sprigs branch out in every direction at once."[16]

A few years after the war, after the affair with Dominique had ended, Édith got to know Anne-Marie Bauer, an extraordinary woman who had become her neighbor on the rue Pierre-Nicole and with whom she enjoyed an enduring friendship as well as mutual admiration, without the volatile complexities of passion that defined her relationship with Dominique. "When we met," Anne-Marie said, "we both knew right away we were going to be very close. I had the sense of an encounter in the deepest sense of the word, a connection where one finds oneself. It was a great joy for me to know her, to talk with her. I knew I could always count on her, as she could always count on me."[17] The two women had long conversations about literature, a love they shared.

In the Resistance Bauer had been active in coding and decoding messages, transporting arms, and assisting escapes. She worked primarily with people who were right-wing but also with others who were Communists ("that was of no importance to me"), acting as a liaison between the group Libération Sud and London and checking terrain in the region from Savoie to the Massif Central for possible parachute landings. Although she wanted to participate in a parachuting operation, de Gaulle categorically refused to allow women to be involved. When she was captured in 1943, she was arrested "like a man this time" and given over to Klaus Barbie, who said to her, "You look Aryan and you have a German name. You will work with us." When she refused she was tortured by Barbie, shot with a blank bullet, and deported to Ravensbrück.[18] The ordeal left her with serious health problems for the rest of her life.

In certain respects, Thomas seems to have been a mentor for Bauer as well as a friend. Born into a family of boys, Bauer resented being a girl. Édith would say to her, simplifying her own ambivalent feelings about the question: "You're the opposite of a feminist. To be a feminist means to feel proud of being a woman, in all the meanings of that word. It doesn't make any sense to want to be a man." Anne-Marie also rejected her Jewishness. Blond and blue-eyed, she did not know she was Jewish or even that Jews existed until she was twelve years old.

Both her parents were from Alsace-Lorraine and like her Protestant friends, she wanted to become a missionary. Édith would reproach her: "I have two Jewish friends, Clara Malraux, who's proud of being Jewish, and you, who don't look Jewish and have no sense of what Jewishness means." Anne-Marie remembered an anecdote that Édith told her about an experience on a train after the war. She had found herself in a compartment with two women who, according to Édith, appeared semitic and were speaking loudly, and a third woman who observed them. When the first two got off the train, the other woman remarked to Édith: "You can certainly tell they're kikes, the way they carry on." Very calmly Édith replied: "But I too am Jewish, Madame," thoroughly enjoying the woman's discomfort.[19]

Although Édith often spoke to Anne-Marie about her passion for Dominique, she liked to see her friends separately, in tête-à-tête, and so Dominique did not meet Anne-Marie Bauer until Édith was dying at St. Antoine hospital. After Édith's death, Dominique offered to drive Anne-Marie to the funeral service in Sainte-Aulde, and they subsequently became friends. Dominique was intensely moved by Anne-Marie: "It is intolerable that this woman is still paying for the courage she showed as a young woman in her twenties." They discovered they were both anglophiles, and every Friday evening she would pick up Anne-Marie on the rue Pierre-Nicole to take her to rue Malakoff in the suburbs where they would have dinner in Dominique's apartment and read English poetry together. Shortly after I met Dominique for the first time, she told me they had discovered an astonishing American writer and wondered if I knew her work: a nineteenth-century poet by the name of Emily Dickinson.

Édith Thomas always felt too close to the events of the occupation and the Resistance to write about them as a historian. She transferred her passion for those years to the history of the Paris Commune, another period of repression and insurgency after a traumatic defeat inflicted on France by the Germans (1870–71). During the 1960s Édith Thomas wrote three studies which focused on that time, Les "Pétroleuses," translated as *The Women Incendiaries, Rossel,* and *Louise Michel,* all published by Gallimard and extensively reviewed.

The term *pétroleuses,* which Thomas puts in quotation marks in her title, was invented in 1871 as an epithet directed at the women who were accused of setting fire to Paris with cans of kerosene. In the preceding ten weeks, the people of Paris had taken charge of the city. During what the French call the *semaine sanglante,* the bloody week, from May 21 to 28 when military forces of the Thiers government in Versailles crushed the Paris uprising, women as well as men made a desperate defense against the troops whose firearms overwhelmed them.

The Communards burned many buildings, in order to deprive Versailles troops of shelter from which they could attack the barricades. Artillery shells fired by the forces of Versailles also caused a number of conflagrations. In neighborhoods occupied by Versailles forces, any woman who was poor and carrying a container of any kind, whether it was a bottle or a shopping basket, was accused of being a *pétroleuse* and sometimes killed on the spot. Although partisans of the Commune categorically denied the existence of *pétroleuses*, Thomas concludes from the available documentation that women of the Commune as well as men probably set fires. Often the same women participated in clubs and committees, cared for the wounded, and were soldiers on the last barricades. The full name of l'Union des femmes was the Women's Union for the Defense of Paris and the Care of the Wounded. The Women's Union clearly envisioned kerosene as a means of combat along with weapons. Thomas does not find evidence, however, to prove an organized participation of women in the fires.

Thomas uses the term *pétroleuses*, without any pejorative connotation, for all the women involved in the revolutionary social movement of 1871. In that sense, the English title *The Women Incendiaries*, without quotation marks, translates the symbolic as well as literal meaning she wanted to convey. All the contemporaries of the Commune uprising, whatever their politics, were struck by the massive and extraordinary importance of women's participation, whether the women were admired as heroines or deplored as viragos. Thomas seeks to determine who these women were, why they got involved in the uprising, which roles they played, and what they sought to achieve.

In contrast to her introductory remarks in *Pauline Roland*, which highlight history as art, she emphasizes here the "rigorous science" that is a necessary part of the historical method. At the same time, she insists on the inevitability and legitimacy of subjective interpretation, especially for a period as controversial as the Commune. As she specifies elsewhere, "historians are also witnesses, although once removed [*au deuxième degré*]." Historical interpretation will be different depending on whether the uprising is considered a justified revolt against the defeat of France and against social injustice, or as a criminal subversion of the established order. However, she makes clear that the historian's commitment, no matter how passionate, can never be an authorization to keep silent about embarrassing documents, or to mask the truth, which, "like Janus, always has two faces."[20]

Édith Thomas's family history was linked to both sides of the conflict. Her paternal grandmother supported the government in Versailles; on her mother's side, her grandmother approved the Commune, although she does not seem to have played an active role. In Thomas's introduction, for the first time in her historical writing, she brings to bear her own experience, specifically her participation in 1944 in the Union of French Women, for which she wrote tracts and prepared demonstrations, as helping her to understand the women of the Commune: "The barricades of 1944," she writes, "replied to the barricades of 1871."[21] It should be added, however, that the barricades in 1944 were barricades of liberation after four years of occupation; the barricades of 1871 were barricades of despair.

Elsewhere in the book she notes "a reversal of position of which we have seen other examples," by those who had rejected war but found themselves, "when their country was invaded, fighting in the front ranks."[22] Although she does not offer examples, the analogy she has in mind is clear. The people of Paris considered the Franco-Prussian War of Napoleon III against Bismarck a dynastic conflict that was not worth fighting. After the war ended with Bismarck's victory, Parisians at the forefront of the Commune opposed the national government, then headed by Thiers and the National Assembly at Versailles, as both reactionary and too ready to accept a humiliating peace with Prussia. In 1940, after France was defeated and invaded by Nazi Germany, many of the leftist pacifists of the 1920s and early 1930s were among the first ranks of combatants in the Resistance.

Women identified the social revolution of the Commune with their own emancipation, although the two movements were often at odds. One of the mentors for male Communards was the misogynist socialist Proudhon, who defined women as "housekeepers or courtesans." In that spirit, the French section of the Internationale presented a memorandum in 1866 against women working outside the home. Women participating in the Commune consisted primarily of working women who earned barely enough to survive. Many needed to resort to prostitution to supplement their daytime income and feed their children. Among the measures they drafted were a transformation of work conditions; recognition of free unions (unmarried couples living together); rights for all children, including those born outside marriage; equal salaries for men and women; day care for children of working mothers; and free, obligatory and secular education for all, whatever the social position of the parents.

Édith Thomas draws vivid portraits of many individuals in the women's groups. Along with her focus on a collective movement, she brings to life particular persons behind the statistics, each one "unique and irreplaceable in her own single being." One of the most flamboyant characters is the milliner Blanche Lefebvre, who made eloquent speeches at the club for social revolution wearing a red scarf, with a pistol at her waist. Tall, thin, and dark-skinned, she loved the revolution "as others love a man."[23] During the bloody week of May 21–28, Blanche Lefebvre was killed on the barricades by government forces. Thomas is equally sympathetic to a far more ambiguous and less known figure, the brilliant journalist André Leo (her masculine pseudonym), who did not hesitate to criticize the errors and excesses of the Commune, in spite of her devotion to its goals.

Édith Thomas's last biography, completed just before her death and published posthumously in 1971, was devoted to Louise Michel, leader and symbol of the Commune. Thomas had been intrigued by the figure of Louise Michel at least since 1939, when she wrote an extended article about her for the pro-Communist journal *Commune*. In protest against the signing of the Nazi-Soviet pact a few months later, she asked the editor, Jacques Decour, to withdraw her article from plans for publication. The manuscript of 1939 presents Louise Michel as unambiguously heroic in her revolutionary ardor and her lifelong commitment to the idea of anarchism. When Thomas returned to Louise Michel thirty years later, her own political evolution during that time, reinforced by her reading of the mass of documents available, led her to a more ambivalent point of view. While all the evidence confirms her perception of Louise Michel's courage and unshakable convictions, what changed was Thomas's relation to a revolutionary faith that never questions and never reflects on its assumptions. "Hagiography," she declares in the introduction, "is always unsatisfactory."[24] Indeed her book, unlike the 1939 article, gives no indication that she was even slightly tempted to engage in heroine worship.

She does see Louise Michel as the grandmother of the French revolt of May 1968, which she enthusiastically supported, notwithstanding her reservations after the abrupt end of that extraordinary month during which everything seemed possible. She imagines Louise Michel on the barricades encouraging the protesting students, although most of them "did not know that their protest (which they thought they were inventing) was in fact the continuation of an old tradition." With inevitable vagueness she defines anarchy as "the absence of government, the direct administration by people of their own lives."[25] Since anarchy, in contrast to communism, was never incarnated anywhere, the hope for freedom it represented could remain intact.

An attentive reader cannot help being aware that Thomas's irritation with her protagonist is at least equal to her admiration. Comparing Louise Michel's voluminous memoirs with documents by her contemporaries, she discovered the extent to which Michel fictionalized her life when it did not fit her self-image, eliminating everything in her early life that might seem to contradict what she subsequently became—although Thomas pointedly insists on the "inner logic" between her early religion and later revolutionary faith. Michel chose to remain silent about the fervently pious young girl who was deeply involved with her church, and presented herself instead as a revolutionary since childhood. Louise Michel's sentimental romanticism found expression in an exalted writing style replete with hyperbole and imprecation, unchastened by any trace of nuance or self-doubt. In her speeches as well as her writing she was intoxicated with the persona she incarnated, the vanquished Commune and the revolution eternally reborn. She became an anarchist in the name of the credo that government should be by all the people for all the people; that human beings are good and power is bad. However, Thomas points out, the Commune died not because "power is a curse," in Louise Michel's formulation, but the contrary, because of "its own inability to organize revolutionary power with which to fight the power of Versailles. The Commune died of the impotence that resulted from its own petty squabbles and disorganization."[26] All her adult life, Michel's Manichean moral universe remained unchanged, a world that consisted of oppressors and victims, traitors and martyrs to the cause.

Thomas still found much to admire in Louise Michel, who had the positive qualities that were the counterpart of her faults. Throughout her life she showed an unfailing solidarity with those who were poor and oppressed. During the Commune, she helped the wounded, organized food distribution, and took up arms. She was a fearless combatant, inspiring others by her example. When the Commune was defeated and the forces of Versailles arrested her, she brazenly demanded the death sentence; instead she was condemned to be deported to New Caledonia. Although efforts for a pardon were made on her behalf in France by her numerous friends and allies, Louise Michel refused to consider special treatment and stayed in New Caledonia until 1880, when a total amnesty was promulgated for the Communards. She returned to Paris in triumph and launched a new career as a speaker for the revolution. Her charisma attracted huge crowds all over France, made up of those who adored her and those who hated her, until her death twenty-five years later. After one of her lectures, when she was wounded by a would-be assassin's bullet, she refused to press charges, declaring, "I admire him, because he is a man who, for once in his life, acted on his convictions." At the end of her life, she was horrified by the new Marxist church she saw being born, a new papacy with its own "infallible hierarchy." She predicted its consequence: "the best, the wisest of men will turn out to be worse than those they seek to replace in power."[27]

Thomas reserves her unqualified admiration for Louise Michel's actions in New Caledonia. In prison, waiting for the sentence to be carried out, she prepared for her voyage as if it were a scientific mission she was undertaking voluntarily, and learned as much as she could about the region. While she was there, she studied the customs and languages of the indigenous New Caledonians and taught them how to read. She became a friend of El Mokrani, the Algerian chief who had led the Kabyle insurrection in 1871. In 1878, during the New Caledonians' revolt, she took their side against the French, seeing in their rebellion another version of the struggle of workers in the Commune—in contrast to the racist views of most of the Communards deported with her, who rallied to the side of the whites. In that situation, Thomas notes, Louise Michel was a precursor: "In her day, when people 'of the left' looked at colonization, they saw only the benefits being given a primitive people by a superior civilization."[28]

14

WARTIME TRUTHS

La Question and Algeria; *Rossel*

In 1956, after the Soviet intervention in Hungary, Thomas became vice-president of a group founded by Louis Martin-Chauffier which they called Union des Écrivains pour la Vérité (Writers' Union for the Truth). "Truth" was taken in its meaning of opposition to propaganda that was demonstrably false, whether it came from the French government, the USSR, or elsewhere. The Union, which defined itself as a leftist group against fascism, consisted largely of people who had been fellow travelers or members of the Communist Party. Their former allegiance led to divergent positions: there were those who refused common action with the Communists, those who were convinced that no leftist politics could be effective without the significant popular support the Party represented, and those who found themselves sometimes on one side, sometimes on the other. After her own experience with Communist methods, Thomas felt at home in a pluralist group that emphasized individual freedom to make decisions.

Although the initial impetus to form such a group came from opposition to Soviet actions, the major concern of its members soon became Algeria, where the French government fought a traumatic and bloody war from 1954 to 1962 against Algerian independence. For the majority of the French, Algeria was not a colony but a part of France and could not be "abandoned." In a climate of increasing government distortions of the truth produced by the contradictions of that war, the Writers' Union focused on what it considered ethical rather than political issues. Some in the group, like Édith Thomas, supported Algerian independence from the beginning; others gradually evolved in that direction. Group members saw their role as protecting essential freedoms of information, research, and expression, in the name of which they protested against the frequent seizure of newspapers, journals, and books in France as well as in Algeria. Thomas became part of the steering committee, which prepared a monthly notebook of previously unpublished material about the war.

In the summer of 1957 Aury wrote a letter to Thomas from her country home praising an article Thomas had written, "which is creating quite a stir." However, she wants to make this "slight addition" to what Thomas has said:

> No, the minor bureaucrats, the minor colonists [in Algeria] are not as racist as the major ones, they are ten times more so. As are the anti-Spanish, anti-Czech, anti-Polish, anti-Italian peasants here. The woman we found to do housework ... who used to be married to a Parisian butcher, left him for one of the Tahitians in de Gaulle's security guard, whom she married and went away with ten years ago. She came back with a ravishing little girl who looks like a Gauguin painting, and the husband, as nice as you could wish. The poor fellow is despised and hated by all your good local communists—a dirty Negro, that's what he is. They all read *l'Huma*[*nité*] and consider us, of course, exploiters of poor working people.[1]

It is difficult to imagine that Édith would have quarreled with Dominique's observations.

In her anticommunist focus, Aury makes no reference to the subject of Thomas's article "De la torture" (On torture), a passionate and eloquent polemic against what had become institutionalized practice in France's colonial war. Thomas's article was one of a growing number of protests published that year in the press by intellectuals of all political and religious persuasions. The "stir" to which Aury refers was in all likelihood occasioned by the unexpected context in which Thomas began her denunciation of torture: the French Resistance. She notes that she and others entered the Resistance not only in revulsion against German occupiers on French land but also in revulsion against Nazi ideology. She then reveals publicly for the first time what she had previously confided only in her unpublished memoir: her discovery, during a trip to the maquis, that certain *résistants* had been guilty of torturing members of the militia to "make them talk." The article also evokes her own eye-opening discovery, in Algeria during the 1930s, of French settlers' contempt for the Arabs and Kabyles they had colonized.

Thomas's criticism of French workers—as well as the Communist Party—is far stronger than Aury's letter suggests. The Party, concerned about alienating its constituency of working families whose sons were fighting in Algeria, remained hesitant and equivocal in its position on independence, especially since the war continued to have widespread popular support. Workers in metropolitan France showed little solidarity with the Algerians who labored with them in factories and menial jobs but were treated as pariahs in French society. "I fear," Thomas writes, "that racism is not just the vice of a few of the privileged, but that it has deeply infected our entire people." The sentence that follows is the one alluded to by Aury: "In Algeria the minor bureaucrats, the *petits colons*, are just as racist as the major ones." Thomas concludes her article with a plea to "the people who invented human rights," whatever their politics, to agree on at least one point, the absolute refusal of recourse to "that method of government" called torture.[2] Several months later Thomas wrote a more extended article about torture, giving it the same title, in which she repeats her maquis story and the reaction of the Communist official to whom she reported it. Her article, which begins with the war in Algeria, is a study of the history of torture, from Antiquity to the contemporary period.[3]

Thomas's public protest against torture dates from 1946, long before the beginning of the Algerian war, although she did not disclose then the Resistance incident in the maquis that so dismayed her. She calls her 1946 article "Si nous montions d'un degré" (Suppose we moved up a step), alluding to a poem by Paul Éluard. The article recounts a conversation she happened to overhear between two boys about sixteen or seventeen years old. They were not discussing what she would have expected in the immediate postwar period, with its shortages of almost everything: the black market, or how to get a good deal exchanging sugar for cigarettes or bicycle tires. They were debating with great seriousness whether it was all right to use torture and under what conditions, a conversation that would have been unthinkable ten years earlier.[4] In Thomas's biography of *Louise Michel*, describing the interrogation after Michel's arrest by the forces of Versailles, she will caustically note: "In that period, people had not yet reinvented torture, which had been abolished at the end of the eighteenth century in all civilized countries. In the meantime we have reestablished these methods and made great progress in applying them."[5] The conversation Thomas overhears in 1946 demonstrates to her the contagion of Nazi methods, which has made torture something that can be considered, as long as it is applied to the enemy.

Early in 1958 the Éditions de Minuit published *La Question* by Henri Alleg, a journalist and member of the Algerian Communist Party. The "question" of the title is that of torture. In addition to its cognate meaning in English, *la question* in French has the historical meaning of torture inflicted to obtain a confession. Alleg's book, an exposé of France's systematic policy of torture in Algeria, recounts his own ordeal of arrest and torture by French parachutists. Government authorities seized *La Question* shortly after it appeared; its publisher, Jérôme Lindon, was accused of offending the morale and honor of the army. The French government suspended news magazines of broad circulation, including *L'Express* and *France Observateur,* which had discussed *La Question* and urged people to read it, in an attempt to halt the book's distribution. As a result, the book circulated clandestinely.

One of Édith Thomas's functions, as director of the scholarly library for personnel of the Archives nationales, was to acquire books of historical interest. She ordered *La Question* as soon as it was published and exhibited the book on the special display table for new acquisitions. A colleague, furious that she had the nerve not only to buy such a book for the Archives but then to put it on display, ripped *La Question* into pieces and left it, in its mangled state, on the table. Thomas immediately bought a second copy. This time she displayed it in a glass cabinet with bars, to which she had the key.[6]

Thomas had always been ambivalent about Charles de Gaulle. Her underground poem cited by de Gaulle in Algiers in 1943 evokes the Resistance hero who has crossed the sea to lead "a triumphant army." At the same time, like many on the left, she resented the assumption of all those in France and abroad who believed that without de Gaulle, the Resistance would have had no credibility and no impact. She was also deeply suspicious of de Gaulle's imperious style, and she feared that once in power, he might move the country to dictatorship. However, his actions after the liberation showed the left's fundamental misunderstanding of his relation to power. Although he was unanimously elected provisional president of France in November 1945, he chose to resign a few months later when it became clear that his views against a regime controlled by political parties would not prevail in the new constitution for the Fourth Republic.

In 1958 the crisis in Algeria brought France to the brink of what many thought would be civil war. Enraged by rumors of possible French negotiations with the FLN (the Algerian revolution's Front de Libération Nationale), a group of generals took over power in Algiers, formed a Committee of Public Safety, and demanded a government of Public Safety in Paris that could be led, they declared, only by de Gaulle. A few days later, paratroopers in Algiers threatened to land on Paris. Although there was no actual coup d'état, de Gaulle came to power as a result of the army's sedition. By a significant majority, the National Assembly voted to grant him the right to govern by decree for six months and the authority to write a new constitution for what would become the present Fifth Republic.

Although most intellectuals on the left were hostile to de Gaulle's return, fearing a fascist takeover, a letter written by Thomas to her mother during the week of June 19, 1958, gives expression to a paradoxical analysis that proved to be correct.

> I do not rejoice any more than you do [she writes] at the dictatorship of the generals. But one fact is certain: de Gaulle is settling our relationship with Tunisia [by the evacuation of French military forces] as the "left" wished would happen and in spite of the declarations of the "right." If ever Mendès-France had done that, we would have heard the troublemakers screaming about "abandonment"! Perhaps this man of the right, brought to power by its most extreme elements, will carry out a policy acceptable to the left, whereas the men of the left sent to Parliament by the elections of January 1956 are carrying out a colonial policy with special powers given to them by—the Communists."[7]

The men of the left to whom she refers are those in the Socialist government of Guy Mollet who proclaimed that the ties between France and Algeria were "indissoluble." The National Assembly, including the Communist deputies, granted Mollet special powers after his election in 1956 to reestablish "order" in Algeria.

In another letter to her mother during the same week of June 1958, Thomas speaks of her "mitigated confidence" in de Gaulle.[8] She believed that antifascists should support rather than attack him, to prevent his becoming the prisoner of the right-wing extremists who brought him to power and whom she saw as representing the real danger of fascism in France. A year later, de Gaulle proposed self-determination to the Algerians, a decision that ran counter to the wishes of three quarters of the people who had supported him. His declaration accelerated the radicalization of those elements in the army who were determined to keep Algeria French, whatever the cost.[9] The mutinous OAS (Organisation de l'Armée Secrète), led by high-ranking officers, launched a campaign of terrorist attacks in Algiers.

On the left, militant support for Algerian independence took the form of a network that gave material assistance to the FLN. In September 1960 the "Manifesto of the 121" was signed by well-known writers and intellectuals, including Sartre and Simone de Beauvoir. They proclaimed the "right to insubordination," justifying those who refused to fight against the Algerians and those who gave aid and protection to the FLN. A number of militants, called *porteurs de valises* (literally, suitcase carriers, a metaphor for those who sought to assist the FLN in any capacity), had already been tried and imprisoned. Earlier that year, Édith Thomas became involved in a new group, Vérité-Liberté (Truth-Freedom), specifically committed to distributing seized documents about the Algerian war.

Government authorities had forbidden publication of the manifesto, or "any text concerning the situation in Algeria which they considered inopportune for the public to see."[10] Vérité-Liberté decided to publish the Manifesto of the 121. Following an investigation and a police search in the offices of the journal *Esprit,* Thomas and others on the steering committee were briefly arrested as they were preparing a meeting of the group. Along with many others in Vérité-Liberté, for diverse reasons, Thomas had chosen not to sign the manifesto. Her own decision was based on the conviction that one does not have the right to sign a document that creates risks for others when minimal risk is involved for oneself. By signing that paper, she felt she would be encouraging young men to refuse to fight in Algeria, with serious consequences for them, while she herself would not suffer comparable punishment.[11]

The war did not officially come to an end until the conference at Evian in March 1962 when France finally recognized the sovereignty of the Algerian state. Even as the accords were being signed, the OAS staged a putsch against de Gaulle's authority, unleashing a bloody battle in the hope that the FLN would respond in kind and force the French army to intervene alongside the OAS, rekindling the war. Their strategy failed. On de Gaulle's orders, the army intervened against the OAS. In the referendum in France a month later, over 90 percent expressed their approval of Algerian independence. In Algeria, virtually the entire population of Europeans, distrustful of the guaranties of Evian, fled to France in an exodus of panic, ending 130 years of colonial rule in what they had considered their North African French homeland.

Édith Thomas wrote only one biography of a man, *Rossel (1844–1871),* a military officer who also became a figure of resistance during the period that is the focus of most of her historical writings. Colonel Louis-Nathaniel Rossel deserted the army in indignation after France's defeat in the Franco-Prussian War. He then joined the Commune, resigned a few months later, and was executed by the government in 1871 at the age of twenty-seven. It is Édith Thomas's most astonishing biography, in both the choice and the treatment of its subject. As we shall see, some reviewers of Thomas's book compared Rossel to de Gaulle, the *résistant* of 1940: Rossel was a de Gaulle who failed.

In addition to published work and material available in public archives, Thomas's biography of Rossel is based on private documents she was able to obtain from descendants of his family. In her introduction she records an imaginary dialogue with his mother, father, and two sisters, who want to know what she's going to do with all this information about their beloved "Lisé," his nickname in the family. They are suspicious of her as a historian of the Commune, concerned that she will use him, try to make of Rossel a Communard, have him follow her own sympathies. She reassures them that she will not make Rossel say anything he did not say himself, that she is interested in who this man was, even if he leads her in directions she does not want to go. What initially attracts her to Rossel is what she calls the "style" of his successive resignations, which seem contradictory but express a consistent fidelity to his conscience. Ultimately, both sides in the conflict rejected him. The Versaillais and their inheritors rejected him because he betrayed their class and their army. Communards and their descendants didn't like him any better, since he left them.

Rossel was born into a Protestant family of career military officers, from Nîmes on his father's side, from Scotland on his mother's side, and was trained in engineering at the École Polytechnique. He read widely in literature, history, and philosophy but, strikingly, given the turn in his destiny, showed no interest at all in any of the socialist theories of the time, Marxist or utopian. Although he was indifferent to religion, Thomas sees Rossel as very much a Protestant: scrupulous, puritanical, constantly questioning his conscience, hard on himself, and reliant on his own interpretations of texts, sacred or not. He was promoted to captain and then colonel, but superiors noted his Protestantism with suspicion: "In the [French] army," she remarks, "being Protestant or Jewish is a presumption of dissidence."[12] Liberal and reformist in his thinking, he was hostile to the Emperor Napoleon III, an opinion he kept to himself. For the pleasure of perfecting his English and deepening his knowledge of liberal philosophy, he translated John Stuart Mill's *On Liberty*. He did not particularly like the military and thought of resigning so he could claim his political rights as a citizen and develop his many other talents.

In family letters, Rossel showed his brilliance and often a playful humor. However, his puritan upbringing made him stiff and awkward with women other than his sisters. When he began to think about marriage, his aunt suggested Suzanne Paulhan, the daughter of a family from Nîmes, also Protestant. Both families decided she would be a good match for Louis-Nathaniel. Suzanne, Thomas tells us, was the aunt of the writer Jean Paulhan. Rossel felt neither affection nor antipathy for her, and the idea of an arranged "good match" chilled him. But he did want to marry, especially since he found himself increasingly concerned about his tendency to be a loner. A few months later, he met the first young woman who warmed his heart. In the eyes of his family, however, she had a terrible flaw: she was Catholic. Although they were liberal in their views in many other respects, they were appalled at the idea of a "mixed" marriage and remained unconvinced by Louis-Nathaniel's argument that every marriage is mixed in one way or another, since there are always differences on important issues. When his mother finally agreed, in good faith or bad, to write to Marie's family, her mother responded politely that Marie was still too young to be married. It is not clear whether Marie was aware of Louis-Nathaniel's feelings or his desire to marry her.

On July 19, 1870, the Emperor Napoleon III, ill and faltering, declared war against Bismark's Prussia, although in comparison to the Germans, French military preparation was inferior and its arms were inadequate. Colonel Rossel, garrisoned in Bourges, requested active duty with the engineering regiment in Metz. When he arrived, the succession of French defeats had already begun. Disgusted with the generals, Rossel wrote a memorandum that called for a change of military strategy to a form of guerrilla warfare that would enable the struggle to continue. Meanwhile, after news of the disaster of Sedan on September 1 reached Paris, a bloodless revolution occurred which deposed Napoleon III and proclaimed a new republic with a government of national defense. In Metz General Bazaine, finding his garrison surrounded by the Prussians, handed over the city and the army.

When Bazaine decided to remain loyal to the Empire of Napoleon III, Rossel chose to take sides with the new republic and, in his words, "sacrifice my duty as a soldier for my duty as a citizen."[13] Refusing to accept French defeat, furious at Bazaine's capitulation, he made a number of journeys to try to enlist the support of other generals for his plans. At the same time, he briefly reconsidered a project he had been thinking about since his student days at the École Polytechnique: to leave the army and go to America, where he could start a new career as a railroad engineer.

On January 28, 1871, the new government of Louis-Adolphe Thiers signed an armistice with Prussia ceding most of the provinces of Alsace and Lorraine. In Paris, the Prussians were to occupy the forts and take over war material. The Thiers government, more worried about the people of Paris than about the Prussians, decided to seize the cannons that the population had taken from the *beaux quartiers* to hill sites of the working-class neighborhoods in Montmartre, Belleville, and the Buttes Chaumont. The army entered Paris during the night of March 18, but housewives had given an alert that morning. A strange spectacle ensued, which Édith Thomas had described in detail in *The Women Incendiaries:* the line of soldiers let itself be disarmed by women and fraternized with the Parisian National Guard. The cannons remained with the people and the army was given the order to leave Paris, while Thiers fled to Versailles.

Rossel, who had still been hesitating in his plans, decided to join the insurgents in Paris. On March 19 he wrote a letter of resignation to the Ministry of War in Versailles in which he declared that with two parties engaged in struggle, "I place myself without hesitation on the side of that party which did not sign the peace and which does not count in its ranks generals guilty of capitulation." All of Rossel can be found in that letter, Édith Thomas remarks, with his rectitude, his courage, and the insolence of his conventional closing formula: "I have the honor of being, my general, your very obedient and devoted servant."[14] When he arrived in Paris, this liberal republican immediately offered his services to the revolutionary socialists who made up the Commune.

From the beginning Rossel was caught up in intrigues that undermined the movement, impeded its struggle against Versailles, and finally led to its destruction. In spite of his sympathies, he found himself as a military man frustrated by this army of citizens, which was incapable of disciplined action because they endlessly discussed each order they received. When he wanted to exclude a disorderly group in the battalion he was given, the Commune officers arrested him, then decided they needed him and named him chief of staff in their War Ministry. Although the Commune gave him titles, it did not allow him real power. Many Communards suspected him of harboring dictatorial ambitions. On May 9, 1871, after numerous attempts at reorganizing the army, when it became clear to Rossel that the revolution was lost and the military situation had deteriorated too far for any hope of victory, he wrote a letter of resignation to the Commune as remarkable as his letter to the government of Versailles: "Provisionally charged by you to be War Delegate, I feel incapable of bearing any longer the responsibility of a command in which everyone deliberates and no one obeys." The situation left him with only two options, "to break the obstacle which blocks my action or to withdraw." He would not break the obstacle "because the obstacle is you" and he would not violate public sovereignty. Therefore he chose to withdraw.[15]

While the Commune deliberated on his case, he took refuge in a hotel on the boulevard St. Germain under a pseudonym. On June 7, after a denunciation, the Versailles police found Rossel in his hiding place and arrested the man they considered to be War Delegate of the Commune. He was accused of desertion to the enemy, participation in an attempt to excite civil war, and bearing arms against France. Édith Thomas's narrative of Rossel's imprisonment, his trial, the appeal for a pardon, his death sentence, and his execution are among the most moving pages she wrote, bringing together her best talents as a novelist and a historian.

Like *The Women Incendiaries*, *Rossel* was widely and sympathetically received. Many reviews as well as a number of personal letters evoke a name that is strikingly absent from her study: Charles de Gaulle. Rossel, they point out, is reminiscent of the attitude of the man of June 18, 1940, in his patriotism, his stubbornness, and his pride. Both men were accused of being motivated by personal ambition and dictatorial desires. A sense of honor drove Rossel in 1871, like de Gaulle in 1940, to continue the struggle against the Germans and a dishonorable, cowardly French government (Thiers or Pétain) considered illegitimate. In other circumstances, and with more allies, Rossel might have emerged as a highly effective resistance leader. De Gaulle, who was condemned in absentia by Pétain for treason, would have suffered a fate analogous to that of Rossel had his resistance failed. In prison Rossel read intensively about Joan of Arc, a heroine for de Gaulle as well, in whom he found a fellow warrior and a sister. As one reviewer put it, Rossel at twenty-seven years old "thought he was Joan—or, if one prefers, de Gaulle."[16]

A recurring subtext of *Rossel* suggests its protagonist as a *résistant*. Thomas's chapter "In the Service of the Resistance" tells the story of Rossel's "no" to the army of Thiers and his attempts to find a way of continuing the struggle after France's acceptance of defeat by the Germans. Édith Thomas embraces him in his failures: he failed as a Versailles officer, failed as a revolutionary, and succeeded only in saving his conscience. In prison, in notes for himself and his family, Rossel writes: "I have to say that I prefer, in spite of everything, . . . to have fought with the vanquished of the Commune rather than the victors of Versailles." In her conclusion she describes Rossel as first of all a free conscience, a Protestant who continued the tradition of the Camisards, those "who refuse the constraints of powers and laws when they undermine the inalienable right to freedom." In that tradition Rossel would not continue to serve a cause when it became no more than "an appearance without content," which she sees as an experience he lived through twice in his military career. In Rossel's eyes, the government of Versailles did not defend France and the government of the Commune did not defend its revolution. Therefore, she argues, a deeper fidelity to the cause he thought he had chosen led him to his two resignations, contradictory only in appearance.[17]

That fundamental paradox of Rossel, which underlies the entire book, speaks to Édith Thomas's own experience and her need to see her actions as coherent. In an interview following the publication of *Rossel* she comments: "To remain in accord with oneself, simply to be logical from one day to the next, it is necessary, more than once, to 'resign' and to risk appearing, in the eyes of others, incoherent."[18] After Thomas wrote her first novel in the early 1930s, she received a literary prize from a right-wing jury and immediately decided to join a revolutionary writers' group. A few months later she resigned, having found her commitment as a writer in contradiction with the demand for ideological orthodoxy. However, the traumatic and defining experience that crystallized the paradox of Rossel in her own life was her resignation from the Communist Party. In order to break the intolerable contradiction of belonging to a party that claimed to embody the truth of the times but constantly lied, and to remain faithful to the need for truth that had inspired her to join that party in the first place, she needed to resign. Resigning in the name of a fundamental commitment thus became for Thomas, as it did for Rossel, an expression of both fidelity and coherence.

She was also attracted to Rossel's support for women's equality. In contrast to many partisans of the Commune who were as imbued with misogyny as their bourgeois adversaries, he did not hesitate to call on women's energy and skills to help the cause. Just before the end, early in May, when the journalist André Leo (her masculine pseudonym) urged women to fight for the Commune, Rossel responded to her personally with a number of specific suggestions. Before the war, he was supportive of his sister Bella's desire to pursue higher education at a time when the Sorbonne was closed to women. He provided the moral and financial support for Bella to enroll in courses that gave her a teaching diploma, along with only two other young women, although he was too traditional to accept the idea of her earning her own living. Édith Thomas clearly heard personal echoes of her own relationship with Gérard in the abiding fraternal love between Louis-Nathaniel and Bella.

The particular quality of Édith Thomas's intimacy with Rossel, this young puritan who never loved a woman outside his family, is unlike that of any of her other biographies. When Colonel Rossel was executed at the age of twenty-seven, he was probably still a virgin. Her interpretation of his life, while remaining faithful to the historical record, projects both romantic admiration and maternal tenderness. Many passages convey a desire to protect and rescue him from the slander of those who did not understand him. Previously inaccessible personal documents, along with the extensive public record, allow her to create an image of Rossel that makes him into an unlikely soul mate. In Rossel she found the ideal lover, child, and brother she could imaginatively have to herself.

15

ENDINGS

Among the many responses Thomas received after the publication of *Rossel* was a letter from Jean Paulhan in December 1967, his first direct communication to her since he ended their relationship fifteen years earlier. He begins: "I should have found a better way to tell you how much I liked your introduction, and the entire book."[1] The allusion contained in that conditional past tense is unclear; it could refer to remarks he asked Dominique to convey to Édith or to an awkward encounter. Although there is no mention of the long silence between them, Paulhan's letter is his way of ending their quarrel.

A few months earlier, in August, Dominique had written Édith to invite her for a weekend at the country home in Boissise that Paulhan had bought for her, a place where they often spent weekends and vacations together. She wanted Édith to be aware that the invitation came from Paulhan, "who really wants to be reconciled." "I let him know," Dominique adds, "that he took his time about it."[2] She thinks his change of heart came about because of *Rossel,* and because of news, in June 1967, of the sudden death of Gérard. Enclosed in Paulhan's December letter about *Rossel* is a note about Gérard, which begins with the same grammar, a past conditional tense of guilt or regret: "I should have told you earlier that I was saddened by the death of your brother. I had always heard about him as a man who was just and fine: infinitely rare."[3]

Gérard had been plagued with severe health problems all his adult life. For twenty years, from 1937 to 1957, his Pott's disease, a progressive deterioration of the bones of the vertebral column, made it impossible for him to exercise his profession as a lawyer. Parts of his lungs and some of his ribs had to be removed to help him breathe. His son Daniel remembers the draconian hygiene precautions observed by the family to avoid the risk of infection. The two boys were never embraced or even touched by their father, since children were considered to be especially vulnerable to the contagion of tuberculosis. Although Gérard lived with recurrent pain and constricted breathing, he refused to talk about what he suffered. "My personal misfortunes are of no interest to anyone," he said to Daniel.[4] Stoicism in everyday life was his way of mastering his illness.

For Édith, with the exception of his stern disapproval when she resigned from the Communist Party, Gérard was someone to whom she could always turn for moral support. After her initial bout with tuberculosis of the bone and until she met Dominique, this austere man of uncompromising integrity was her closest confidant, even for her romantic and sexual dilemmas. When she lost her virginity in 1941, she wrote gleefully to Gérard: "I took the plunge!"[5] Gérard's letters to his mother about Édith from Arcachon in 1939, as well as those to his sister just before he died in 1967, show a constant affection and concern for her well-being.

Gérard's legal career in Grenoble was devoted to workers' rights. In June 1967, as he was pleading a case, he suddenly could no longer speak and fell to the floor. A massive stroke left him close to death, in a coma and brain damaged. Madeleine, Gérard's wife, later recalled speaking to Édith during the preparations for the funeral: "We are the two people who loved him the most. From now on we will have to live without him. I know your pain is as great as mine. In memory of our love for Gérard, we should be very close to each other." When she approached her sister-in-law to embrace her, Édith recoiled. "No. Don't kiss me. There will always be between us what you said to me, in 1934 or maybe 1935. I haven't forgotten."

During those prewar years, Madeleine worked as a librarian at the Ministry of Foreign Affairs on the quai d'Orsay in Paris. In Madeleine's telling, when she returned home after a long day, looking forward to being alone with her husband, as often as not Édith would be in the house, visiting her brother. One evening the two women argued over the priority of their intimacy with Gérard. Exasperated, Madeleine had the last word: "I'm his wife. I can give him what you cannot." Édith never forgave her, even thirty-two years later at her brother's funeral.[6]

Yet the two women had just shared an extraordinary if ambiguous complicity. When Édith learned her brother had been stricken, she immediately went to Grenoble to be with him at the hospital. Gérard, in a coma, was under a tent, breathing in hisses, his face contorted in what looked to both women like unbearable pain. Madeleine was terrified that her husband would survive diminished, no longer himself. Édith pressed her: "He can't stay like this. We must do something for him. You have to make a decision." But it was Édith who made the decision, insisting that her sister-in-law persuade the nurse to administer an extra dose of morphine. Madeleine, in a fog, complied. A few tears ran down Gérard's cheek when he died, which may have been physiological, but Madeleine was deeply affected. She was angry with herself and with Édith, feeling that Édith had forced her hand.[7] It is revealing that in Édith's version of the story, as she recounted it to Dominique, it was she rather than the nurse who gave Gérard the second injection of morphine, to end his suffering. "It takes courage to kill the person one loves the most," Dominique said to me.

Édith's mourning for her brother took the form of a long, imaginary letter she wrote to him a few months after his death, adding to it periodically until the following summer. She begins with an epigraph from the Baal-Shem-Tov, the Russian Jew who founded modern Hasidism in the eighteenth century: "In memory lies the secret of redemption." That quote ties her letter to *Le Témoin compromis* and to her historical biographies as well. "Haven't I given many years," she notes, "to bringing the dead back to life—Pauline Roland, the women of the Commune, Rossel? Why shouldn't I do for you, for me, for this time in which we have lived, what I have tried to do for others?"[8]

However, in the handwritten pages she addresses simply "To my brother," pages even more difficult to decipher than her diary, she makes no attempt to shape her memories and does not imagine a reader other than herself. She writes to revive her brother's presence and pretend he is still alive, in the hope that she will occasionally be taken in by her fiction. Although she describes the free association that characterizes the letter as "a little repellent" to what she thinks of as her Cartesian mind, she writes as therapy to avoid recourse to a psychoanalyst or a "miracle worker"—the two being hardly different to her mind, each partaking in the illusion of a magic cure.

Those who knew Gérard or knew about him, from Jean Paulhan to close friends, considered him a man of exceptional integrity and selflessness: "Your brother was one of those men who honor the causes they serve," one of Gérard's colleagues said to Édith.[9] In a rare tribute to her sister-in-law, Édith notes that for the funeral service Madeleine refused to allow the spectacle of the black and red robes of his profession, deciding that it would have seemed like a masquerade in La Bâtie, the village in the Vercors Mountains where the family lived. She opted instead for a service with a minimum of ceremony. When I interviewed Madeleine Thomas in 1991, she was eighty-five years old, a sprightly, alert woman who lived alone with her dogs in the same mountain village and still belonged to the Communist Party. She spent her time reading Charles Dickens, E. R. Tolkien, Icelandic sagas, and *L'Humanité*.

In her letter to her brother Édith compulsively returns to his allegiance to the Communist Party and her own reasons for resigning, as if she is still defending herself in a trial she cannot quite win in her own mind. The deepest pain of her break was the estrangement it threatened with Gérard, which they avoided by not confronting it, both of them fearful that talking would intensify their disagreement. She remained grateful that when Gérard was told to write an article against her that would disassociate him from her, his loyalty to his sister took precedence and he refused, writing instead a self-criticism that did not implicate her.

Édith recalls the Communist Party official, formerly a worker-priest, who led the service at her brother's grave. She finds in his eyes and his words the same inner flame she imagines he used to have as a priest, dedicated to a faith that remained intact although it changed content. His passion, so close to what used to be her own, helps her come to terms with Gerard's choice to remain in the Party. Immobilized for two decades by his illness, Gérard wanted to use whatever life he had left to serve as an advocate for the poor and the unions, the working-class clients from whom he would have been cut off had he resigned from the Party. During the Algerian war many of his clients were North Africans, whom the police were only too eager to find guilty. The former priest speaking eloquently at her brother's funeral gives voice to Gérard's unwavering faith in the communist ideal, which provided support and solidarity for his desire to serve.

In temperament Gérard seems to have been able to enjoy the simple pleasures of the moment, as his sister could not. When his illness improved, he liked going down to the river in the early mist to find his boat and go fishing among the bulrushes, or weed his alpine garden in the Vercors where he had planted edelweiss and gentians. He was able to bear the adversity of illness with patience, equanimity, and remarkable optimism. Unlike Édith, he seems never to have been tempted by suicide, even during the long years of immobility on his back. He willed to survive and he survived. For Édith his refusal to complain showed a tenacious courage as worthy and "perhaps more difficult than courage on the battlefield." She uses another military image to evoke his political combat, choosing an analogy that also suggests a romanticized link to the *Rossel* she has recently completed: "You died like the soldier you wanted to be, in spite of everything."

"I admired you, my brother," Édith writes, "and I was never able to equal you." In moments when life seemed too unbearable to continue, she remembers Gérard there for her as always, refusing to let her drown in depression. She could manage to give "a good kick" and come up to the surface because she knew he was waiting at the edge of the pond, to "pull me by the hair" out of despondency. The bond between them was forged from early childhood when they usually played alone together, since the village children were too young or too old. In her reconstruction of the past, being with each other was what mattered; they did not need anyone else: "We were a couple you and I."[10]

In adulthood Édith's admiration for her brother's forbearance and integrity informed her love for him and served as an ethical model. In 1937, the year he was stricken with his disastrous illness, she wrote a rare diary entry about Gérard: "The only exceptional being I know is in agony. Gérard, my dear beloved, my only beloved whose name has never appeared in this notebook because I have never had to unburden myself of you, our friendship—our love. . . . I want so much to meet him, the person who would be your equal."[11]

After Gérard's death, he became in Édith's imagination the first and last incarnation of the impossible love she was seeking all her life. She borrows the words of Montaigne's explanation of his love for the friend he mourns, transposing his words into a direct address to Gérard, "because it was you, because it was I, my brother." Gérard is an idealized object and a kindred spirit, the perfect lover and brother fused into one. When she thinks back to their times alone together, what she remembers is the impression of encountering "that other half of myself I had sought in vain elsewhere." After his death, she reinvents the meaning of her love for her brother: "It is because of the admiration I had for you that I was never able to meet a man who counted for me as much as you did. No one who was worthy of you." In the parentheses that follow, she dismisses a psychoanalytic interpretation of those words in favor of an ethical one: "Plutarch is more important to me than Freud."[12] Her love for Gérard became the explanation for the failure of other loves, in defiance of the complexities and contradictions revealed in her diaries, her letters to Dominique Aury, and her narrator's self-analysis in Le Jeu d'échecs.

Thomas's last years life were a time of devastating losses, beginning with that of her brother. A year after his death, Gérard's six-year-old granddaughter died. Marianne, the daughter of Daniel and Andrée, was a special favorite among the grandchildren for Édith, who identified with her energetic independence and found in the child's closeness to her brother Gilles a mirror of her own intimacy with Gérard. At the age of three Marianne became ill with leukemia but the following summer her illness was in remission, allowing the family to visit in Sainte-Aulde with Édith for a few weeks. She was grief stricken when Marianne died in 1968, after bouts of intense suffering that recalled her own struggles with tuberculosis. For Gérard, it was only in his anguish over his granddaughter's illness that he was able to reveal the depth of his own ordeal over the years, which he had not allowed himself to express directly.

Like Édith's father, mother, and then her brother, Marianne died in the summertime. Before Marianne's death in August 1968 Édith had raged, thinking about Gérard: "All those I loved have died in the summertime and that's doubtless why I hate the sun and vacation time." Her preferred landscape was always northern, in particular Brittany, "where the sea dashes ceaselessly against the

melancholy rocks: always, never, always."[13] Dominique shared Édith's dislike of
the sun and her affinity with the brooding ocean landscape of Brittany. After
Paulhan's death Dominique imagined the two of them retiring in Brittany,
where together they would watch the sea and listen to the sound of the waves.

The last years of Édith Thomas's life, a time of private loss and premonitions
of her own imminent death, were also years when she began to emerge from obscurity in her professional life as a historian. Les "Pétroleuses," subsequently
translated into English as The Women Incendiaries, won the Femina-Vacareso
prize in 1963, awarded each year by a jury of women to the best nonfiction work
by a man or a woman. Rossel won the Gobert prize for the best work of history
that year (1967), awarded by the Académie Française. In 1968 Dominique Aury,
who was vice-president of the Prix Femina jury, nominated her to be a member
and she was unanimously elected. The last of Thomas's historical biographies,
Louise Michel, published posthumously in 1971, was translated into English a
decade later.

In Louise Michel Thomas's desire to write an exhaustive study, taking into account all the archival material she had discovered, often becomes a problem,
overwhelming her narrative and leaving the impression that the book is too long
because she didn't take the time to make it shorter. When her young editor at
Gallimard suggested that she make a number of cuts, Thomas indignantly refused and had sufficient authority to prevail.[14] But the editor, Pierre Nora, who
subsequently emerged as one of the leading historians of his generation, was
right in his criticism.[15]

Édith Thomas's finest achievement in her last years, along with Rossel, is Le
Jeu d'échecs (1970), a novel that crystallizes recurring themes in her life and her
writing. Although she contextualizes her personal obsessions within the catastrophic historical events of the mid-century, an intimate autobiographical focus remains dominant. Le Jeu d'échecs follows the quest of the narrator, an
archaeologist, to find a love commensurate with her desire for meaning. As she
approaches middle age, Aude seeks to uncover and put together the pieces of her
failed relations to those she has loved. The novel is addressed to her first love,
Stevan, as an imaginary letter, the form that served as a therapeutic strategy for
so many of Thomas's personal writings. In Le Jeu d'échecs the imaginary letter
becomes a formal device, loosely weaving together four stories and four names,
"Stevan," "Claude," "Esther," and "Anne."

Through Stevan, Thomas returns to the theme of the elusive love her narrator has been seeking with "astonishing perseverance" and expectations that
make its realization impossible. Aude's narrative distills the lifelong contradictions of Thomas's yearnings as a woman in love. The character of Stevan is inspired not by her brother but by her image of Stefan, the phantom lover who

had been her obscure object of desire for many years. Aude meets him in an unnamed country of Eastern Europe that resembles Yugoslavia, where she is attending a conference on the history of art. They go on a moonlight walk under
the olive trees to the ocean one warm evening, take a long swim, and "all the rest
was just as simple."[16] That idyllic moment is a transcription of the beginning of
Édith's relationship in 1950 with a Yugoslav diplomat, of whom Dominique had
written her: "Don't be too much in love with the handsome Dalmatian."[17] In
literature and in life, he abruptly withdraws, without explanation.

Some years later Aude finds herself convalescing for a few months, having been
hospitalized for reasons far more appealing to Thomas's imagination than the recurrent tuberculosis she suffered since her early twenties. Aude was on a skiing
trip and at one point ventured down the slope alone, away from the usual trails.
After a night in the vast expanse of snow, uncertain whether she will be found before she dies of cold, she lands in the hospital with a broken leg and pulmonary
congestion. Among those who come to see her during her long convalescence is
Danilo, a young historical researcher sent by his compatriot and mentor Stevan.

Danilo tells her the story of Esther, which clarifies the mystery of Stevan's elusiveness and mirrors her own obsession with the failure of love. Esther Schwartz,
an artist whom Stevan had met in Vienna in the 1930s, enchanted him with her
free spirit and a poetic universe utterly different from his own world of work,
the Communist Party, and his mother, a sturdy peasant woman completely dependent on him. When Esther comes to live with him in his country, he finds
himself unable to bridge the gap between their worlds and cannot bring himself to marry her. Lonely and desperate, she returns home to an Austria controlled by Hitler. After the outbreak of war, Stevan is in despair that if Esther is
dead, he has killed her, and that if they had married, he could have hidden the
fact she was Jewish. Danilo ends his narrative with Stevan learning that Esther
had joined the Resistance, was deported, and died in Auschwitz. In a later chance
encounter, Aude meets a woman who survived Auschwitz and knew Esther
there, whom she remembers vividly as a figure of grace in hell. Sometime after
this revelation, Aude learns from Danilo that Stevan has married a woman who
looks like the double of Esther.

Esther's unearthly ability to transcend the evil inflicted on her could have
been inspired by one of the many narratives of the camps that Édith Thomas
heard after the war. It is also possible that this ethereal, idealized figure is an expression of Thomas's philosemitism. Like Thérèse Levy in Thomas's wartime
story "L'Étoile jaune," whose physical appearance "recalled the faces of certain
medieval virgins," the spiritual radiance of Esther Schwartz in the face of bar-
barism counters racist stereotypes.

"Claude," the most fully realized section of *Le Jeu d'échecs,* recreates the emotional resonance of Édith Thomas's experience with Dominique Aury. In the months following the liberation, Aude meets the androgynous Claude at a resort in the French Alps, where Aude has come to write and recuperate from the extreme stress of the war years. Walking in the mountains, she sees coming down the slopes what she takes to be a boy in a blue pullover, his hands in his pants pockets. As he approaches, she recognizes him as the new guest she had noticed the previous evening at the hotel, who is in fact a woman about her age. Aude, like Édith in 1945, is writing a book on the liberation of Paris; Claude, an artist whose name seems to complete that of Aude, is preparing illustrations for *Alice in Wonderland*—the subject of one of Dominique Aury's literary essays. Aude is struck by Claude's beauty, "like certain drawings of Clouet," "strange and out of place in this century, like encountering a Renaissance face in the metro."[18]

In Paris, as they begin to see each other frequently, becoming friends and confidantes, Claude tires of her male lover, whose conversation she finds far less enjoyable than his lovemaking: "Claude was not one of those women who don't dare admit their pleasure and who hide erotic desire under the veil of sentiment."[19] When Claude declares her love for Aude, the latter reacts without the shock recorded in Édith's diary when Dominique did the same, but with the same caution, realizing that she had never thought of Claude erotically. When the two women become lovers, their union is described in a language of idyllic happiness rare in Édith Thomas's work. Some months later Claude falls in love with a male painter and Aude's affair becomes for the narrator one more *jeu d'échecs:* another game of chess or, literally, of failures.

In the last section of the book Aude is tempted by thoughts of suicide, from which she emerges with the abrupt desire to affirm life by having a child. Walking through Montmartre, she happens to meet Philippe, her first lover, who is now married with two children. The character of Philippe, as well as their initial and subsequent relationship, closely follows Édith Thomas's experience with Renaud. In contrast to Édith, however, Aude becomes pregnant and gives birth at the end of the novel to a daughter, Anne, the name of Thomas's autobiographical heroine in *Le Champ libre* and the name she chose for herself in her clandestine Resistance poems. Fictionally, Thomas was giving birth to a new self, a new generation, new possibilities.

At the age of sixty-one Édith Thomas became violently ill with hepatitis and died a few days later without regaining consciousness, on December 7, 1970. She had gone to her beloved Brittany for a couple of weeks and then taken a trip to Lorraine with her friend Yvonne Lanhers. When she returned she caught a chill and was forced to stay in bed. Her doctor, who was also Dominique Aury's doctor and who diagnosed viral hepatitis, did not administer the usual hepatitis remedy out of concern for its effect on her tuberculosis.

Édith's death remained for Dominique a painfully vivid memory that she related to me, always in the same terms, a number of times.

In the morning her housekeeper, Anna, found her flailing about on the floor, the lamp knocked down beside her. She was completely delirious. Anna called the doctor, who had Édith taken immediately to St. Antoine Hospital, the best there was. But nothing could be done. When I came to see her in the afternoon, they wouldn't let me go into her room; the hepatitis was too contagious. She was in a tiny room, huddled naked on a bed with tubes in all directions; she couldn't speak, didn't recognize anyone. At a certain moment she moved and cried out. "She's suffering, help her," I said. "No, no, she's completely unconscious, she's not suffering," the doctors said. But what do they know? And the next day she was dead. I had to identify her body at the morgue. She had been put in a drawer, just like in the detective novels.

Dominique Aury's obituary article reveals her intimate understanding of who Édith was. "Under an appearance of perfect control," she writes, "Édith Thomas was a passionate being who all her life sought for a way to use that passion, for what she called a reason to live." She describes Édith's quest for such a reason in literature, and in the struggle for an ideal of justice and freedom. She speaks of her underground writings during the Resistance, "the most ardent years of her life," and her "very personal" conception of women in life and society, defined by the expression *humanisme féminin*. Moreover, she adds, there was in Édith Thomas "a singular mixture of rebellion, stoicism, and humor."[20]

Édith's last surviving letter—one she actually sent—was written to her nephew Daniel Thomas three months before she died. In Daniel's telling, he felt close enough to his aunt and sufficiently confident of the trust between them so that he could playfully provoke her, calling her an "anti-male racist." In the long letter she wrote to him in response, she reflects on being a woman and a feminist in terms that are inextricably personal and historical, as these few passages make clear:

My dear Daniel,

    If I am a "racist," it's the way black people are. And if white racism seems odious to me, that of blacks seems to me in part justified. . . . For centuries, women have had no option other than marriage, prostitution, or the cloister: society rejected them if they did not have, in one way or another, a mediator. "Housewives or harlots," said the pseudo-socialist Proudhon. That is why I am a "feminist," even if it's ridiculous. The problems that concern women have not been transcended or resolved. And so much the better if I can, in a very small measure, call to mind that they exist and that "l'humanisme féminin" remains to be invented. . . . In politics we've theoretically had equal rights for twenty-five years. How many women deputies are there? Or ministers? . . . Don't think, by the way, that I am embittered at being a woman. On the contrary. It's much more difficult to be a woman than a man, and I've always liked difficult contests and lost causes."[21]

In the postscript to her letter she mocks her convictions, "this long feminist harangue," and mocks as well her need for healing, as if only a belief in magic could make it happen. Noting that she finds herself tired and tense after completing *Louise Michel,* she comments: "If things don't get better I'll go see my neuropsychiatrist and have him give me some magic powder, *perlimpinpin*: all that's needed is to believe in it."

The cause of women championed by Thomas continued to be difficult but certainly not lost. In hindsight the birth at the end of her last novel can be read as enacting what was to become a metaphor of the women's movement, which was just then being born in the French social and political world. A journalist who had interviewed Thomas about *Rossel* and reviewed *Le Jeu d'échecs,* writes in her obituary for *Le Monde:* "The work and life of Édith Thomas, as they were, as they are, bear witness to an exceptional personality but also to woman's situation at a particular time in our society: she brought the weight of her work and her courage to moving that society toward a more just equilibrium."[22] The idea that women could lead an autonomous existence without a male mediator between themselves and society would come to seem less radical than it did in her lifetime—when there was no legitimacy given to women intellectuals who also spoke as women—but a problem nevertheless. Several decades later, Thomas's issues concerning women in their public and private lives remain very much alive.

Her last novel reflects a split that characterized the life of Édith Thomas, Simone de Beauvoir, and many other pioneering intellectual women in the mid-twentieth century: they were torn between their determination to participate as equals in public life and their emotional dependency. In *Le Jeu d'échecs,* the narrator is pulled between incompatible needs for fusion and autonomy, unable to reconcile her warring identity as a woman and a person. In her life as in her novel, Thomas found it impossible to heal that self-division, as if the modern, socially committed intellectual and the woman yearning for a great love belonged to different generations. Only the passion of the Resistance provided a struggle powerful enough to engage heart, mind, and imagination. Édith Thomas's writings testify to a life in resistance, both personal and political, against a world she found unacceptable.

Édith Thomas's published books are cited by title only:

La Mort de Marie. Novel. Paris: Gallimard, 1934.

L'Homme criminel. Novel. Paris: Gallimard, 1934.

Sept-Sorts. Novel. Paris: Gallimard, 1935.

Le Refus. Novel. Paris: Éditions sociales internationales, 1936.

Contes d'Auxois. [Auxois, pseud.]. Stories. Paris: Éditions de Minuit clandestines, 1943.

"Le Professeur et les moules." In *Contes d'Auxois.* 1943. Translated by Maria Jolas under the title "The Professor and the Mussels," in *Bedside Book of Famous French Stories,* ed. Belle Becker and Robert Linscott. New York: Random House, 1945.

"F.T.P." In *Contes d'Auxois.* 1943. Translated under the title "F.T.P.," in *Defeat and Beyond: An Anthology of French Wartime Writing, 1940–1945,* ed. Germaine Brée and George Bernauer. New York: Pantheon Books, 1970.

Étude de femmes. Novel. Paris: Éditions Colbert, 1945.

Le Champ libre. Novel. Paris: Gallimard, 1945.

La Libération de Paris. Essay. Paris: Éditions Mellottée, 1945.

Jeanne d'Arc. Essay. Paris: Éditions Hier et Aujourd'hui, 1947. Reprint, Paris: Gallimard, 1952.

Les Femmes de 1848. Essay. Paris: Presses Universitaires Françaises, 1948.

Ève et les autres. Stories. Paris: Gizard, 1952. Reprinted Mercure de France, 1970. Translated by Estelle Eirinberg under the title *Eve and the Others.* Sioux City, Iowa: Continental Editions, 1976.

Pauline Roland: socialisme et féminisme au XIXe siècle. Essay. Paris: Librairie Marcel Rivière, 1956.

George Sand. Essay. Paris: Éditions Universitaires, 1960.

Les "Pétroleuses." Essay. Paris: Gallimard, 1963. Translated by James and Starr Atkinson under the title *The Women Incendiaries.* New York: George Braziller, 1966.

Rossel (1844–1871). Essay. Paris: Gallimard, 1967.

Le Jeu d'échecs. Novel. Paris: Grasset, 1970.

Louise Michel ou la Velleda de l'anarchie. Essay. Paris: Gallimard, 1971. Translated by
   Penelope Williams under the title *Louise Michel.* Montreal: Black Rose Books, 1980.

Pages de Journal, 1939–1944, suivies de Journal intime de Monsieur Célestin Costedet.
   Edited by Dorothy Kaufmann. Éditions Viviane Hamy, 1995.

Le Témoin compromis, mémoires. Edited by Dorothy Kaufmann. Paris: Éditions Viviane
   Hamy, 1995.

Note: All translations, both of interviews and written texts, are my own, unless otherwise
indicated.

Throughout the book, quotations of Dominique Aury that are not otherwise attributed come from our conversations in Paris between 1990 and 1995: October 2, November 8, December 12, 1990; July 23, 1991; June 30, 1992; January 19, June 29, 1993; March 9,
March 24, May 10, June 14, 1994; May 16, 1995.

Abbreviations such as AN318AP13 refer to items in the fourteen cartons of the Édith
Thomas dossier, AN (Archives Nationales), 318AP (Archives Privées), 13 (here carton 13).

Introduction

1. I take this phrase from Susan Rubin Suleiman's question after she summarizes the
heroic Resistance plot of *The Blood of Others:* "Shall we call this a compensatory fantasy
on Beauvoir's part?" *Risking Who One Is: Encounters with Contemporary Art and Literature* (Cambridge: Harvard University Press, 1994), p. 194.

2. In her analysis of Jean-Paul Sartre's unparalleled celebrity in mid-twentieth-century France, Anna Boschetti discusses the extraordinary prestige in the 1930s of the École
Normale Supérieure and especially the *agrégation* in philosophy within the hierarchical
universe of the French educational system. *Sartre et "Les Temps modernes"* (Paris: Éditions de Minuit, 1985), p. 23. The most notable women at the École Normale Supérieure
in Édith Thomas's generation were the religious philosopher Simone Weil (*agrégation*
1931) and Simone de Beauvoir. In 1929, at the age of twenty-one, Simone de Beauvoir became the youngest *agrégé* in France. She placed second in the *agrégation* of philosophy,
just after Sartre, who had failed the examination the previous year.

3. Vercors (pseudonym for Jean Bruller), *The Battle of Silence* (New York: Holt, Rine-
hart, and Winston, 1968), p. 12.

4. *Témoin compromis,* p. 35.

5. Ibid., pp. 177, 228.

6. *Pages de journal,* December 1, 1942, p. 189.

7. Ibid., June 5, 1942, p. 179.

8. *Jeu d'échecs,* p. 76.

9. I have taken the "life/lines" metaphor from *Life/Lines: Theorizing Women's Autobiography,* ed. Bella Brodzki and Celeste Schenck (Ithaca, N.Y.: Cornell University Press,
1988). Reflecting on the metaphor's multiple meanings in her foreword to this book, Germaine Brée evokes "lifelines, ropes that link the deep-sea diver to the mother-ship" (p. ix).
My interpretation of Édith Thomas's autobiographical writings depends on preserving

the tension described by the editors of *Life/Lines* "between life and literature, between politics and theory, between selfhood and textuality, which autobiography authorizes us to enjoy" (p. 14).

10. Béatrice Didier, *Le Journal intime* (Paris: Presses Universitaires de France, 1976), p. 12.

11. Unpublished diaries, January 4, 1933, AN318AP13.

12. *Pages de journal,* September 27, 1940, p. 97.

13. Philippe Lejeune, *Le Pacte autobiographique* (Paris: Éditions du Seuil, 1975), pp. 13–46.

14. *Pages de journal,* January 7, 1940, p. 54; March 1, 1941, pp. 123–124; September 25, 1939, pp. 49–50.

15. Ibid., June 5, 1942, p. 178.

16. *Louise Michel* (Eng. trans.), p. 11.

17. Odile Krakovitch, interview by author, Paris, October 15, 1990.

18. Yvonne Lanhers, interview by author, Paris, November 5, 1990.

19. Dossier Édith Thomas, AN318AP1–14.

20. Édith Thomas, "L'Humanisme féminin," AN318AP3.

21. *Jeu d'échecs,* pp. 68–69.

22. In an article about the publishing house Gallimard, *Le Monde* feels free to refer to Dominique Aury as "the author of the sulfurous erotic novel *Story of O*" (November 23, 1990).

23. See John de St. Jorre, "Une Lettre d'Amour: The True Story of *Story of O*," in *Venus Bound: The Erotic Voyage of the Olympia Press and Its Writers* (New York: Random House, 1994), pp. 202–236; and St. Jorre, "The Unmasking of O," *New Yorker,* August 1, 1994, pp. 42–50. There are some errors in his account, notably the year when Dominique Aury and Jean Paulhan became lovers. They began their affair in 1947, not during the occupation. Although St. Jorre "unmasks" Dominique Aury for an American readership, in Paris her identity was known for a long time, far beyond "a small inner circle."

24. The anecdote about de Gaulle and *O* was recounted to me by Dominique Aury's son from her early (and only) marriage. Philippe d'Argila, interview by author, Boissise-le-Bertrand, June 14, 1997.

25. These documents now constitute carton 13 in Édith Thomas's dossier, AN318AP.

26. The correspondence between Édith Thomas and Dominique Aury, along with the letters from Jean Paulhan to Édith Thomas, now constitute carton 14 in Édith Thomas's dossier, AN318AP.

27. Pauline Réage [Dominique Aury], "A Girl in Love," preface to *Return to the Château,* trans. Sabine d'Estrée (New York: Grove Press, 1971), p. 17.

28. AN318AP1.

29. *Jeu d'échecs,* p. 74.

1. A Daughter of the Republic

Unattributed quotations of Édith Thomas and her family in this chapter are taken from her letter to her brother after his death, "À mon frère," AN318AP13.

1. Quoted in James E. McMillan, *Housewife or Harlot: The Place of Women in French Society, 1870–1940* (New York: St. Martin's Press, 1981), p. 13.

2. Julien Kravtchenko, letter to author, May 10, 1991.

3. *Témoin compromis,* p. 96.

4. Simone de Beauvoir, *Memoirs of a Dutiful Daughter,* trans. James Kirkup (New York: Harper Colophon Books, 1974), p. 27.

5. Unpublished diaries, August 20, 1939, AN318AP13.

6. My thanks to Daniel and Andrée Thomas for showing me this inscription in Georges Thomas's copy of *L'Homme criminel.*

7. *Témoin compromis,* pp. 31–32.

8. Ibid., p. 32.

9. Ibid., p. 37.

10. Archives of Lycée Victor Duruy, Paris.

11. Françoise Mayeur, *L'Enseignement secondaire des jeunes filles sous la troisième république* (Paris: Presses de la Fondation Nationale des Sciences Politiques, 1977), pp. 392–399.

12. *Témoin compromis,* pp. 39–40.

13. AN318AP1.

14. Édith Thomas to Daniel Thomas, September 14, 1970, Dossier Daniel Thomas.

15. Édith Thomas, "Promenade au Villaret," *Lettres,* no. 2 (1945): 49–53.

16. Édith Thomas, "Un Sanctuaire de l'Histoire: Les Archives Nationales," *Les Lettres françaises,* March 18, 1946.

17. Maurice Prou, *L'École des Chartes* (Paris: Société des Amis de l'École des Chartes, 1927), p. 20. My thanks to the École des Chartes for giving me this brochure.

18. Quoted in Hélène Gosset, "À l'École des Chartes," *L'Oeuvre,* May 2, 1934.

19. Madeleine Thomas, interview by author, La Bâtie, July 8, 1991.

20. Unpublished diaries, February 1932, AN318AP13.

21. Madeleine Thomas, interview, July 8, 1991.

2. Illness and Phantom Lovers

1. Unpublished diaries, October 1931, AN318AP13. Subsequent quotations from the unpublished diaries will be indicated by their date of entry.

2. February 1932.

3. January 1932.

4. The phrase "propitiatory incantation" comes from Daniel and Andrée Thomas, who are certain that Édith was not treated for tuberculosis of the bone in a sanatorium. The known dates of her studies and examinations do not leave room for a stay, which would necessarily have been lengthy. Moreover, they point out, such information would have been part of the family's oral history, which includes all the major episodes of her career.

5. Pierre Guillaume, *Du désespoir au salut: les tuberculeux aux 19e et 20e siècles* (Paris: Aubier, 1986), p. 230.

6. April 1932.

7. March 1932.

8. October 1931. There are a number of entries for that month, dated simply October 1931.

9. *La Mort de Marie,* pp. 48, 163.

10. Béatrice Didier, *Le Journal intime* (Paris: Presses Universitaires de France, 1976), p. 105.

11. Letter from Librairie Plon to Édith Thomas, January 5, 1934, AN318AP1.

12. January 3, 1934.

13. André Frank, *Les Nouvelles littéraires*, December 30, 1933.

14. Ramon Fernandez, *Marianne*, February 7, 1934. Widely respected during much of the 1930s as a literary critic for the *Nouvelle Revue française* and as a philosopher with moderate leftist political views, Fernandez turned to literary collaboration with the Germans during the following decade.

15. Robert Brasillach, *Action française*, March 8, 1934. Brasillach later became editor of *Je suis partout*, the most virulently pro-Nazi and antisemitic newspaper of the occupation years. He was the only French writer condemned to death and executed as a traitor after the war.

16. *Témoin compromis*, p. 46.

17. Madeleine Thomas, interview by author, July 8, 1991.

18. Julien Kravtchenko, letter to author, May 31, 1991.

19. March 1934.

20. *Jeu d'échecs*, pp. 67–68.

21. November 28, 1933.

22. "Monsieur C." gave me permission to quote his remarks about Édith Thomas on the condition that he remain anonymous.

23. March 27, 1936; December 20, 1934.

24. *Sept-Sorts*, p. 135.

25. May 25, 1934; August 15, 1936.

26. Louis Parrot, *Les Lettres françaises*, February 1, 1946.

27. June 30, 1938.

28. June 22, 1937; January 30, 1936.

29. Night of September 14, 1936.

30. June 6, 1937.

31. July 1933.

3. *"To Rediscover a Reason to Live"*

1. Jacques Soustelle was an ethnologist who did groundbreaking work in the 1930s on Indian culture in Mexico. He is more widely known for his later political trajectory. Refusing to accept the armistice with Germany in 1940, Jacques Soustelle immediately contacted General de Gaulle in London, who put him in charge of coordinating information services for Free France, first in London and then in Algiers. In 1955 Pierre Mendès-France appointed him governor-general of Algeria. Although Soustelle initially favored a reformist policy of integration for the Algerians, he became an increasingly militant supporter of keeping Algeria French as the Algerian revolt intensified. After de Gaulle returned to power in 1958 and decided to support Algerian self-determination, Soustelle broke ranks with him. In 1961 Soustelle became one of the leaders of the extreme right-wing military group that organized an insurrection against de Gaulle's policies, the Organisation de l'Armée Secrète (OAS). Soustelle went into exile until the amnesty of 1968, when he returned to France and resumed his academic career. He died in 1990.

2. Julien Kravtchenko, interview by author, Grenoble, July 12, 1991.

3. *Témoin compromis*, p. 42.

4. See especially David Caute, *Communism and the French Intellectuals, 1913–1960* (New York: Macmillan, 1964).

5. *Témoin compromis*, p. 47.

6. "La Position sentimentale," letter from Édith Thomas to Vaillant-Couturier, and his response, "Votre place est à nos côtés," letter from Vaillant-Couturier to Édith Thomas, *Commune*, no. 9 (May 1934).

7. Unpublished diaries, January 1, 1934; May 1, 1934, AN318AP13.

8. *Témoin compromis*, pp. 50–53.

9. Maria Van Rysselberghe, "Les cahiers de la petite dame," 1929–1937, *Cahiers André Gide 5* (Paris: Gallimard, 1974), p. 386.

10. Alistair Horne, *A Savage War of Peace: Algeria, 1954–1962* (New York: Viking Press, 1978), p. 35.

11. Unpublished diaries, September 1934.

12. Letter of resignation from AEAR, November 30, 1934, AN318AP1.

13. Unpublished diaries, May 1936; "Passage," *Europe*, no. 174 (June 15, 1937).

14. Later, she will see the Resistance as part of that continuum. When she congratulated her friend Joël Schmidt, editor of the Protestant newspaper *Réforme*, on the publication of his book about the early Christians, *Le Christ des profondeurs* (Paris: Balland, 1970), she said to him: "You are speaking about us." Joël Schmidt, interview by author, October 24, 1990.

15. Unpublished diaries, March 23, 1935; October 3, 1935.

16. See Susan Rubin Suleiman's analysis of Bakhtin in *Authoritarian Fictions* (New York: Columbia University Press, 1983). Suleiman refers to *Le Refus* as an example of the monological novel.

17. Claude Morgan, review of *Le Refus*, by Édith Thomas, *Vendemiaire*, January 13, 1937.

18. Henry de Montherlant to Édith Thomas, Dossier Daniel Thomas.

19. Unpublished diaries, July 2, 1937.

20. Édith Thomas, review of *Le Démon du bien*, *Commune* 48 (August 1937), pp. 1515–1516.

21. Among recent studies in French intellectual history that have begun to change that perception, see especially *Intellectuelles: du genre en histoire des intellectuels,* ed. Nicole Racine and Michel Trebitsch (Brussels: Éditions Complexe, 2004), which includes a chapter by Dorothy Kaufmann on Édith Thomas, "L'Humanisme féminin."

22. Paul Nizan, review of *Le Refus*, by Édith Thomas, *L'Humanité*, March 20, 1937.

23. Édith Thomas, review of *Le Démon du bien*, *Commune* 48 (August 1937).

24. *Témoin compromis*, pp. 58–59.

4. Fellow Traveling and Its Discontents

1. "Et toi, qu'as-tu fait pour la victoire?" *Regards*, December 31, 1936.

2. David Caute points out that there was no French *Homage to Catalonia* even among the idealists: "Possibly Orwell's experiences in Barcelona had no counterpart among any of the major French writers, and reports of the fighting were so distorted and contra-

dictory that they could be quietly discounted by those for whom the fascist threat and the need for Republican unity remained the overriding considerations." Caute, *Communism and the French Intellectuals* (New York: Macmillan, 1964), p. 120.

3. Dominique Borne and Henri Dubief, *La Crise des années 30 (1929–1938)*, (Paris: Éditions du Seuil, 1989), pp. 166–169.

4. *Ce Soir,* March 2, March 7, 1937; *Regards,* March 18, 1937.

5. Paul Nizan, review of *Le Refus,* by Édith Thomas, *L'Humanité,* March 20, 1937.

6. *Ce Soir,* September 9, September 10, 1937.

7. Ibid., January 13, 1938.

8. Ibid., April 13, 1938.

9. Ibid., April 16, 1938.

10. *Cahiers de la jeunesse,* April 15–May 15, 1938.

11. Unpublished diaries, July 1, 1938.

12. *Regards,* August 11, 1938.

13. *Femmes,* September 1938.

14. *Témoin compromis,* p. 72.

15. Unpublished diaries, October 3, 1938.

16. Ibid., May 25, 1939.

17. Ibid., June 2, 1939.

18. *Témoin compromis,* p. 76.

19. Édith Thomas, "Promenade au Villaret," *Lettres,* no. 2 (1945): 49–53.

20. Unpublished diaries, July 9, 1935; October 31, 1938.

21. Édith Thomas, "Lettres à Ariane," AN318AP13.

22. A month later, after France's declaration of war against Germany, Paul Nizan was drafted into the military and resigned from the Communist Party. He was killed in 1940 during the battle of Dunkirk. Gabriel Péri was executed in 1941 by the Nazis.

23. *Témoin compromis,* p. 78.

24. *Pages de journal,* August 24, 27, and 28, 1939, pp. 37–39.

25. Ibid., August 29, 1939, pp. 40–41. Jacques Decour was a writer and a professor of German literature who later became the founder, with Jean Paulhan, of *Les Lettres françaises.* Decour was putting together the first issue when he was arrested in 1942. He was sentenced to death and executed by the Nazis on May 30, 1942, along with two other Communist intellectuals, the physicist Jacques Solomon and the philosopher Georges Politzer.

26. Stefan P. to Édith Thomas, AN318AP13.

27. *Pages de journal,* August 28–September 14, 1939, pp. 40–48.

28. Ibid., May 8, 1940, p. 59.

29. It is now estimated that by June 20 at least eight million French people, including Belgians and Luxembourgeois, had abandoned their homes and fled south. Jean-Pierre Azéma, *1940, l'année terrible* (Paris: Éditions du Seuil, 1990), pp. 119–128.

30. *Pages de journal,* June 16–June 24, 1940, pp. 72–76.

5. Diary of Resistance, Diary of Collaboration

1. *Pages de journal,* June 25–26, 1940, pp. 77–78. Subsequent references to *Pages de journal* in this chapter will be indicated by the date and page number of their entry in Édith Thomas's diary.

2. Philippe Burrin, *France under the Germans: Collaboration and Compromise*, trans. Janet Lloyd (New York: The New Press, 1996), pp. 4, 177–190.

3. August 19, 1940, p. 88.

4. According to the research service of the Bibliothèque nationale, roasted beechnuts can serve as a substitute for coffee, and oil extracted from the nuts can be used for cooking, "possibilities that were not insignificant during a period of shortages." Beginning in October 1940, schoolchildren and the Chantiers de Jeunesse participated in outings to gather beechnuts, considered to be at their best at that time of year. My thanks to Christine Patoux, who assisted me in deciphering and transcribing Édith Thomas's diaries, for pursuing this information.

5. October 1940; October 28, 1940, pp. 104–106.

6. The name Costedet evokes Costals, the hero of Montherlant's *Young Girls*. The first name Célestin speaks for itself. Ladies' Paradise (Le Paradis des Dames) ironically updates the great department store of Emile Zola's novel *Au bonheur des dames*.

7. Stanley Hoffmann, *Decline or Renewal? France since the 1930s* (New York: Viking, 1974), p. 3.

8. *Pages de journal*, November 7, 1940, p. 242. Subsequent references to *Le Journal intime de Monsieur Célestin Costedet* will be noted as *Célestin Costedet*.

9. *Célestin Costedet*, January 28, 1941, p. 300.

10. July 8, 1940, pp. 81–82.

11. *Célestin Costedet*, November 27, 1940, p. 264.

12. July 9, 1940, p. 83.

13. October 4, 1940, p. 98.

14. October 18, 1940, p. 102.

15. *Célestin Costedet*, October 18, 1940, p. 227.

16. November 9, 1940, p. 108.

17. See in particular Robert Paxton, *Vichy France: Old Guard and New Order, 1940–1944* (New York: Alfred A. Knopf, 1972), p. 51: "Collaboration was not a German demand to which some Frenchmen acceded, through sympathy or guile. Collaboration was a French proposal that Hitler ultimately rejected."

18. October 6, 1940, p. 99.

19. *Célestin Costedet*, October 19, 1940, p. 229.

20. November 15, 1940, p. 108.

21. October 27, 1940, pp. 105–106.

22. June 30, 1940, p. 79.

23. February 24, March 5, 1941, pp. 123–125.

24. July 23, 1941, p. 142. Aragon's poem, which Thomas transcribes in its entirety in her diary, was published in 1941 by Gallimard in Aragon's *Le Crève-Coeur*.

25. December 7, 1940, pp. 113–116.

26. August 27, 1940, p. 90.

27. Herbert Lottman, *The Left Bank* (Boston: Houghton Mifflin, 1982), p. 141.

28. My thanks to Madame Maison and the research services at the Archives nationales for providing this information.

29. October 8, 1941, p. 155.

30. Unpublished diaries, October 20, October 25, November 7, December 6, 1941, AN318AP13.

31. Gilbert Joseph, *Une si douce Occupation* (Paris: Albin Michel, 1991), p. 118.

32. October 5, 1941, pp. 153–154.

33. June 6, 1942, p. 179.

34. Édith Thomas, "L'Étoile jaune," *Les Étoiles*, September 25, 1945.

35. Night of September 9, 1940, p. 94; November 27, 1939, p. 53.

36. Thomas, "L'Étoile jaune," September 25, 1945.

37. June 6, 1942, pp. 179–180.

38. June 24, 1942, pp. 181–182.

39. Jean-Paul Sartre, *Anti-Semite and Jew,* trans. George J. Becker (New York: Schocken Books, 1995), p. 68. For a reading of Sartre's portrait of the Jew in light of Édith Thomas's reflections on the yellow star, see Dorothy Kaufmann, "Réflexions sur l'étoile jaune: Jean-Paul Sartre, Édith Thomas, et Jean Paulhan," in *Sartre et les juifs,* ed. Ingrid Galster (Paris: Éditions de la Découverte, 2005).

40. Ibid., p. 152.

6. Writing Underground

1. Édith Thomas, *Les Lettres françaises,* March 1, 1946.

2. Conversations with Daniel and Andrée Thomas, St. Marcellin, Novemebr 17–18, 1990.

3. *Pages de journal,* June 30, 1940, p. 79.

4. René Luynes [Édith Thomas], "Littérature, clandestine," AN318AP13.

5. René Luynes, "Littérature interdite," AN318AP13.

6. Quoted in Claude Bellanger, *La Presse clandestine, 1940–1944* (Paris: Armand Colin, 1962), p. 34.

7. *Témoin compromis,* p. 103.

8. *Pages de journal,* December 25, 1941, p. 163.

9. Ibid., August 31, 1942, p. 188.

10. Michael R. Marrus and Robert O. Paxton, *Vichy France and the Jews* (New York: Basic Books, 1981), p. 265.

11. "Crier la vérité!" *Les Lettres françaises,* no. 2 (October 1942). Édith Thomas's editorial is quoted in Claude Lévy and Paul Tillard, *Betrayal at the Vel d'Hiv,* trans. Inea Bushnaq (New York: Hill and Wang, 1967), p. 182, and in Robert O. Paxton, *Vichy France, Old Guard and New Order, 1940–1944* (New York: Alfred A. Knopf, 1972), p. 183.

12. Jean-Paul Sartre, *"What Is Literature?" and Other Essays,* trans. Bernard Frechtman (Cambridge: Harvard University Press, 1988), p. 37.

13. René Luynes [Édith Thomas], "Juifs," AN318AP13.

14. *Témoin compromis,* pp. 106–107. See also Jacques Debû-Bridel, *La Résistance intellectuelle* (Paris: Julliard, 1970), pp. 58–59.

15. Louis Aragon, "La Rose et le Réséda," in *La Diane française* (La Bibliothèque Française, 1945). Aragon dedicated his poem to four Resistance fighters, two of them Catholics, the other two Communists.

16. Debû-Bridel, *Résistance intellectuelle,* p. 48.

17. Quoted in ibid., p. 35.

18. Anne Simonin, *Les Éditions de Minuit (1942–1955): le devoir d'insoumission* (Paris: IMEC, 1994), p. 13.

19. *Témoin compromis*, p. 110.

20. Édith Thomas, "Sous l'Occupation," *La Quinzaine littéraire*, July 1, 1967.

21. Vercors, *The Silence of the Sea*, ed. James W. Brown and Lawrence D. Stokes (Oxford: Berg, 1991), p. 92.

22. In spite of the success and influence of Vercors's story, the enemies of Nazi Germany, in France and abroad, did not always receive it with approval. By the time the book was widely circulated at the end of 1942, killings and destruction by the occupying forces had greatly intensified and many people found it difficult to accept Vercors's main character or even to understand the point of the story. Some thought that *The Silence of the Sea*, far from being a call to resistance, encouraged an attitude of accommodation. Others, like the Soviet journalist Ilya Ehrenburg, writing in the midst of the horrors of the campaign against Russia, found this affable and decent German officer simply unbelievable.

23. Édith Thomas, "Les Années noires," *La Quinzaine littéraire*, November 15, 1966.

24. Gerhard Heller, *Un Allemand à Paris, 1940–1944* (Paris: Éditions du Seuil, 1981), p. 72.

25. Gérard Loiseaux, *Littérature de la défaite et de la collaboration* (Paris: Fayard, 1995), pp. 507–508.

26. "The Professor and the Mussels," from *Contes d'Auxois*, was translated by Maria Jolas and appears in Belle Becker and Robert Linscott, eds., *Bedside Book of Famous French Stories* (New York: Random House, 1945), pp. 415–419.

27. See *Pages de journal*, May 11, 1941, p. 130.

28. "Le Tilleul," in *Contes d'Auxois*, p. 33.

29. Roger Bacuet, interview by author, Sainte-Aulde, July 17, 1991.

30. "F.T.P.," from *Contes d'Auxois*, appears in English in *Defeat and Beyond: An Anthology of French Wartime Writing, 1940–1945*, ed. Germaine Brée and George Bernauer (New York: Pantheon Books, 1970), pp. 224–230.

31. Charles de Gaulle, "Clairvoyance de la pensée française," in *Discours et Messages* (Paris: Plon, 1970), pp. 332–333.

32. Charles de Gaulle to Édith Thomas, July 23, 1970, Dossier Daniel Thomas.

33. Édith Thomas, "Femmes françaises," in *Almanach des Lettres françaises* (Paris: Éditions de Minuit, March 1944), pp. 55–57.

34. Édith Thomas, "Sous l'Occupation," *La Quinzaine littéraire*, July 1, 1967. Julien Cain, director of the Bibliothèque nationale from 1930 to 1940, was instrumental in instituting public readings and book buses, in order to make library books more widely available. As a Jew, he was dismissed from his position by the Vichy authorities in 1940. He became actively engaged in the Resistance and was deported to Buchenwald. He survived the camps and after the war was reinstated in his position at the Bibliothèque nationale, where he served from 1945 to 1964.

7. Uses of the Past

1. *Pages de journal*, October 1940, p. 103.

2. Édith Thomas, "Révélation du Moyen-Age," *Les Lettres françaises*, January 27, 1945.

3. *Pages de journal*, August 14, 1940, p. 87.

4. Pierre Drieu la Rochelle, *Gilles* (Paris: Gallimard, 1939), p. 658.

5. *Pages de journal*, March 18, 1943, pp. 189–191.

6. Georges Sadoul, *Histoire du cinéma mondial* (Paris: Flammarion, 1949), p. 288. The historian Natalie Zemon Davis has underscored a further irony. The sets for *Les Visiteurs* were designed by Alexandre Trauner, a Communist and a Jew who had immigrated to France in 1928 from fascist Hungary and went into hiding after the exodus. Another name was credited for the set designs (Natalie Davis, note to author, 1998).

7. The material difficulties of producing *Les Visiteurs du soir* are detailed in Marcel Carné, *La Vie à belles dents* (Paris: Éditions Jean-Pierre Ollivier, 1975), pp. 195–216.

8. Evelyn Ehrlich, *Cinema of Paradox: French Filmmaking under the German Occupation* (New York: Columbia University Press, 1985), p. 108.

9. Jean-Pierre Bertin-Maghit, *Le Cinéma sous Vichy* (Paris: Éditions Albatros, 1980), p. 91.

10. Quoted in Deirdre Bair, *Simone de Beauvoir* (New York: Summit Books, 1990), p. 248.

11. Ingrid Galster, "Simone de Beauvoir and Radio-Vichy: About Some Rediscovered Radio Scripts," *Simone de Beauvoir Studies* 13 (fall 1996): 109.

12. I am thinking in particular of Bianca Bienenfeld Lamblin's testimony in *Mémoires d'une jeune fille dérangée* (Paris: Balland, 1993).

13. Simone de Beauvoir, *Pour une morale de l'ambiguïté suivi de Pyrrhus et Cinéas* (Paris: Gallimard, 1944), p. 249.

14. Jean Lescure, ed. *Domaine francais. Messages* (Geneva: Éditions des Trois Collines, 1943), p. 12.

15. The first stanza of Whitman's poem (seventeen lines are quoted in the epigraph of *Messages)*, reads as follows:

O star of France,
The brightness of thy hope and strength and fame,
Like some proud ship that led the fleet so long,
Beseems to-day a wreck driven by the gale, a mastless hulk,
And 'mid its teeming madden'd half-drowned crowds,
Nor helm nor helmsman.

Walt Whitman, *Leaves of Grass and Other Writings*, ed. Emory Holloway (Garden City, N.Y.: Doubleday, 1926).

16. Édith Thomas, "Christine de Pizan," in Lescure, *Domaine francais*, pp. 263–271. See the analysis of Angus J. Kennedy and James Steel, "L'Esprit et l'Épée ou la Résistance au féminin: Christine de Pizan, Jeanne d'Arc et Édith Thomas," in *Une Femme de lettres au Moyen Age: Études autour de Christine de Pizan*, eds. Liliane Dulac and Bernard Ribémont (Orléans: Paradigme, 1995). I wish to thank Assia Djebar for calling my attention to this article and the medieval scholar Helen Solterer for sending it to me.

17. *Jeanne d'Arc*, p. 267.

18. Ibid., p. 8.

19. Ibid., pp. 19, 210.

20. Ibid., quoted on pp. 248–249.

21. Ibid., p. 8.

22. According to the Bibliothèque Protestante in Paris, the last few files concerning the Huguenots were not returned until January 26, 1988. During the Cold War the files had been kept in what became East Berlin.

23. Édith Thomas, "Les Religionnaires fugitifs," *Réforme,* February 5, 1949.

24. Recent scholarship has explored more carefully the historical and geographic context of Le Chambon's extraordinary rescue effort. For example, given the nature of clandestine work, it has proved impossible to discern exactly how many of the five thousand forged identities were for Jewish refugees. Some seem to have been for STO *réfractaires* and members of the Resistance. Christine van der Zanden, "The Plateau of Hospitality: Jewish Refugee Life on the Plateau Vivarais-Lignon," Ph.D. diss., Clark University, 2003.

25. Madeleine Thomas, interview by author, La Bâtie, July 8, 1991.

26. Édith Thomas, "Un seul et même people," *Les Lettres françaises,* no. 17 (June 1944).

27. Édith Thomas, "J'ai visité le maquis," *Femmes françaises,* no. 2 (September 21, 1944); no. 3 (September 28, 1944).

28. Unpublished diaries, May 28, 1937.

29. *Pages de journal,* June 6, 1944, p. 200.

8. The Liberation of Paris and the End of the War

1. *Libération de Paris,* p. 7.

2. Ibid., pp. 11–15.

3. Ibid., pp. 16–39.

4. *Témoin compromis,* p. 155.

5. *Libération de Paris,* p. 94.

6. Jean-Paul Sartre, "La Délivrance est à nos portes," *Combat,* September 2, 1944. The Forces Françaises de l'Intérieur were created by the Comité Français de Libération Nationale (CFLN) to confer on the *résistants* the legal status of soldiers. The CFLN was the predecessor of the provisional government of the French Republic.

7. Charles de Gaulle, *Discours et Messages, Juin 1940–Janvier 1946* (Paris: Plon, 1970), p. 440.

8. *Pages de journal,* August 20, 1944, p. 210.

9. Ibid., August 23, 1944, pp. 214–215.

10. *Libération de Paris,* p. 29.

11. See Miranda Pollard, *Reign of Virtue: Mobilizing Gender in Vichy France* (Chicago: University of Chicago Press, 1998), pp. 42–70.

12. Claude Chabrol's film is based on Francis Szpiner, *Une Affaire de femmes* (Paris: Balland, 1986).

13. Jean-Paul Sartre, "Qu'est-ce qu'un collaborateur?" *La République française,* no. 8 (August 1945): 14–17, reprinted in Sartre, *Situations III* (Paris, Gallimard, 1949), pp. 43–62.

14. Robert Brasillach, "Lettre à quelques jeunes gens," *Révolution nationale,* February 19, 1944, reprinted in Brasillach, *Oeuvres complètes* (Paris: Club de l'Honnête Homme, 1964), 12:612. Quoted in Alice Kaplan, *The Collaborator: The Trial and Execution of Robert Brasillach* (Chicago: The University of Chicago Press, 2000), p. 162.

15. Laurent Gervereau and Denis Peschanski, eds. *La Propagande sous Vichy, 1940–1944* (Paris: La Découverte, 1990), p. 123.

16. Charles de Gaulle, *The Call to Honour, 1940–1942* (New York: Viking Press, 1955), p. 3.

17. Roy Rosenstein, "Resistance Literature and the Exilic Imagination: Wartime Readings in Medieval Poetry for Occupied Europe," *Journal of Medieval and Renaissance Studies* 27, no. 3 (fall 1997): 530.

18. Louis Aragon, "The Reseda and the Rose," in *Defeat and Beyond: An Anthology of French Wartime Writing, 1940–1945,* ed. Germaine Brée and George Bernauer (New York: Pantheon Books, 1970), p. 200.

19. Édith Thomas, "Vieilles Pierres précieuses," *Les Lettres françaises,* November 3, 1945.

20. *Pages de journal,* August 23, 1944, pp. 213–214.

21. The statistic is cited in Fabrice Virgili, *La France "virile"* (Paris: Payot, 2000), p. 7.

22. Henry Rousso, "L'Épuration en France," *Vingtième Siècle. Revue d'Histoire,* no. 33 (January–March 1992): 85.

23. *Pages de journal,* August 25, 1944, p. 219.

24. *Témoin compromis,* pp. 169–170.

25. Ibid., p. 173.

26. Édith Thomas, "Le Professeur Wallon nous parle de l'enfance," *Femmes françaises,* October 5 and 12, 1944. Henri Wallon (1879–1962) is the author of a number of influential works on child development. A member of the Communist Party, he was appointed minister of national education in 1944 in the provisional government of de Gaulle.

27. "L'Union des Femmes Françaises groupe 200.000 femmes," *Femmes françaises,* November 16, 1944.

28. Renée Rousseau, *Les Femmes rouges: chronique des années Vermeersch* (Paris: Albin Michel, 1983), p. 48.

29. *Témoin compromis,* p. 175.

30. Édith Thomas's initial observations are recorded in the following articles, all from 1946: "Au pays des Soviets," *Le Parisien libéré,* June 26 and July 12; "La Campagne soviétique," *Regards,* June 7; "Choses vues en URSS," *Lettres françaises,* May 24 and 31; "La Famille en URSS," *Regards,* July 26; "La Femme en Union Soviétique," *La Marseillaise,* May 23–29; "Leningrad," *Femmes françaises,* May 18; "Usines d'URSS," *Regards,* May 29.

31. *Témoin compromis,* p. 194.

32. Ibid., p. 186.

33. Édith Thomas, "A travers l'Allemagne occupée," *Le Parisien libéré,* August 11, 1945.

34. Cyril Buffet, "1945: L'Allemagne sous occupation française," *L'Histoire,* February 1999. My thanks to Daniel Thomas for calling my attention to this article.

35. Édith Thomas, "Deux Morts parlent des Allemands," *Les Lettres françaises,* May 12, 1945.

36. *Témoin compromis,* pp. 188–189.

37. Édith Thomas, review of *Convoy to Auschwitz,* by Charlotte Delbo, *Le Droit de Vivre,* February–March 1966.

9. Story of Two Women: Édith Thomas and Dominique Aury

1. Jean Paulhan to Édith Thomas, November 16, 1944, AN318AP14.

2. Dominique Aury, interview by author, December 12, 1990.

3. Dominique Aury, review of *Étude de femmes*, by Édith Thomas, *Femmes françaises*, September 7, 1945.

4. Dominique Aury, "Par delà tout espoir," *L'Arche*, February 1946.

5. Unpublished diaries, October 27 and 28, 1946, AN318AP13.

6. Dominique Aury to Édith Thomas (hereafter DA to ET), October 27, 1946, AN318AP14. Letters cited below are in this same carton.

7. Régine Deforges, *O m'a dit: entretiens avec Pauline Réage* (Paris: Jean-Jacques Pauvert, 1975), p. 72.

8. Ibid., p. 42.

9. Benserade, "On the love of Urania and Philis," AN318AP13.

10. DA to ET, September 1947.

11. Unpublished diaries, November 1, 1946; November 2, 1946.

12. Ibid., February 15, 1947; April 26, 1947.

13. Ibid., November 3, 1946; August 1, 1947.

14. Deforges, *O m'a dit*, p. 48.

15. Édith Thomas, "La Fin de Gomorrhe," *Europe*, October 1947.

16. Unpublished diaries, November 5, 1946.

17. Édith Thomas to Dominique Aury (hereafter ET to DA), undated, postmarked 1947 (otherwise illegible).

18. DA to ET, December 20, 1947.

19. ET to DA, September 10, 1947; ET to DA, July 30 (no envelope: year uncertain); ET to DA, August 12, 1948.

20. Pauline Réage [Dominique Aury], "A Girl in Love," preface to *Return to the Château*, trans. Sabine D'Estrée (New York: Grove Press, 1971), p. 6.

21. DA to ET, October 5, 1950.

22. ET to DA, October 10, 1950.

23. DA to ET, August 3, 1954.

24. Réage, "Girl in Love," p. 20.

25. Pauline Réage, *Story of O*, trans. Sabine d'Estrée (New York: Ballantine Books, 1965), p. 159. Sabine d'Estrée's translation reads "like some mighty nobleman in exile." The phrase of Pauline Réage is "un grand seigneur exilé." Pauline Réage, *Histoire d'O* (Paris: Jean-Jacques Pauvert, Livre de Poche, 1954), p. 258. I have chosen a literal rendering of her phrase, which I think is more faithful to her meaning.

26. Réage, *Story of O*, p. 152, 159.

27. Dominique Aury, "Fénelon: le pur amour," in *Lecture pour tous* (Paris: Gallimard, 1958), p. 20. In addition to this collection, Dominique Aury wrote hundreds of literary essays and reviews, published in the *Nouvelle Revue française* and elsewhere. Of particular interest as a counterpoint to *Story of O* is her essay "La Révolte de Madame de Merteuil," *Cahiers de la Pléiade*, no. 12 (spring–summer 1951), a reading of the protagonist of *Les Liaisons dangereuses* in relation to the position of women of her class in pre-Revolutionary France. My thanks to Anne Simonin for calling my attention to this essay. In 1999, in commemoration of the first anniversary of Dominique Aury's death, Gallimard published two books: another selection of her literary essays, under the title *Lecture pour tous, II,* and an extended interview she gave to Nicole Grenier in 1988 about her literary life, to which Gallimard gave the title *Vocation: clandestine* (although there is no mention of *Story of O*).

28. DA to ET, September 25, 1954.

29. *Pages de journal,* June 10, 1944, p. 200.

30. Simone de Beauvoir, *The Second Sex* (Vintage Books, 1989), p. 652.

31. Réage, "Girl in Love," p. 13.

32. DA to ET, October 19, 1954.

33. Nancy K. Miller, "The Text's Heroine: A Feminist Critic and Her Fictions," *Subject to Change: Reading Feminist Writing* (New York: Columbia University Press, 1988), p. 72.

34. *Jeu d'échecs,* p. 133.

10. Feminine Humanism versus Existentialism

1. Unpublished diaries, July 18, 1934.

2. Édith Thomas, "Sappho," AN318AP5.

3. Édith Thomas, "Eve and the Serpent," in *Eve and the Others.* Some translations are my own.

4. Édith Thomas, "L'Humanisme féminin," p. 3, AN318AP3.

5. Édith Thomas, "Pourquoi 'l'éternel féminin' serait-il seul à être éternel?" *Action,* November 26–December 2, 1947.

6. Thomas, "L'Humanisme féminin," pp. 320–321.

7. Simone de Beauvoir, *The Second Sex* (Vintage Books, 1989), p. 731.

8. *Champ libre,* p. 147.

9. Thomas, "L'Humanisme féminin," p. 314.

10. Édith Thomas, "Des vessies et des lanternes," review of *Tous les hommes sont mortels, La Marseillaise,* January 2–3, 1947.

11. In contrast, Dominique Aury was one of the few women who wrote a review article that defended *The Second Sex* when it was first published, describing it as a "milestone, less in its content than in its accent of freedom." Aury, "Le Visage de Méduse," review of *Le Deuxième Sexe, Contemporains,* November 1950. My thanks to Sylvie Chaperon for sending me this article.

12. Édith Thomas, "A propos de Pyrrhus et Cinéas," *France Soir,* November 24, 1944.

13. Michael Kelly, "Humanism and Unity," *History of European Ideas* 20 (1995): 923–928. Kelly notes the durability of humanism even now, in spite of "more cogent" arguments by structuralists, poststructuralists and postmodernists. "From the massacre of the Master-narratives," he argues, "the humanist frame has emerged at worst as a necessary myth, at best as a shared hope for the future of the planet." While "it tends to live a quiet and unobtrusive life," he concludes, "reports of its death have been greatly exaggerated." He is referring to the philosophies of antihumanism put forth since the 1960s by theorists—including Marxists—opposed to the humanist idea of autonomous consciousness.

14. Henri Lefebvre, *L'Existentialisme* (Paris: Éditions du Sagittaire, 1946), p. 215. Lefebvre's book was written before the publication in France of "Letter on Humanism," in which Heidegger differentiates his own *Existenzphilosophie* from that of Sartre. He rejects the idea of humanism, which he views as giving priority to the human being rather than Being, thus succumbing to "metaphysical subjectivism."

15. Henri Lefebvre, quoted in Dominique Aury, "Qu'est-ce que l'existentialisme? Bilan d'une offensive," *Les Lettres françaises,* November 24, 1945.

16. Édith Thomas, "De l'avilissement," *Les Lettres françaises,* January 4, 1946.

17. Albert Camus to Édith Thomas, January 7, 1946, Dossier Daniel Thomas. I wish to thank Catherine Camus for her kind permission to reproduce her father's letter in its entirety.

18. Quoted in Édith Thomas, unpublished diaries, November 15, 1943.

19. Édith Thomas "La Littérature de la Résistance," handwritten lecture given in USSR, May 1946, AN318AP1.

20. Jean-Paul Sartre, *"What Is Literature?" and other essays,* trans. Bernard Frechtman (Cambridge: Harvard University Press, 1988), p. 71.

21. Édith Thomas, "Prométhée" (1940), radio play, AN318AP5.

22. Jean-Paul Sartre, *The Flies,* in *No Exit and Three Other Plays* (New York: Vintage International, 1989), p. 119.

23. Édith Thomas, "Une Étudiante dans la Résistance," review of *L'Épreuve,* by Annie Guéhenno, *La Quinzaine littéraire,* February 16, 1969.

24. Édith Thomas, "Lettre à mon frère," AN318AP13.

25. Unpublished diaries, January 4, 1948.

26. Dr. René Wolfromm to Édith Thomas, October 3, 1967, AN318AP12.

27. Unpublished diaries, January 12, 1949.

11. The Compromised Witness: Leaving the Communist Party

1. *Pages de journal,* June 5, 1942, p. 178.

2. David Caute, *Communism and the French Intellectuals, 1914–1960* (New York: Macmillan, 1964), p. 38.

3. Édith Thomas, "De l'emploi du pronom personnel," AN318AP13.

4. Édith Thomas, "Le Roman, chemin de la culture," *Les Lettres françaises,* September 10, 1947.

5. Édith Thomas, "Discours au Parti Communiste," typed, undated, probably 1948, AN318AP1.

6. See Louis Aragon, "Jdanov et Nous," *Les Lettres françaises,* September 9, 1948.

7. Unpublished diaries, February 26, 1948; September 24, 1948.

8. Ibid., February 2, 1950.

9. Édith Thomas, "Critique et Autocritique," *Combat,* December 16 and 17, 1949.

10. *L'Humanité,* December 19, 1949.

11. Letter from the Royer-Collard cell (5th arrondissement), French Communist Party, January 4, 1950, AN318AP1.

12. *Témoin compromis,* p. 206.

13. Dominique Desanti, *Les Staliniens* (Paris: Fayard, 1975), p. 168.

14. Édith Thomas, review of *Autocritique,* by Edgar Morin, *La Nouvelle Revue française,* June 1959.

15. Edgar Morin to Édith Thomas, June 7, 1959, Dossier Daniel Thomas.

16. *Témoin compromis,* pp. 166–168.

17. Ibid., pp. 115–117.

18. Ibid., p. 210.

19. Ibid., pp. 149–151.

20. Ibid., p. 172.

21. Édith Thomas, "Voyage au maquis," May 1944, AN318AP1.

22. Édith Thomas to Jean Paulhan, 1950, Archives Paulhan, now in Paris at the IMEC (Institut Mémoires de l'édition contemporaine).

23. My thanks to Monsieur Guillot, curator at the Archives nationales, for making available to me the correspondence of Édith Thomas with the Éditeurs français réunis and the Société des gens de lettres.

24. *Témoin compromis*, pp. 222–223.

25. Édith Thomas, "Une Française en Yougoslavie," *Franc-Tireur*, April 5, 1950.

26. Yvonne Dumont, "Choisir Tito c'est choisir le camp de la guerre," *L'Humanité*, April 1, 1950.

27. Clara Malraux, *Le Bruit de nos pas*, vol. 6, *Et pourtant j'étais libre, 1940–1968* (Paris: Grasset, 1979), p. 238.

28. Anne-Marie Bauer, interview by author, November 20, 1990.

29. Édith Thomas, "Esquisse pour un humanisme féminin," undated, about 1965, p. 1, AN318AP3.

30. Édith Thomas, "Vers un humanisme féminin," undated, probably 1952, pp. 22–23, AN318AP3.

12. The Compromised Witness: The Quarrel with Jean Paulhan

1. Jean Paulhan, *Lettre aux directeurs de la Résistance* (Paris: Éditions de Minuit, 1952), p. 9.

2. Jean Paulhan to Édith Thomas (hereafter JP to ET), January 24, 1940, AN318AP14.

3. *Témoin compromis*, p. 99.

4. Louis Guilloux, *Carnets, 1921–1944* (Paris: Gallimard, 1978), entry dated June 22, 1941.

5. *Témoin compromis*, p. 100.

6. Ibid., p. 105

7. Jacques Debû-Bridel, *La Résistance intellectuelle* (Paris: Julliard, 1970), p. 57.

8. JP to ET, September 1, 1942, AN318AP14. After the war Édith Thomas scribbled on the envelope: "CNE."

9. JP to ET, February 8, 1943, AN318AP14.

10. Édith Thomas to Jean Paulhan (hereafter ET to JP), undated (February 9, 1943), Archives Paulhan, now at IMEC.

11. JP to ET, February 10, 1943, in *Choix de lettres*, vol. 2, *1937–1945*, ed. Dominique Aury and Jean-Claude Zylberstein (Paris: Gallimard, 1992), p. 300. The letters from Jean Paulhan to Édith Thomas in *Choix de lettres* were selected from the packets that Dominique Aury seems to have taken from Édith Thomas's apartment after her death.

12. JP to ET, February 13, 1943, AN318AP14.

13. JP to ET, February 23, 1943, in *Choix de lettres*, 2:301.

14. In the speech of Count Stanislas de Clermont-Tonnerre, on December 23, 1789, he famously declared, "To the Jews as a Nation, nothing; to the Jews as individuals, everything. They must renounce their judges; they must have none but ours. . . . They must not form a political corps or an Order in the state; they must be citizens individually." Quoted in Paula E. Hyman, *The Jews of Modern France* (Berkeley: University of California Press, 1998). Jews officially became French citizens in September 1791.

15. JP to ET, April 20, 1943, AN318AP14.

16. Édith Thomas and Claude Morgan, "L'Agonie de la NRF," *Les Lettres françaises,* July 1943.

17. JP to ET, July 27, 1943, *Choix de lettres,* 2:323.

18. Thomas and Morgan, "Agonie de la NRF."

19. *Les Lettres françaises,* September 16, 1944.

20. *Témoin compromis,* p. 177.

21. Jean Guéhenno, *La Foi difficile* (Paris: Grasset, 1957).

22. Jean Paulhan to Vercors, December 18, 1946, in *Choix de lettres,* vol. 3, *1945–1968,* ed. Dominique Aury and Jean-Claude Zylberstein (Paris: Gallimard, 1996), p. 39.

23. Jean Paulhan to Vercors, December 23, 1946, in *Choix de lettres,* 3:40.

24. Jean Paulhan to Marcel Jouhandeau, September 7, 1944, in *Choix de lettres,* 2:374.

25. Jean Paulhan to Henri Pourrat, August 19, 1940, in *Choix de lettres,* 2:181.

26. Jean Paulhan, *Les Incertitudes du langage: Entretiens à la radio avec Robert Mallet* (Paris: Gallimard, 1970), pp. 154–155.

27. The metaphor of the shield and the sword, Pétain and de Gaulle in complementary patriotic functions, was developed by Robert Aron in his *Histoire de Vichy* (Paris: Fayard, 1954). Cited in Henry Rousso, *The Vichy Syndrome: History and Memory in France since 1944,* trans. Arthur Goldhammer (Cambridge: Harvard University Press, 1991), p. 66.

28. Stanley Hoffmann, *Decline or Renewal? France since the 1930s* (New York: Viking Press, 1974), p. 47.

29. JP to ET, September 3, 1945, in *Choix de lettres,* 2:437.

30. ET to JP, September 7, 1945, Archives Paulhan, Paris, IMEC.

31. JP to ET, February 17, 1947; May 4, 1947; October 9, 1947, AN318AP14.

32. Draft of ET to JP, October 13, 1947, included in Dominique Aury's packet of letters from Jean Paulhan to Édith Thomas. It is not clear whether this letter was mailed, AN318AP14.

33. JP to ET, October 25, 1947, in *Choix de lettres,* 3:55.

34. JP to ET, January 11, 1948, AN318AP14.

35. Jean Paulhan and Dominique Aury, *La Patrie se fait tous les jours* (Paris: Éditions de Minuit, 1947), p. 22.

36. JP to ET, July 1, 1947, AN318AP14. The cover of Édith Thomas's *Jeanne d'Arc* is taken from a miniature in a series that illuminates the 1484 manuscript of Martial d'Auvergne's poem *Les Vigiles du Roi Charles VII,* which celebrates Joan's greatest exploits. Thomas chose for the cover of her book only the left side of the miniature. (The right side shows the prostitutes that Joan is driving from the army camp.) My thanks to the Joan of Arc scholar Nadia Margolis for identifying the source of Édith Thomas's cover illustration.

37. ET to JP, undated, probably 1950, AN318AP14.

38. JP to ET, December 22, 1951, AN318AP14.

39. Anne Simonin, *Les Éditions de Minuit (1942–1955): le devoir d'insoumission* (Paris: IMEC, 1994), p. 401.

40. Paulhan, *Lettre aux directeurs,* p. 12.

41. Henry Rousso, "L'Épuration en France: une histoire inachevée," *Vingtième Siècle, Revue d'Histoire,* no. 33 (January–March 1992): 72–106.

42. Anne Simonin, "La *Lettre aux directeurs de la Résistance* de Jean Paulhan," *Les*

Écrivains face à l'histoire (Paris: Bibliothèque Publique d'Information en Actes, 1998), pp. 45–69.

43. Louis Martin-Chauffier, "Lettre à un transfuge de la Résistance," *Figaro littéraire*, February 2, 1952; reprinted in *Lettre aux directeurs de la Résistance* (Paris: Jean-Jacques Pauvert, 1968), pp. 45–55.

44. Jean Paulhan, "Réponse de Jean Paulhan à Louis Martin-Chauffier," *Figaro littéraire*, March 15, 1952; reprinted in *Lettre aux directeurs de la Résistance (1951) suivie des répliques des contre-répliques*, pp. 56–70.

45. JP to ET, March 14, 1952, AN318AP14.

46. ET to JP, draft of letter, undated, AN318AP14.

47. JP to ET, undated, 1952, AN318AP14.

48. Dominique Aury to Édith Thomas, undated, 1952, AN318AP14.

49. Draft of ET to JP, undated, 1952. Included in packet of letters from Jean Paulhan to Édith Thomas, AN318AP14.

50. Ibid.

51. Dominique Aury to Édith Thomas, undated, 1953 or 1954, AN318AP14.

52. *Témoin compromis*, pp. 95–98.

53. Rousso, *Vichy Syndrome*, pp. 15–59.

54. *Témoin compromis*, p. 136.

55. Édith Thomas, "Au Comité National des Écrivains (1941–1944)," *Vie intellectuelle*, August 1956.

56. *Témoin compromis*, p. 136.

13. From Novels to Women's Histories

1. *Pauline Roland*, p. 7.

2. Simone de Beauvoir, *The Second Sex* (New York: Vintage Books, 1989), p. xix.

3. *The Women Incendiaries*, p. vii.

4. Édith Thomas, "Un Voyant," *La Quinzaine littéraire*, January 1, 1967.

5. Quoted in *Pauline Roland*, p. 64.

6. Ibid., p. 90.

7. Ibid., p. 85.

8. *George Sand*, p. 100.

9. Dominique Aury, "Les Femmes de lettres," in *Les Femmes célèbres*, ed. Lucienne Mazenod (Paris: Éditions d'Art Lucien Mazenod, 1960), 1:176. My thanks to Joël Schmidt for calling my attention to the existence of this encyclopedia and especially to Philippe d'Argila, who gave me the encyclopedia in his mother's library as a gift.

10. Aury, "Les Femmes de lettres," p. 177.

11. Édith Thomas, "Les Femmes et le pouvoir," in Mazenod, *Femmes célèbres*, p. 97.

12. Édith Thomas, "L'Humanisme féminin," in Mazenod, *Femmes célèbres*, p. 233.

13. "Les Fleurs du temps," AN318AP2.

14. Lucien Mazenod to Édith Thomas, November 16, 1960, AN318AP2.

15. Sonia Madrona, "Édith Thomas: la quête inlassable de l'absolu" (D.E.A. thesis, University of Orléans, 1996). Mme Madrona's thesis is an invaluable resource for the study of the writings by Édith Thomas at the Archives nationales.

16. Édith Thomas to Dominique Aury, September 22, 1948, AN318AP14.

17. Anne-Marie Bauer, interview by author, November 20, 1990.

18. See *Les Femmes dans la Résistance. Actes du colloque tenu à l'initiative de L'Union des Femmes Françaises* (Monaco: Éditions du Rocher, 1977), pp. 52–53.

19. Anne-Marie Bauer to author, February 26, 1991.

20. Édith Thomas, "Clio elle-même doit choisir," *Les Lettres françaises,* January 6, 1945.

21. *Women Incendiaries,* p. xiv.

22. Ibid., p. 37 (my translation).

23. Ibid., p. 134.

24. *Louise Michel* (Eng. trans.), p. 11.

25. Ibid., pp. 12–13.

26. Ibid., p. 361.

27. Ibid., pp. 288, 344.

28. Ibid., p. 159.

14. Wartime Truths: La Question *and Algeria;* Rossel

1. Dominique Aury to Édith Thomas, August 10, 1957, AN318AP14.

2. Édith Thomas, "De la torture," *La Commune,* June 1957.

3. Édith Thomas, "De la torture," *La Nouvelle Réforme,* January–February 1958, pp. 281–286.

4. Édith Thomas, "Si nous montions d'un degré," *Front National,* August 9, 1946.

5. *Louise Michel,* p. 113 (my translation).

6. Monique Pouliquen, interview by author, October 16, 1990; Monsieur Guillot, interview by author, October 30, 1990, Archives nationales. After Thomas's death, the personnel library (in which this incident took place) was named the Salle Édith Thomas, to honor her memory.

7. Édith Thomas to Fernande Thomas, June 19, 1958, Dossier Daniel Thomas.

8. Édith Thomas to Fernande Thomas, June 25, 1958, Dossier Daniel Thomas.

9. See Jean Lacouture, *De Gaulle,* vol. 2, *The Ruler, 1945–1970,* trans. Alan Sheridan (New York W. W. Norton, 1990–92).

10. *Le Monde,* October 12, 1960.

11. Yvonne Lanhers, interview by author, December 14, 1990.

12. *Rossel,* p. 111.

13. Ibid., p. 208.

14. Ibid., p. 259.

15. Ibid., pp. 358–360.

16. Dominique Jamet, review of *Rossel,* by Édith Thomas, *Figaro littéraire,* November 13–19, 1967.

17. Ibid., pp. 411, 475.

18. "Édith Thomas parle de Rossel," *La Quinzaine littéraire,* October 1–15, 1967.

15. Endings

1. Jean Paulhan to Édith Thomas, December 29, 1967, AN318AP14.

2. Dominique Aury to Édith Thomas, August 21, 1967.

3. Jean Paulhan to Édith Thomas December 29, 1967.

4. Daniel and Andrée Thomas, conversations with author, La Bâtie, July 8, 1991.

5. Ibid.

6. Madeleine Thomas, interview by author, July 8, 1991.

7. Ibid.

8. "Lettre à mon frère," AN318AP13.

9. Ibid.

10. Ibid.

11. Unpublished diaries, July 15, 1937, AN318AP13.

12. "Lettre à mon frère."

13. Ibid.

14. Édith Thomas to Pierre Nora, October 2, 1970, AN318AP12.

15. Pierre Nora to Édith Thomas, October 19, 1970, AN318AP12.

16. *Jeu d'échecs*, pp. 13, 69.

17. Dominique Aury to Édith Thomas, October 5, 1950, AN318AP14.

18. *Jeu d'échecs*, p. 69.

19. Ibid., p. 95.

20. Dominique Aury, "Une Femme de sagesse," *Nouvelles littéraires*, December 17, 1970.

21. Édith Thomas to Daniel Thomas, September 14, 1970, Dossier Daniel Thomas.

22. Josane Duranteau, "Mort d'Édith Thomas: Une oeuvre au service de la vérité," *Le Monde*, December 10, 1970.

Index

Note: For the sake of clarity, entries under "Thomas, Édith" have been kept to a minimum. See also entries under relevant names and categories. See notes for complete references to Édith Thomas's directly autobiographical texts: "À mon frère"; *Pages de journal; Le Témoin compromis*; unpublished diaries.